"So has a Daisy vanished"

"So has a Daisy vanished": Emily Dickinson and Tuberculosis

GEORGE MAMUNES

McFarland & Company, Inc., Publishers
Jefferson, North Carolina, and London

Emily Dickinson's poems reprinted by permission of the publishers and the Trustees of Amherst College from *The Poems of Emily Dickinson: Reading Edition*, Ralph W. Franklin, ed., Cambridge, Mass.: The Belknap Press of Harvard University Press, Copyright © 1998, 1999 by the President and Fellows of Harvard College. Copyright © 1951, 1955, 1979, 1983 by the President and Fellows of Harvard College.

Emily Dickinson's letters reprinted by permission of the publishers from *The Letters of Emily Dickinson*, Thomas H. Johnson, ed., Cambridge, Mass.: The Belknap Press of Harvard University Press, Copyright © 1958, 1986, The President and Fellows of Harvard College; 1914, 1924, 1932, 1942 by Martha Dickinson Bianchi; 1952 by Alfred Leete Hampson; 1960 by Mary L. Hampson.

LIBRARY OF CONGRESS CATALOGUING-IN-PUBLICATION DATA

Mamunes, George, 1938–
  "So has a Daisy vanished" : Emily Dickinson and tuberculosis / George Mamunes.
    p.   cm.
  Includes bibliographical references and index.

  ISBN-13: 978-0-7864-3227-1
  softcover : 50# alkaline paper ∞

  1. Dickinson, Emily, 1830–1886—Criticism and interpretation.
  2. American poetry—Women authors—History and criticism.
  3. Tuberculosis and literature. 4. Poetry—Authorship—Psychological aspects. 5. Women and literature—United States—History—19th century. I. Title.
  PS1541.Z5M2158   2008
  811'.4—dc22   2007034732

British Library cataloguing data are available

©2008 George Mamunes. All rights reserved

No part of this book may be reproduced or transmitted in any form or by any means, electronic or mechanical, including photocopying or recording, or by any information storage and retrieval system, without permission in writing from the publisher.

On the cover: Emily Dickinson (Wikimedia Commons); Window ©2007 Shutterstock

Manufactured in the United States of America

McFarland & Company, Inc., Publishers
  Box 611, Jefferson, North Carolina 28640
    www.mcfarlandpub.com

For Lee,
wife,
research partner,
editor
and best friend

Acknowledgments

For their guidance and courtesies, the author is grateful to

Tevis Kimball, Special Collections, Jones Library, Amherst, MA
Robert Ellis, Historian, Northborough (MA) Historical Society
Ethan Tarasov, Emily Dickinson International Society
Frances O'Donnell, Andover-Harvard Theological Library, Cambridge, MA
Leslie Perrin Wilson, Special Collections, Concord (MA) Free Public Library
Meredith Paine Sorozan, Rhode Island Historical Society, Providence, RI
Maggi Humbertson, Connecticut Valley Historical Museum, Springfield, MA
Jack Eckert, Francis A. Countway Library of Medicine, Boston, MA
American Antiquarian Society, Worcester, MA
New York Academy of Medicine Library, New York City, NY
New York Public Library, New York City, NY
Local History Room, Goodnow Library, South Sudbury, MA
Local History and Genealogy Room, Worcester (MA) Public Library
Manhattanville College Library, Purchase, NY
George T. Potter Library, Ramapo College, Mahwah, NJ
SUNY Rockland Community College Library, Suffern, NY

My thanks to those Dickinson scholars who graciously offered their comments on the original version of this book, self-published in 2006 as *"So has a Daisy vanished": Emily Dickinson's Tuberculosis*. That edition, circulated privately for comment, was the starting point for the present version and has benefitted from the comments I received.

*And a special thanks to Stuart and Joanne Hollis,
keepers of the quest from beginning to end*

Hope

I want to let go—
so I don't give a damn about fine writing,
I'm rolling my sleeves up.
The dough's rising...

Oh what a shame
I can't bake cathedrals...
that sublimity of style
I've always yearned for...
Child of our time—
haven't you found the right shell for your soul?

Before I die I *shall*
bake a cathedral.

EDITH SÖDERGRAN

Edith Södergran (1892–1923) was born in St. Petersburg, Russia. In 1907, her father died of pulmonary tuberculosis, and the next year Edith was diagnosed with the disease. She was sent to a sanatorium but did not feel at ease there. The feelings of captivity caused by the disease are a recurring theme in her poetry. In 1912, her condition improved and she returned home. Sadly, the disease returned and she died at home in Raivola, Finland, at age 31.

Contents

Acknowledgments vii
Introduction 1

1. The Omitted Center 5
2. Dread Disease 22
3. Impenitence 41
4. Ben Newton 56
5. First Love 80
6. Spirit-Bride 100
7. Queen Recluse 110
8. Terror 128
9. Afterlife 148

Appendix A: Novel Excerpts 161
Appendix B: List of Poems 171
Chapter Notes 175
Bibliography 185
Index 193

Introduction

Why am I so caught up in reading Emily Dickinson's poems? No one should have to work this hard! I suppose the payoff comes in jolts of insight, deep or delicious, or when I suddenly laugh aloud in recognition. But there are also moments when I *don't* get it, when I stumble over a poem's starting point, or the density of its images, or its complex syntax, as if I were in a labyrinth. The guideposts I look for in poetry—*titles*, for instance—are simply not there.

Jay Leyda, one of the hardest-working of all Dickinson scholars, knew what Emily was up to: "A major device of Emily Dickinson's writing, both in her poems and in her letters, was what might be called the 'omitted center.' The riddle, the circumstance too well known to be repeated to the initiate, the deliberate skirting of the obvious—this was the means she used to increase the privacy of her communication; it has also increased our problems in piercing that privacy."[1] In other words, what is *missing* in Dickinson's poetry is far more important than what is there. She seems to know that a select audience will understand her completely, and leaves it at that.

The rest of us are left to fend for ourselves. And perhaps that is all to the good. T. S. Eliot once observed that "a knowledge of the springs which released a poem is not necessarily a help toward understanding the poem," and that "there is, in all great poetry, something which must remain unaccountable however complete might be our knowledge of the poet."[2] Eliot makes sense; genuine poetry transfixes the reader even as conscious understanding lags behind. But it's equally plain that Emily Dickinson attracts attention, and not only because of her poems. The Dickinson Homestead in Amherst has become a beacon, if not a shrine, for thousands.

And so, when I learned in *The New England Quarterly* in 1999 of the probability that Emily Dickinson was tubercular, I decided to give the poems a fresh look. I was surprised. Time and again, Dickinson seems to touch upon disease and its impact. One poem in particular caught my eye:

567

It knew no Medicine—
It was not Sickness—then—
Nor any need of Surgery—
And therefore—'twas not Pain—

It moved away the Cheeks—
A Dimple at a time—
And left the Profile—plainer—
And in the place of Bloom

It left the little Tint
That never had a Name—
You've seen it on a Cast's face—
Was Paradise—to blame—

If momently ajar—
Temerity—drew near—
And sickened—ever afterward
For Somewhat that it saw?[3] [1863]

Dickinson was being coy, or perhaps caustic. She knew, of course, that "the little Tint / That never had a Name," the bright red spot on a pallid cheek, was called *hectic*, and that it signaled the presence of the dread disease, *consumption*. Consumption was then the household word for pulmonary tuberculosis, a disease that can kill quickly, but one that often takes many years to work its damage, "A Dimple at a time." A 2005 article in *New England Ancestors* laid out TB's symptoms:

> The disease can be severely painful and physically devastating, causing persistent coughing; throat irritation; pains in the chest and shoulders; fast pulse rate; severe weight loss; fevers; difficulty in breathing; ulcers of the throat; emaciation; death rattle coughs; night sweats; diarrhea; choking and sometimes suffocating; slight to profuse hemorrhaging; sunken eyes; and exhaustion and swollen joints.[4]

In 1858, at the age of 27, Dickinson set out to "Tell all the truth but tell it slant." She's so good at her game that scholars sometimes miss or minimize her anguish. In his 1974 Dickinson biography, for instance, Richard Sewall describes the mutual admiration flowing between Emily and Joseph Lyman, a family friend who spent many hours with Emily when both were in their teens and early twenties. After Lyman moved out of Massachusetts, the two maintained their connection in long and introspective letters. Shortly before his marriage, Lyman wrote to his fiancée for permission to continue to write to "such sweet friends as Mintie and to Emily Dickinson."[5] He linked Emily with Araminta Wharton, "one of those to whom God gave a white soul ... who have been made perfect through suffering."[6]

Sewall observes that Lyman enclosed in the letter "a blue slip on which he had written the famous verses from Revelation (III: 4–5) which may have had some bearing on Emily's later habit of wearing white: 'and they shall walk with me in white: for they are worthy.'"[7] No one knew Emily Dickinson in the 1850s better than Lyman, and yet Sewall looked right through the implications of his data: "Lyman thought of both Emily and Araminta as in the 'white company' of those born pure and made perfect through suffering, *although Emily's suffering was surely not from physical causes like Mintie's, who died of tuberculosis when she was twenty-seven*."[8]

Emily Dickinson died at age 55 in 1886. Ten years later, when officials in Amherst set down their town's history, they were silent on the tuberculosis that had devastated the area. Perhaps they thought of consumption as unremarkable, commonplace. Though the disease was dubbed "the great white plague," it intruded on one person at a time; health often shaded into prolonged illness, and consumptives sometimes lived with their symptoms for years or even decades. It's likely the historians in Amherst were thinking of more *overt* epidemics—cholera, for one, struck with terrifying suddenness, quickly turning victims into wizened caricatures of their former selves, their skins black and blue. Another possibility is that the town historians feared the stigma that accompanied TB, and simply wanted Amherst to look good. There must be multiple reasons why we need to look away from or through chronic illness, rather than at it. Even so, it seems odd that *The History of the Town of Amherst* (1896) included not one mention of tuberculosis: "Amherst has suffered but little from epidemics of disease. The favored location of the town, its healthful climate and the lack of tenement-house population have proved unfavorable to the spread of contagious disease."[9]

Pulmonary tuberculosis now runs beneath our radar. Only 14,093 TB cases were reported nationwide in 2005 (4.8 cases per 100,000 people, the lowest U.S. rate since 1953).[10] Our reference points to consumption are gone. *Hectic* is used only as an adjective. Casinos go up where sanatoriums once stood. "Lunger stories" no longer circulate among families, and Boy Scouts have left off singing "My Bonnie has tuberculosis, my Bonnie has only one lung / My Bonnie can cough up raw oysters, and roll them around on her tongue." Unless one is close to a person with active TB or HIV or AIDS, one might think of TB as a "conquered" disease.

It is not. In other regions, TB is pandemic, infecting a third of the world's population and killing 2 million a year. This breaks down to 228 deaths each hour. "Tuberculosis has escaped to the places where its victims once sought refuge, the one-time colonies of Western nations," writes David Morens of the National Institute of Health. "The disease destroys the poor and underprivileged as it once destroyed the wealthy—95 percent of cases and 98 percent of deaths occur in the developing world. Its ravages are worst in the Pacific Islands."[11] Most Americans do not take notice of this suffering, and Morens thinks he knows why: "How can we grasp such statistics of misery? Reduced to numbers stacked up in columns and cut up in pie charts, tuberculosis patients don't seem like us. They live in faraway places, come from obscure cultures, speak incomprehensible languages, have disreputable co-morbid disease, or exhibit antisocial behavior. They are 'the other.' Maybe they do not even exist."[12]

It was different for Emily Dickinson's generation. Then, it was a family member or neighbor or schoolmate who developed TB, someone known to Amherst's 3,000 residents, someone very much like them, someone who *did* exist. Someone's diminished lung capacity, or persistent cough, or need for an exotic diet to roll around on the tongue was never a target for humor. And yet, in subtle and less subtle ways, that someone was expendable, a part of *the other*. Amherst's formulaic response to the sick and dying did not sit well with Dickinson. She raised her objections, not in public, but in the private code of her poems.

EXCERPTS FROM NOVELS, 1850–1876

The opening of each chapter in this book is preceded by a brief excerpt from an American novel published between 1850 and 1876, that is, between Emily Dickinson's twentieth and forty-sixth year of life. Each excerpt sets a chapter theme and, more importantly, speaks to us of a time when Americans were caught up in a disease that would come to be known as tuberculosis.

A more extensive excerpt from each of the novels can be found in Appendix (A).

> "Were you really in earnest, mother," said Margaret ... "when you spoke about parents transmitting to their children a predisposition to the particular diseases from which they suffered?" ... "Deeply in earnest," replied Mrs. Ellis. "...My mother died of consumption; I have a marked predisposition to that fatal disease; and I need not tell you that your lungs are peculiarly sensitive."
> —T. S. Arthur, *Seed-time and Harvest*, 1851

1. The Omitted Center

In 1999 an article appeared in *The New England Quarterly*, "Was it Tuberculosis? Another Glimpse of Emily Dickinson's Health." In sixteen detailed and carefully reasoned pages, Dr. Norbert Hirschhorn laid his case before the academic community:

> Between 1846 and 1852 Emily Dickinson suffered distinct episodes of ill health for which she was treated just as she was embarking on her poetic career. By matching clinical clues extracted from her correspondence with medical information available to and used by her physicians, it is apparent that her symptoms suggested to observers at the time that she was suffering from tuberculosis.
>
> Surely that diagnosis would have been troubling to an individual as sensitive as Dickinson—indeed to a family as sensitive as hers—and the effects such an experience may have had on her poetry have yet to be plumbed.[1]

"Perhaps it was her own close brush with consumption that served to organize Emily Dickinson's thoughts on the topic of death," Hirschhorn mused, "for she almost surely imagined herself, at one time or another, as among the victims she saw passing by her window"[2] in funeral processions. Dr. Hirschhorn's comments make sense. When one's life is taken over by chronic illness, everything changes: self-image, priorities, social interaction—one's entire outlook on life (and death). For instance, Emily suspected something was lacking in the accommodations at Amherst's West Cemetery:

100
What Inn is this
Where for the night
Peculiar Traveller comes?
Who is the Landlord?

> Where the maids?
> Behold, what curious rooms!
> No ruddy fires on the hearth—
> No brimming tankards flow.
> Necromancer! Landlord!
> Who are these below? [1859]

Dr. Hirschhorn's thesis was endorsed by Alfred Habegger in his meticulous 2001 Dickinson biography, *My Wars Are Laid Away in Books*: "Norbert Hirschhorn is surely right in arguing that ... Dickinson had pulmonary tuberculosis."[3] Prior to Hirschhorn and Habegger, there had been only one Dickinson critic, Cynthia Wolff, curious about TB. Wolff detailed the presence of consumption on the Norcross side of Emily's family, leading to the early deaths of a number of her mother's siblings, nieces and nephews. Wolff suspected there was something significant in this, and she was right. Emily Dickinson in her early twenties was, like Margaret Ellis in *Seed-time*, pale, thin, subject to coughing. In *Seed-time*, Margaret's grandmother dies of consumption, and Margaret's mother has "a marked predisposition to that fatal disease." This scenario was almost a cliché in the mid–1800s. Emily's grandmother, Betsy Fay Norcross, died of TB in 1829, the year before Emily was born, and for years Emily's mother, Emily Norcross Dickinson, showed signs of a TB-like illness, a formless affliction variously characterized by Wolff as "obscure,"[4] "vague,"[5] "ephemeral,"[6] "nameless,"[7] "disabling,"[8] "intractable"[9] and "persistent."[10] Did the Dickinson family fear to give it a name?

Wolff reacted to the poems of disease and death. Citing Dickinson's line "A Cheek is always redder / Just where the Hectic stings!," she identified *hectic* as the fever of consumption, as one of the "signs of visible decay embedded even in feminine beauty ... [that] still haunted the Norcross family when the poet was at the height of her powers."[11] Lines in another poem, "Narcotics cannot still the Tooth / That nibbles at the soul," revealed, for Wolff, a "flourish of the macabre ... Americans of the nineteenth century had a homely nickname for tuberculosis: it was 'the mouse in the breast,' gnawing away at breath and finally at life."[12] It would seem that Wolff was able to detect a poet *of* consumption, but not a poet *in* consumption.

One can discern a TB subtext couched in Dickinson's "slant," in her use of the *daisy*, the *mouse*, the cheek's *hectic* red. *Winter*, *midnight*, or the *moon* might be read as disease or despair; *spring*, *summer*, *noon* or the *sun* as remission or hope. A *volcanic eruption*, a *violent storm*, an *earthquake*, or even an *avalanche* might symbolize a gush of blood from the lungs. Dickinson's favorite bird, the *robin*, departs in autumn for the balmy South, in company with hundreds of Yankee consumptives flocking to Florida or New Orleans or the West Indies in search of a cure.

Emily was the robin who never went South, except for a trip of several weeks to Washington, D.C., and Philadelphia in 1855, at the time her father, Edward Dickinson, served a term in Congress. Father never thought of sending Emily to Florida or Louisiana during the cold New England winters. This was consistent with the norms then in place: consumptive *men* traveled South in search of healthier climates; consumptive *women* were commonly told to remain with their families, to hunker down in New England.[13] The reasons were patriarchal and practical; in Edward Dickinson's case, Emily was needed at home to minister to her invalid mother, a task that would occupy her, daily, for three decades. Dickinson, the poet, seemed aware of the gender gap:

> 528
>
> 'Tis not that Dying hurts us so—
> 'Tis Living—hurts us more—
> But Dying—is a different way—
> A kind behind the Door—
>
> The Southern Custom—of the Bird—
> That ere the Frosts are due—
> Accepts a better Latitude—
> We—are the Birds—that stay.
>
> The Shiverers round Farmer's doors—
> For whose reluctant Crumb—
> We stipulate—till pitying Snows
> Persuade our Feathers Home [1863]

Dickinson parses the rhythms and moods of consumption (without once *naming* it in the poems), hinting at pain, difficult breathing, chills, rivers of blood. So much blood that critics are caught short. Camille Paglia, for one, sees the blood as evidence of sadism, labeling Dickinson "Amherst's Madame de Sade": "Dickinson relishes blood and is lavish with her red palette. 'Sang from the Heart, Sire, / Dipped my Beak in it, / If the Tune drip too much / Have a Tint too Red / Pardon the Cochineal— / Suffer the Vermilion–'.... The poet is a self-maiming pelican, tearing clots of flesh from her breast to feed her song.... 'Whole Gulfs of Red, and Fleets of Red / And Crews of solid Blood'.... Who else but Dickinson could think of autumn leaves as blood clots, 'great Globules in the Alleys'?"[14] Paglia derides the poet's "theatricality," and her "ostentatious withdrawals," and floats a joke at Dickinson's expense: "A mass murder seems to have been committed in Amherst. The red streams of blood recall the curse upon Pharaoh."[15]

Running all the stop signs, Paglia pictures Dickinson as "a vampire hunting female prey."[16]

Paglia is too quick to blame the victim. Her image—a mass murder in Amherst—is, in fact, the sad truth. Dickinson was no vampire, but instead, a *veteran of war*. One out of every four people taken to West Cemetery had been destroyed by pulmonary tuberculosis. In her poetry, Dickinson identifies with them, and with their struggles. The earliest poems in R. W. Franklin's 1999 edition hint at grief, anger and survivor guilt. The poems can be seen as *grief therapy*, Dickinson's attempt to climb out of a slough of depression. In one of the earliest, she pictures a life ending—"Oozed so, in crimson bubbles." In the context of a poem describing death, line 5 can be read as a nod to TB: a hemorrhage of frothy blood escaping the lungs and oozing from the lips.

19

So has a Daisy vanished
From the fields today—
So tiptoed many a slipper
To Paradise away—
Oozed so, in crimson bubbles
Day's departing tide—
Blooming—tripping—flowing—
Are ye then with God? [1858]

Dickinson's very next poem seems to express her frustration at not being able to know the final resting place of those snatched away and, more importantly, whether or not she will ever be able to meet up with them again:

20

If those I loved were lost
The Crier's voice w'd tell me—
If those I loved were found
The bells of Ghent w'd ring—
Did those I loved repose
The Daisy would impel me.
Philip—when bewildered
Bore his riddle in! [1858]

Emily found herself in West Cemetery more frequently than she might have wished. Apparently, she did not give herself over emotionally at these solemn rituals; her poems are written from the perspective of an outsider or, at the very least, an onlooker:

22

> A brief, but patient illness—
> An hour to prepare—
> And one below, this morning
> Is where the angels are—
> It was a short procession—
> The Bobolink was there—
> An aged Bee addressed us—
> And then we knelt in prayer—
> We trust that she was willing—
> We ask that we may be—
> Summer—Sister—Seraph!
> Let us go with thee! [1858]

From the beginning, Emily Dickinson seemed to be fully aware of the therapeutic value of the *singing* that she had entered into. One cannot help but wonder at which word or phrase she intended in the second stanza of "Distrustful of the Gentian" (Fr26), before removing it and substituting a blank line.

> Weary for my _____
> I will singing go—
> I shall not feel the sleet—then—
> I shall not fear the snow. [1858]

To say that Dickinson was *obsessed* with death misses the point. Death *overwhelmed* her. "Death was much of mob as I could master,"[17] she later said of the early 1850s, when 33 young adults in Amherst died, almost all by TB. Religionists in Amherst celebrated each loss, thanking God for his role in what must have seemed, to her, a gruesome lottery. If others in Amherst saw them as *daisies*—commonplace to the point of invisibility—she memorialized them as singular, and lovely, and suddenly mute, a "noiseless noise in the Orchard."[18]

The peak years of the TB pandemic in Europe and America coincided with Emily Dickinson's first 20 years of life. She was seven when Charles Dickens in 1838 wrote in *Nicholas Nickleby* of the eerie qualities of a disease called consumption:

> There is a dread disease which so prepares its victim, as it were, for death; which so refines it of its grosser aspects, and throws around familiar looks, unearthly indications of the coming change—a dread disease, in which the struggle between soul and body is so gradual, quiet, and solemn, and the result so sure, that day by day, and grain by grain, the mortal part wastes and withers away, so that the spirit grows light and sanguine with its lightening load, and,

feeling immortality at hand, deems it but a new term of mortal life; a disease in which death and life are so strangely blended that death takes the glow and hue of life, and life the gaunt and grisly form of death; a disease which medicine never cured, wealth never warded off, or poverty could boast exemption from; which sometimes moves in giant strides, and sometimes at a tardy sluggish pace, but, slow or quick, is ever sure and certain.[19]

This death-in-life scourge crested in 1850, before beginning its long decline. Almost every family in the Connecticut River Valley was victimized or, at the very least, knew of consumptives up the road. The 1850 U. S. Census revealed that, of the 4415 deaths in the five westernmost counties in Massachusetts in the 12 months leading up to June 1, 1850, 916 were due to "consumption." Perhaps as many as 150 other TB-induced deaths were subsumed under other categories: "congestion," "hemorrhage," "bronchitis," "disease of the lungs," and "unknown." All in all, pulmonary consumption brought on about 1 in every 4 deaths.[20]

The census further tabulated the 916 TB deaths by the "duration" of the illness: only 6 percent of the victims were taken in the first week, 7 percent between 1 week and 1 month, 16 percent between 1 and 3 months, and 71 percent at some point in time subsequent to 3 months, often many, many years later. Of interest are the corresponding numbers for death by cholera, a hideous but efficient disease: 73 percent gone in 1 week, 25 percent between 1 week and 1 month, 2 percent between 1 and 3 months, and 0 percent after that. Cholera, unlike consumption, never overstayed its visit.[21]

TB hit hardest at those in the prime of life: of the 916 victims, 11 percent were under 10 years of age, 12 percent were age 10–19, 49 percent were age 20–49, and 28 percent were age 50–99. Because this was a time when no man or woman could maintain a farm without a spouse to shoulder half the burden, the Connecticut River Valley was dotted with serial widows and serial widowers.[22]

The disease was on everyone's mind. Americans argued the causes of consumption, and newspaper and magazine ads regularly hawked the latest "remedies." *Medico*tourism became the fashion for those who could afford it; sufferers traveled to the American South or across the Atlantic, and later to the American West, in search of healthier climes. Care for the terminally ill became an obsession for the religiously devout; deathwatches were common, in which volunteers (almost always females) sat at the bedside of a relative or neighbor, attending to physical needs, at times cleaning up blood, repeatedly asking if the patient was right with Christ. More attention needs to be paid to the link between the 1820–1850 spike in consumptive deaths and the intense religious revivals that boiled up again and again in Connecticut River Valley towns. The faithful gathered to celebrate death and resurrection. There were no losers; each victim was proclaimed a victory for God. Americans looked more regularly to religion than to medicine for comfort and solace in the face of death.

Popular culture played its part. Scores of novels and countless magazine stories featured TB-related scenes and plot lines. A case can be made that pulmonary tuberculosis and Gothic literature share the same motifs: ancestral curses; an aura of vampires; feelings of entrapment or imprisonment; the threat of pain and destruction; questions without answers; blood. *Jane Eyre* and *Wuthering Heights* come quickly to mind. Charlotte and Emily Brontë, victims of TB, were two of Emily Dickinson's very special daisies—"Queens," she called them.

Remarking on the "strong sense of mortality that oppressed Amherst," Alfred Habegger assigns special significance to "the first half of 1844, when a series of deaths made a dramatic impact on the town and precipitated the poet's most serious childhood crisis."[23] Emily was barely thirteen when she attended the 1844 funeral of Deborah Vinal Fiske. The mouse inside Mrs. Fiske's breast had gnawed and gnawed—she weighed but 70 pounds at the end. Weeks before, in December, Deborah Fiske had planned a birthday party for her daughter Ann, and among those invited were the two Dickinson sisters. (Ann's older sister, Helen Maria Fiske, would in later years achieve fame as the poet and novelist Helen Hunt Jackson. She was born in Amherst two months before Emily Elizabeth Dickinson; the girls played with each other in childhood, connected up again in later life, when Helen repeatedly urged Emily to publish, and asked to be her literary executor. They died only months apart. Two lives, coterminous, and darkened by tuberculosis.) The birthday party never came off, because Mrs. Fiske found herself "too feeble" to bear the noise of children at play.[24] Now she was dead of consumption, the subject of a funeral oration, "The Woman that Feareth the Lord," delivered by the president of Amherst College, Heman Humphrey. Listen in on some of what Emily heard in Humphrey's 48-page eulogy:

> A wife, a daughter, a mother, a sister, a friend, has finished her course, and fallen asleep, at the age of thirty-seven. She is now at rest. The coughing and panting and sinking are all over.... With the seeds of that most insidious and wasting of all diseases, in her constitution, which made her motherless at two years of age, Mrs. Fiske lived much longer than she expected to live. Ten years ago, she looked upon herself as in a sure decline; and as she said, was greatly surprised when she found, as the spring opened, that she was slowly recovering.... But the "last enemy," though kept at bay, was not to be foiled.[25]

Deborah Vinal Fiske was no deathbed convert to Christ. Christianity had been her strength and solace even as sickness took one infant son in 1829 and another, Humphrey, in 1833. She wrote to her father that "Humphrey ... is in the hands of an infinitely good and wise Being who cannot but do right, and is constantly aiming at the eternal welfare of his creatures in every event that takes place," and that Humphrey's illness, TB, was a sign and a warning from Heaven: "my sins against God deserve the heaviest judgments, instead of which he has given me innumerable blessing and therefore it is exceedingly unreasonable & wicked to repine & murmur if he but takes one away—although that one may be a beloved child."[26] In 1844, nearing death, Deborah wrote to her aunt: "My earthly house is *failing*, and while we are at home in the body, we are absent from the Lord, and I do hope through the *infinite mercy* of God that ... my soul will find a home in a house not made with hands, eternal in the heavens."[27] This was indeed, a Woman that Feareth the Lord.

Helen Maria Fiske, listening to the Heman Humphrey eulogy, became visibly agitated. *Her mother hadn't received a blessing. She was gone!* In her masterful study of TB and the social experience of illness in America, *Living in the Shadow of Death*, Sheila Rothman notes that Helen "had not been able to contain her rage as her mother's coffin was lowered into the ground. Instead of being subdued by her mother's tranquility, she rebelled. Almost two months later she still refused to find solace through the acceptance of God's will."[28]

Only six weeks later, Emily attended another funeral, this one for Mrs. Harriet Fowler, daughter of Noah Webster (whose dictionary would become Emily's "lexicon," her treasure). Like her devoted companion, Deborah Fiske, Harriet Fowler had also wasted away for years because of tuberculosis. The dead woman's daughter was another of Emily's friends, the beautiful and popular Emily Fowler. Heman Humphrey again presided, and Rothman notes that he once more used the biblical phrase, "The woman who feareth God she shall be praised," and that Humphrey concluded his sermon "by evoking the friendship between Harriet and Deborah. He assured the congregation that Harriet Fowler would be admitted to the community of saints and that Deborah Fiske would be waiting for her.... Surely, some who followed Harriet's coffin to the graveyard and watched as the mourners shoveled the wet earth over it envisioned Harriet and Deborah standing together. And perhaps, as Humphrey intended, the vision gave them energy as well as solace in the face of consumption."[29]

But not Harriet Fowler's daughter. Young Emily Fowler, bitter and unwilling to be consoled, wrote to her aunt: "I dare not look forward to the future. I cannot realize that she is gone never to come again ... that I am motherless for life."³⁰ Both Emily Fowler and Helen Fiske were angry: why would a loving God *will* their mothers' long and agonizing deaths?

None of this was lost on Emily. Her turn was next. Shortly after Mrs. Fowler's funeral, she visited the home of a gravely ill 15-year-old cousin, Sophia Holland, and stole into the sick room moments after Sophia died. Transfixed, she looked into Sophia's face until others pulled her away. Sophia's was the third funeral for Emily in a span of two months—considerable trauma for a girl of 13, even for one living in a town accustomed to the metronome of death. In fact, it proved *too much* for Emily: "I gave way to a fixed melancholy," she later confided to a friend, "I told no one the cause of my grief, although it was gnawing at my very heart strings. I was not well & went to Boston & stayed [at the home of her favorite aunt, Lavinia Norcross Norcross] a month...."³¹

When she returned home from Boston, Emily was again put to a test. She was taken to the funeral of Martha Strong, without being told that Strong had plunged into a well outside her home. The cause of death was entered as "Suicide. Drowned in a state of mental derangement."³² Those taking their own lives were barred by Calvinist doctrine from salvation, but Martha Strong's mental state clouded the question. Writing to Thomas Wentworth Higginson many years later, Dickinson reconstructed the scene: "I was taken to a Funeral which I now know was of peculiar distress, and the Clergyman asked 'Is the Arm of the Lord shortened that it cannot save.' He italicized the 'cannot.' I mistook the accent for a doubt of immortality and not daring to ask, it besets me still."³³ Alfred Habegger sorted out Emily's confusion: "What the young listener surmised was that God might be weaker than he was thought to be and that heaven could be a fable...."³⁴

Near the end of her life, Dickinson thought back upon all those who had been taken too soon:

1632

> Quite empty, quite at rest,
> The Robin locks her Nest, and tries her Wings—
> She does not know a Route
> But puts her Craft about
> For <u>rumored</u> springs—
> She does not ask for Noon—
> She does not ask for Boon—
> Crumbless and homeless, of but one request—
> The Birds she lost—[1884]

Emily's doubts about God and salvation took hold in 1844, that awful year. In 1846, she asked in a letter to her close friend, Abiah Root, "Does not Eternity appear dreadful to you?"[35] Her skepticism did not go unnoticed. At 16, she entered Mount Holyoke Female Seminary, eager to advance her education. But what she learned, right off, was that she was seen as *obdurate*. Mary Lyon, the seminary's founder and director, extolled the *saved* students, the fervent followers of Christ, and urged all girls at Holyoke to follow suit. Miss Lyon had, over her twelve-year reign, organized eleven religious revivals, prompting droves of students to excitedly profess Christ. As part of a small impenitent group in 1847, Emily Dickinson attracted Miss Lyon's unstinting attention. It was probably not by chance that Emily was asked to room with her first cousin, Emily Lavinia Norcross, a final year student who had surrendered herself to Christ the previous term, when religious fervor had swept through the seminary.

In April 1848, Edward Dickinson ordered Emily home from Mount Holyoke after learning of her worsening cough. She missed a month of classes, returned to complete the academic year, then left for good in August. Formal education had ended and Emily, more than likely, felt a sense of relief.

Back home on West Street, she found herself once again in a more relaxed religious setting. Mother (also named Emily) had professed Christ in 1831, but Father and her older brother, Austin, and her sister Vinnie had yet to acknowledge God's grace. Emily was then 17 years old. Father and the doctors were in their third year of fussing over her sickness. We have no way to know what plans she had for her life ahead. We can guess at what she *didn't* want: housekeeping, religious obedience, ordinariness. Her needs were few, but pressing: improved health, self-esteem, recognition, love.

Then she found Ben Newton. Emily Dickinson first met Newton at the time she left for Mount Holyoke, and before returning home for the 1847 Thanksgiving break, she asked if Newton would be there for the holiday.[36] The two may have written after Thanksgiving, and since Edward Dickinson regularly had his law clerks over to the house, Emily surely saw Newton during the two-week winter recess and again in the Spring of 1848, when she came home from the seminary to recuperate from a bad cough. Home for good in August, she and Ben commenced fifteen months of walks and talks and, one suspects, occasional coughing fits. He, too, was consumptive.

Unlike many buttoned-down males of Amherst, Newton was open-minded, warm, enamored of new literature, and enthusiastic about bold female authors such as the Brontës. Emily had been writing and saving poems, and now she shared some of them with Ben. He was dazzled, remarking that, some day, she would be a great poet. *Emily never forgot that comment.*

470

That first Day, when you praised Me, Sweet,
And said that I was strong—
And could be mighty, if I liked—
That Day—the Days among—

Glows central—like a Jewel
Between Diverging Golds—
The Minor One—that gleamed behind—
And Vaster—of the World's. [1862]

The conversations between Emily and Ben were far ranging. They talked of salvation, a concept troubling to Emily. Unitarians like Newton thought of Jesus as an exemplar of human integrity, love and sacrifice, but not necessarily a part of the divine. Most Unitarians felt that people entered the world innocent, not depraved, and deserved a loving God.

Perhaps Emily and Ben shared their uncertainties about heaven—in her wry way, Emily would later use one of her poems to dub heaven "The House of Supposition."[37] She came to think of *eternity* in God's residence as far too stately and static. We can infer that her first preference was life on earth, and after that, it would seem, an *immortality* that would come (for a while) to include Ben, a flight down the ages by entwined spirits.

An age gap separating the two—she was 17, he was 26—was no barrier. Emily and Ben shared a love for literature, nonconforming religious views, and the empathy that flows between any two people who are struggling with similar problems of ill health. Their walks assured privacy, and were *therapeutic*—outdoor exercise was the well-recognized remedy for bad lungs. Ben's playful use of irony must have surprised and delighted Emily; when asked to sign her autograph album, he wrote: "All can write autographs, but few paragraphs; for we are mostly no more than *names.*—B. F. Newton."[38] There was a growing sense of fondness between Emily and Ben, and perhaps something more.

Early in 1849, Emily was given the novel, *Picciola*, the tale of Count de Charney, imprisoned in a fortress named Fenestrella. Charney, hopeless, gives up on religion. One day he spots a plant growing, miraculously, between two paving stones. He carefully tends the flower, naming it Picciola, *little one*. It is a beginning, even in captivity, of his redemption. Emily, at age 18, felt like a prisoner, if prison meant the stuffiness of Amherst, or a life like the one being led by her mother, boxed in by ill health. "I'm a 'Fenestrellan captive,'" she wrote in her thank-you for the book, "if this world be 'Fenestrella,' and within my dungeon yard, up from the silent pavement stones, has come a plant, so frail, & yet so beautiful, I tremble lest it die. Tis the first living thing that has beguiled my solitude, & I take a strange delight in it's society. It's a mysterious plant, & sometimes I fancy that it whispers pleasant things to me—of freedom—and the future."[39]

Writing this, was Emily thinking of Ben Newton?

Did Emily and Ben experience a parting walk and talk in the early Autumn of 1849, during the run-up to Ben's departure for Worcester and a law career? If so, they almost certainly avoided expressions of outright love. Ben had no family pedigree, no college degree, and no immediate income. His health was sub-marginal, and his religious views an affront to almost everyone in Amherst. And even if Ben *had* committed to Emily, it's unlikely that she would have thrown herself into his arms. Life at home had its appeal: Father was seeing to her medical treatment, the ample family library was enlarging, college-age friends of both sexes dropped by regularly. She cherished her playful relationship with her brother, Austin, and she was pleased by the uncomplaining way her younger sister, Vinnie, took on the bulk of the housework.

And then Emily and Ben parted. It is not unusual for any one of us to remember, many years later, the time, the setting, some of the exact words and all of the emotions of the day that someone we loved walked out of our lives. In 1862 Emily Dickinson memorialized a parting scene between two people who apparently meant the world to one another. There's every chance that the poem is autobiographical:

325

There came a Day—at Summer's full—
Entirely for me—
I thought that such—were for the Saints—
Where Resurrections—be—

The Sun—as common—went abroad—
The Flowers—accustomed—blew—
As if no Soul the Solstice passed—
That maketh all things new.

The time was scarce profaned—by speech—
The symbol of a word
Was needless—as a Sacrament—
The Wardrobe—of Our Lord—

Each was to each—the sealed church—
Permitted to commune—this time—
Lest we too awkward—show—
At "Supper of the Lamb."

> The hours slid fast—as hours will—
> Clutched tight—by greedy hands—
> So—faces on two Decks—look back—
> Bound to opposing Lands—
>
> And so—when all the time had failed—
> Without external sound—
> Each—bound the other's Crucifix—
> We gave no other bond—
>
> Sufficient troth—that we shall rise—
> Deposed—at length—the Grave—
> To <u>that</u> New Marriage—
> Justified—through Calvaries of Love! [1862]

Emily read *Jane Eyre* in the weeks before Ben's departure (it's not known if she and Ben discussed the novel). Early in the story, Jane Eyre comes to the realization that her friend, Helen Burns, might be dying. Jane steals into the Lowood School sickroom to be with Helen, who will that night die of tuberculosis. Jane is hard on herself: "Helen was ill … her complaint was consumption … and by consumption I, in my ignorance, understood something mild, which time and care would be sure to alleviate."[40] Charlotte Brontë was warning against denial in the face of grim disease and death, a lesson that Emily Dickinson would learn only after she began to write out her feelings in poems.

Newton left for Worcester that winter. Early on, he sent Emily a handsome volume of Emerson's poems, in which he had marked a number of passages. Writing to a friend, Jane Humphrey, Emily gushed over Newton's gift. Judith Farr intuits that Emily had "a crush on him."[41] Vivian Pollak imagines Jane guessing at "a romance … her thoughts might have reverted to Benjamin Franklin Newton and to the possibility of a secret engagement … Or if Jane's speculations did not extend to a secret engagement, she might have imagined something more tentative, such as an engagement to be engaged, sealed by a series of rapturous embraces."[42] Farr and Pollak are Dickinson scholars, but they're also empaths. A poem (Fr640) written ten years after Newton's death is surely about Newton, and reveals an ongoing grief. It starts off as analysis:

> Death sets a Thing significant
> The Eye had hurried by

and ends in heartache:

> A Book I have—a friend gave—
> Whose Pencil—here and there—

Had notched the place that pleased Him—
At Rest—His fingers are—
Now—when I read—I read not—
For interrupting Tears—
Obliterate the Etchings
Too Costly for Repairs—[1863]

At a time when Emily was entering her twenties, she and Ben exchanged letters for 38 months. One senses Ben lacked the courage to tell Emily he was taking on a wife, Sarah Warner Rugg, for that news in 1851 took her by surprise. Her next letter to Ben must have sizzled, and yet they continued to write. All we know of the contents of the letters (honoring her sister's wishes, Lavinia Dickinson burned the thousands of letters Emily had received over the years) is the gift of Emerson's poems and Ben's promise to join her at the time she proved herself a poet. That promise arrived in the Amherst mail days before Newton died of consumption, in March of 1853. Twenty-three years later, she still remembered the exact wording of Newton's promise: "If I live, I will go to Amherst—if I die, I certainly will."[43]

Ben Newton was gone from her life, but where?

Emily lay low after Newton's death, with one exception. She and Vinnie accepted an invitation to visit Josiah Gilbert Holland in Springfield. Dr. Holland had abandoned medicine to work at the *Springfield Daily Republican*, where Samuel Bowles invited him to become a part owner and co-editor. Holland handled literature and the arts, Bowles political news. Both men became friends to the Dickinson family, and beginning in the late 1850s, Emily wrote often to them and to their wives.

The Hollands were warm, youngish (he was 33, Elizabeth, 27), perceptive and candid. "Emily felt she could speak freely to them," asserts critic David Higgins, "especially since they were neither relatives nor neighbors."[44] Did she open her heart? Did she speak of Newton, of sickness and death, and of God's place in it all? If so, Dr. Holland was the perfect ear. In visits to the Dickinson home, he had occasion to assess, informally, the health of the family, and of the symptoms threatening Emily's mother. And he knew, more sharply than most, the feelings of anguish and bereavement. Eight years earlier, he had witnessed the deaths of all three of his sisters—ages 16, 27, and 29.[45] Two were taken by consumption. Dr. Holland, who had experienced lung problems as a young adult, acted to protect his wife and two daughters from consumption by building "Brightwood" at Springfield's north end, on a hill overlooking the Connecticut River. The chalet was painted in outrageous yellows and reds. An early biographer (ignorant of the infectious nature of consumption), explained Holland's concerns:

... dry soil for a house to stand on, and consequent dry air above it for its inmates to breathe, is a fundamental condition in preventing the development of the seeds of consumption.... Dr. Holland had made up his mind that he would forsake the damp river bank, and so he selected a house on a sandy spot, on which the pine-trees readily grow. As it was not a "fashionable" locality, the remark was made "Who would want to live there, except some hare-brained poet like Dr. Holland?" notwithstanding which remark, his family and himself lived there and thrived.[46]

Emily bonded with the Hollands. Prior to a second visit in 1854, she wrote to Elizabeth Holland: "To live a thousand years would not make me forget the day and night we spent there ... so sweet it means to me."[47] And what did it mean to the Hollands? What did they gain from their discussions with Emily, and from the ensuing correspondence? Dr. Holland could not have known many young women so willing to express doubts about God. Is there some of Emily in "Ruth," his lead character in the long narrative poem, *Bitter-Sweet*, his 1858 best-seller? *Bitter-Sweet* sold 90,000 copies, many in illuminated cloth for six dollars.[48] In 200 pages of blank verse, Holland pictured the Thanksgiving gathering of a New England family, where each person revealed private sorrows and where some wondered why God permitted such pain. He prefaced his tale with a "Song of Doubt":

> The day is quenched, and the sun is fled;
> God has forgotten the world!
> The moon is gone and the stars are dead;
> God has forgotten the world!
>
> Evil has won in the horrid feud
> Of ages with The Throne;
> Evil stands on the neck of Good,
> And rules the world alone.
>
> There is no good; there is no God,
> And Faith is a heartless cheat
> Who bares the back for the Devil's rod,
> And scatters thorns for the feet.
>
> What are prayers in the lips of death,
> Filling and chilling with hail?
> What are prayers but wasted breath
> Beaten back by the gale?
>
> The day is quenched, and sun is fled;
> God has forgotten the world!
> The moon is gone, and the stars are dead;
> God has forgotten the world![49]

The young adult daughter of the family, Ruth, is the poem's principal doubter. "I'm frightened; and I'll never wed unless—I change my mind!"[50] Ruth's ensuing statement is one that Emily Dickinson would have readily endorsed (and perhaps *did* in her talks with Dr. Holland). The reference to God at the conclusion of Ruth's monologue—"if I had His power, / Or He my love, we'd have a different world / From this we live in"—has a Dickinsonian ring:

> I know the world is full of evil things,
> And shudder with the consciousness. I know
> That care has iron crowns for many brows;
> That Calvaries are everywhere, whereon
> Virtue is crucified, and nails and spears
> Draw guiltless blood; that sorrow sits and drinks
> At sweetest hearts, till all their life is dry;
>
> That gentle spirits on the rack of pain
> Grow faint or fierce, and pray and curse by turns;
> That Hell's temptations, clad in Heavenly guise
> And armed with might, lie evermore in wait
> Along life's path, giving assault to all—
> Fatal to most; that Death stalks through the earth,
> Choosing his victims, sparing none at last;
>
> That in each shadow of a pleasant tree
> A grief sits sadly sobbing to its leaves;
> And that beside each fearful soul there walks
> The dim, gaunt phantom of uncertainty,
> Bidding it look before, where none may see,
> And all must go; but I forget it all
> I thrust it from me always when I may;
> Else I should faint with fear, or drown myself
> In pity. God forgive me! but I've thought
> A thousand times that if I had His power,
> Or He my love, we'd have a different world
> From this we live in.[51]

"...the dim, gaunt phantom of uncertainty." When she discloses her thinking in this rush of words, Ruth is alone with her father, Israel, a kind and pious man, a man not unlike Holland himself. He loves his daughter, yet he is disturbed by her unorthodox stance. He attempts to set her straight:

> ISRAEL: These are sinful thoughts,
> My daughter, and too surely indicate
> A willful soul, unreconciled to God.

RUTH: So you have told me often. You have said
That God is just, and I have looked around
to seek the proof in human lot, in vain.
The rain falls kindly on the just man's fields,
But on the unjust man's more kindly still;
And I have never known the winter's blast,
Or the quick lightning, or the pestilence,
Make nice discriminations when let slip
From God's right hand.

ISRAEL: I see that whom God loves
He chastens sorely, but I ask not why.
I only know that God is just and good;
All else is mystery.

RUTH: I know that you are happy; but I shrink
From your blind faith with loathing and with fear.

ISRAEL: God will help you, Ruth.

RUTH: To quench my reason? Can I ask the boon?
My lips would blister with the blasphemy.[52]

Dr. Holland was a genial Christian with little use for rigid Calvinist doctrine. But perhaps with an eye on sales, he ended *Bitter-Sweet* with Ruth reversing her stand and accepting, joyfully, God's will. It was easy—Ruth was an invented character. Emily Dickinson was another matter. Scholars have noted her preference for observed fact. And the facts were stark. Ben Newton died at age 31. Death from pulmonary disease spiked for young adults: although 25 percent of all Massachusetts deaths were attributed to consumption, for those dying between ages 15 and 35, the rate jumped to over 50 percent.[53] The disease—*this ghoul*—feasted on young love, wedding engagements, new marriages, fledgling careers, the joys of parenthood.

What kind of God would so arrange the world?

> Eva ... began to fail rapidly. [Augustine] St. Clare was at last willing to call in medical advice—a thing from which he had always shrunk, because it was the admission of an unwelcome truth.... Marie St. Clare had taken no notice of the child's gradually decaying health and strength, because she was completely absorbed in studying ... new forms of disease to which she believed she herself was a victim....
>
> —Harriet Beecher Stowe, *Uncle Tom's Cabin, or, Life Among the Lowly*, 1852

2. Dread Disease

Emily Dickinson read *Uncle Tom's Cabin* shortly after its publication in March, 1852. The novel's most poignant character, Little Eva, would die of pulmonary tuberculosis. When Emily read of Eva's struggle with disease and death, did she reflect on her own death-in-life circumstance?

> 210
>
> If I should'nt be alive
> When the Robins come,
> Give the one in Red Cravat,
> A Memorial crumb—
>
> If I could'nt thank you,
> Being fast asleep,
> You will know I'm trying
> With my Granite lip! [1861]

It seems that Emily's mother was, like Eva's mother, preoccupied with her own poor health, and apparently unready, unwilling or unable to recognize Emily's consumptive symptoms. This was normal for the times—few people were willing to acknowledge the presence of the malady, either in themselves or in those they loved. Tuberculosis was just too scary. *In fact, it's hard to imagine the rise of Gothic literature in the absence of this iconic disease.* When Harriet Beecher Stowe has Marie St. Clare insist, stridently, that neither she nor Eva is consumptive, she is challenging the reader to recognize a darker truth.

Stowe sees to it that Augustine St. Clare blames his wife. Doting on his adorable only child, he sugarcoats Eva's poor health, blaming her worsening condition on over-rapid growth, a surfeit of excitement and exertion, and extremes in the weather. And to a delicate constitution inherited from her mother. Since these factors are outside his control, he places the responsibility for Eva's decline squarely on his wife, Marie. She has failed, Augustine implies, in her day-to-day supervision of Eva, and in her tainted bloodline. Marie will have none of this, and their marriage, already strained and unpleasant, becomes increasingly rancorous.

Incivility of this sort might have unfolded in the Dickinson household, had Emily's parents been given to caustic comments. But Edward Dickinson was not like the dreamy, loose-mouthed, atheistic, wife-baiting Augustine St. Clare. "My father, you know, came first from New England," cousin Ophelia scolds Augustine, "and he was just such another man as your father,—a regular old Roman,—upright, energetic, noble-minded, with an iron will."[1] Edward Dickinson, too, was a regular old Roman, *upright*, and not the kind to debase a wife in front of the children. Nor was Emily's mother petulant or complaining, like Marie St. Clare. Emily Norcross Dickinson has been labeled a hypochondriac; some critics link her illness to unresolved emotional issues. One portrait, however, a Daguerreotype made in the winter of 1846–47, shows Mrs. Dickinson at age 42, emaciated, skin and bones[2] (the Latin root for consumption is *consumere*, to *use up*, or to *waste away*). At least two of her siblings, and her mother as well, had died of consumption—bringing about a saying in Monson, Massachusetts that the Norcrosses could not raise their girls.[3] Yet no one in Edward Dickinson's household was apparently willing or ready to introduce the C-word, to voice the possibility that Mother might die at any time from a dread disease.

Or, more aptly, from a *condition*. Eva's mother is *in a consumption*. Many doctors then did not see the wasting of the lungs as a separate disease, but a *trap* people fell into, either by hereditary predisposition, constitutional weakness, emotional distress, or in the late stage of another disease. Uncertain of consumption's cause or cure, they were quick to read early symptoms as *anything* else: a cold, "the fever," asthma, a sore throat, weak lungs. A diagnosis of consumption became likely only when the patient began hemorrhaging blood from the lungs. Even then, doctors were reluctant to announce consumption, for their patients sometimes enjoyed remissions—"those deceitful lulls," Stowe observes, "by which her [Eva's] inexorable disease so often beguiles the anxious heart, even on the verge of the grave." Those in remission, clinging to hope, knew the other shoe might fall at any time.

485

> The Whole of it came not at once—
> 'Twas Murder by degrees—
> A Thrust—and then for Life a chance—
> The Bliss to cauterize—

> The Cat reprieves the mouse
> She eases from her teeth
> Just long enough for Hope to teaze—
> Then mashes it to death—
>
> 'Tis Life's award—to die—
> Contenteder if once—
> Than dying half—then rallying
> For consciouser Eclipse—[1862]

Conscious of the Norcross curse and of the deaths by lung disease of his two parents, Squire Dickinson kept a tight rein on his family—no one would fall into consumption on his watch! He was, in vigilance, the opposite of St. Clare. Away from home in 1838, he wrote to his wife: "Don't let Austin be out too much in cold, stormy weather. Emily must not go to school, at all. Keep Lavinia away from croup and fits.... If any of you are unwell, *let me know it*—don't keep it a secret from me. *This I insist upon*...."[4]

This is not to suggest that the family *discussed* the topic of disease. The Dickinson household finessed stress-inducing issues by dividing into five zones of privacy. Deep-seated anxieties were not revealed. "[We] all lived like friendly and absolute monarchs,"[5] Lavinia remembered. Millicent Todd Bingham took this to mean that Dickinson family members each existed "in his own domain.... You were bound to those to whom you gave loyalty and devotion, but with whom you did not share your thoughts."[6] And even if the family *had* talked of illness, what was there to say? Consumption was perplexing: the cause; the cure; reasons why one person died in a week while another lingered on for years, and why a third recovered entirely. "With consumption," Sheila Rothman writes, "there was no way of knowing whether a remission might last for months, years, or decades."[7] In 1856 Emily told Elizabeth Holland: "I ... lay my laughter all away, so that I can sigh. Mother has been an invalid since we came *home*, and ... lies upon the lounge, or sits in her easy chair. I don't know what her sickness is...."[8]

"I don't know what her sickness is...." Perhaps Emily was being frank with Mrs. Holland. No one in New England had a clear picture of consumption, and doctors were genuinely baffled. The *Springfield Republican* reported Deborah Vinal Fiske's death on March 2, 1844. The newspaper's following page displayed an ad for "Mrs. M. N. Gardner's Indian Balsam of Liverwort and Hoarhound," promising to cure "Coughs, Colds, Phthisis, Consumption, Asthma, Whooping Cough, Bronchitis, all Pulmonary complaints and diseases of the Lungs."[9] This clever catalogue of lung diseases (with "Consumption" listed as simply one of many complaints) was standard in all ads for patent medicines, and fixed in the public mind. Doctors were reluctant to diagnose consumption; it was kinder (and more profitable) to treat patients for one of the less alarming lung-related diseases. Physicians knew what Mrs. Gardner knew: there was nothing of real use in their medicine bags.

Consumption's cause was the great guessing game of the 19th century. Everyone knew the list, which included, at the top, heredity, followed (in no particular order) by bad air, common colds, early marriage, stooping, drinking strong liquors, tight lacing, grief, too much or too little exercise, anxiety, bad diet, ill-fated love affairs, chill winter winds, poverty, late weaning, want of rest and sleep, self-abuse, living in cellars, wealth, and (particularly in New England) vampire-like attacks upon living relatives by consumptives recently dead and buried.

Doctors settled on heredity as the root cause—the theory dominated public imagination in America and northern Europe. The frequent occurrence of consumption among members of the same family was "proof" that consumption "ran in families" and was handed down from one generation to another. The children of consumptive parents had the "seeds" of the disease in them; the disease might develop at any time, and could hardly be avoided. An American novel in 1854 featured a consumptive who "had inherited a corresponding delicacy of constitution, and the violent cold resulting from his exposure to the malarious influence of the night, together with the tortures of his mind, tended to hasten the development of the disease lurking in his system.... His step lost its firmness and vigor, his face its fullness, his eye became strangely bright and lustrous, and a crimson spot burned deeply on either cheek. These, with their usual accompaniment, a distressing cough, told of the 'worm i' the bud' wasting its beauty and life."[10]

Giving no thought to infection, relatives and neighbors of Amherst consumptives sat close by their sickbeds, held their hands, and spoke to them of salvation in Christ, all the while exposing themselves to *Mycobacterium tuberculosis*. In England and northern Europe, the response was much the same. In southern Europe the locals took the opposite approach, debunking heredity and believing instead in an earlier theory that people *caught* the disease from those already infected. Frédéric Chopin went South in 1838, seeking the mild climate of Majorca. When the Majorcans learned from his doctors that he was consumptive, they would have nothing to do with him. The novelist George Sand was with him then, and years later she wrote angrily of the humiliation:

> After a month there poor Chopin's disease got worse.... Phthisis [pulmonary TB] is scarce in these climates and is regarded as contagious ... the owner of our small house threw us out immediately and started a suit to compel us to

replaster the house on the pretext that we had contaminated it.... We begged ... a carriage to take us to Palma, from where we wanted to take a ship back home. But even this was refused us, although all our friends had carriages and wealth. We had to go three leagues through deserted side roads in "birlocho," that is, wheelbarrows.

When we arrived in Palma, Chopin had a terrifying hemorrhage; the following day, we boarded the only steamship that comes to the island and which is used to transfer pigs to Barcelona. There was no other way to move out of this wretched country. At the time of leaving the inn in Barcelona, the innkeeper wanted us to pay for Chopin's bed under the pretext that it was infected and that the police had given him orders to burn it.[11]

George Sand, one of Dickinson's "Queens" of literature, was far more robust than the other "queens," Elizabeth Barrett Browning and Charlotte and Emily Brontë. Sand nursed Chopin as he coughed up "basins of blood," yet she lived on to the age of 71, dying in 1876. Had Sand lived on a bit longer, and learned of the German microbiologist Robert Koch's discovery in 1882 of the TB bacillus, she might have realized how lucky she had been, and why the Majorcans had acted as they did.

While it's possible to find a bit of black humor in the Majorcan experience of Chopin and Sand—in the clash of cultures over TB's causes—one can only cringe at the endless list of so-called *cures*. In *Rosedale*, an 1863 novel, a mother rejects advice that she find a doctor for her consumptive daughter: "If we call in our village doctor to see her, he will cup her, and blister her ... till she is scarred from head to foot.... There shall be no murdering done here; so you need not recommend medical advice."[12] John Preston Kellogg (who grew up near Amherst) personified the *Rosedale* story: his first wife, showing signs of consumption, had been bled over and over, and asked to inhale resin fumes sprinkled over live coals—she promptly died. His daughter by a second wife was diagnosed as having *worms*, and was purged—she convulsed and died; an autopsy revealed inflamed lungs. The Kellogg children were purged, cupped, blistered and bled. Disgusted with doctors, Kellogg helped organize and finance a worldwide health reform movement centered in Battle Creek, Michigan.[13] The Kelloggs would come to prefer corn flakes to cupping.

All the treatments for consumption were ineffectual, and some were hideous. There was cod liver oil, chloroform/olive oil for the throat, incessant horseback riding, rest and relaxation, opium (Chopin took his on drops of sugar). Doctors suggested anything: "going South" in search of restorative climates, roughing it in the woods, eating butter made from the cream of cows that grazed in churchyards, wearing flannel, bathing in cold water, smoking cow dung, dancing the waltz, breathing in marine air, etc., etc. Various diets were recommended: some physicians kept their patients starved in order to combat fevers, others tried fattening their patients on a rich diet of eggs and milk (preferably goat's milk or the milk of healthy young women). The poet John Keats was put on a meat-free diet. Losing her battle with TB, Walt Whitman's sister-in-law Mattie alternated between whiskey/raw eggs and lemonade/raw oysters. Worst of all were the *heroic* procedures—bleeding, blistering, cupping, leeching, and purging. Many doctors, fully aware that none of the remedies worked, continued to tout them nonetheless.

Those doing battle with the symptoms of consumption put up with it all. They followed orders, and hoped for the best. Many put their fates in the hands of God. Most, like Emily Dickinson, carried on their lives with quiet courage.

138

To fight aloud, is very brave—
But gallanter, I know
Who charge within the bosom
The Cavalry of Wo—

Who win, and nations do not see—
Who fall—and none observe—
Whose dying eyes, no Country
Regards with patriot love—

We trust, in plumed procession
For such, the Angels go—
Rank after Rank, with even feet—
And Uniforms of snow. [1860]

We know that Emily Dickinson, at age 13, was at the funeral of one of the fallen, Deborah Vinal Fiske. Actively consumptive for half of her 38 years, Deborah Fiske experienced a whipsaw of emotions: *acceptance vs. denial, hope vs. despair, reliance on doctors vs.* frustration at the jumble of medical nostrums. Her letters show TB's impact on decisions, large and small: marriage, number of pregnancies, level of religious commitment, household management, choice of doctors, diet, travel plans, opiate use, and so on. In 1829, Deborah wrote to her father in Boston: "Will you be kind enough to call on Dr. Warren and get him to prescribe something.... I have been troubled with hoarseness morning and evening and slight difficulty of breathing ... inclination to cough.... My diet is beefsteak, rusked bread, rye gingerbread, crush coffee and shells, boiled rice, and wasted apples. I wish you would ask Dr. Warren if he approves of this diet, and whether it would do for me to take bark or something to strengthen me faster.... I ride out; and have walked out since I wrote last, but only a short distance."[14] Dr. Warren's regimen was the customary hodgepodge. He told Deborah that "you have some fever brought on by a cold but ... with careful treatment it will be thrown off in a day or two." Deborah was obedient: "he prescribed a medicine to be taken once in four hours till it operated ... he gave me a powder also to take on going to bed.... I am not allowed to take any meat or broth nothing but porridge or a little tea & ripe fruit...."[15]

It went on, year after year. "Friday I had quite a sick day & ... Dr. Warren came & said it was only owing to the accumulation of phlegm & that an emetic would relieve me.... Today I have applied a blister to my stomach, or rather on my left side. Dr. Warren says I shall be obliged to put one on occasionally for some time.... Aunt Vinal asked him today what he thought of my case & his reply was 'it is nothing critical or peculiar—it is the natural effect of the disease.' ... I am free from pain in my side since the application of the blister & I cough less frequently, but it is such hard work to cough that it creates a pain between my shoulders that is rather uncomfortable & prevents me, on account of increasing it, from doing scarcely any work.... I have written ever so many questions to ask Dr. W.... He says I am better and that going home he thinks will be of decided advantage to me."[16]

Deborah Fiske gave up on Dr. Warren, taking on Dr. Leach in 1836: "I am doing as well as I could expect.... Tomorrow if the weather should be fair, Dr. Leach says I may ride, to go in a hack and go slow.... My cough is about the same. I think Dr. Leach is doing all that can be done ... he says external irritants, proper diet and exercise in the open air will be of more value to me than anything else—the difficulty is a bronchial irritation. I have a blister now upon my chest.... Last night as I lay turning one way and another with my blister, the recollection of those verses 'are not fine sparrows sold for two farthings, and not one of them is forgotten before God' ... did more towards quieting my mind and getting me to sleep than any physician's opiate could have done."[17]

Deborah Fiske died in 1844; the medical merry-go-round spun on for another four decades. Then, on the evening of March 24, 1882, Robert Koch delivered a momentous lecture to the Physiological Society of Berlin. The audience listened intently as he drew their attention to the table in front of him, where he had prepared glass slides of animal and human tissue. "Now—under the microscope the structure of animal tissues, such as the nucleus and its breakdown products, are brown, while the tubercle bacteria are a beautiful blue,"[18] he said. *Blue* because of a new method of staining developed by Koch that revealed what no one had seen before. There, under the microscope, were microscopically small, pickle-shaped bacteria, *Mycobacterium tuberculosis*, the infectious agent of tuberculosis.

Once it became known that people could *catch* consumption from the germs put out by others, debate over its cause ended, the sanatorium movement began, and the long search for an effective cure began. Medical scientists fell into line. Dr. Rudolf Virchow scoffed at hereditary influence. "I dispute this heredity absolutely," he said. "For a course of years I have been pointing out that if we examine the bodies of infants newly born, who have had no life apart from the mother, we find no tuberculosis in them. I am convinced that what looked like tuberculosis in the newly born was none of it tuberculosis."[19] The theory that tuberculosis remained latent in the offspring of consumptive parents was discarded, replaced by the idea that babies were infected in the very acts of maternal love: breast feeding, kisses, the singing of lullabies. In time, medical researchers learned that whenever a person sick with TB coughs, sneezes, or speaks, tiny droplets containing two or three bacteria are released into the air, droplets so small that they can remain air-borne for several hours, some making their way into healthy lungs. To contaminate an area with 3000 *droplets*, an infected person needs only to cough for a bit, sing for a minute, or talk to someone for five minutes. Tuberculosis is contagious only when the infected person is actively sick and showing symptoms: a slight fever, night sweats, weight loss, fatigue, a pain in the chest or side, a dry cough that may lead to a productive cough with blood-stained sputum. Heredity was off the hook; the contagion theory ruled in the 20th century.

Now, a century later, we're learning that heredity may be a factor after all. Researchers at McGill University in 2003 used a mouse model and genome scanning to locate the gene in mice that regulates susceptibility to tuberculosis. McGill scientists infected mice with air-borne bacteria and identified a common gene variant on chromosome 19 in those mice that were susceptible to infection. These mice died before the disease-resilient mice that fought off the bacteria. The hope at McGill is that the same gene will be found in humans who are susceptible to the disease.[20] Perhaps doctors in Emily Dickinson's time were not off base in arguing a hereditary predisposition to active consumption.

Is active tuberculosis both hereditary *and* contagious? If so, Emily Dickinson was early in the crosshairs. After Vinnie was born in 1833, Emily's mother took an unusually long time to recover. It was decided that Mother's younger sister, Lavinia Norcross, would come to Amherst and take Emily, then two years old, back to Monson to live with the Norcrosses for a time. The month-long change may have been of help to Emily's mother, but it placed Emily in a bacteria-rich zone. Lavinia Norcross was in the midst of nursing a widowed sister-in-law, Amanda, who was showing signs of advanced consumption. Amanda's husband, Hiram Norcross, had died of consumption in 1829, leaving Amanda with two children, Emily's playmates for the four weeks in Monson. (The younger of the two playmates, Emily Lavinia Norcross, would later become Emily Dickinson's roommate at Mount Holyoke. Both she and her older brother, William, were among the *daisies* mourned by Dickinson in the early 1850s.) Amanda joined the Norcross family at the supper table until even that became too much. A deathwatch was established, headed by Emily's aunt, Lavinia, who reported back to her older sister in Amherst:

> *May 20* Amanda is as well as when I wrote last—but I am afraid & do believe she will never get well ... she is bled very often—for if there is any change in the weather she is immediately affected—& troubled to breathe—Her lung are very weak—I believe, at heart she thinks it is doubtful how it will terminate.
>
> *May 25* Amanda was not as well—since last Monday she has been confined to her bed & has watches every night.
>
> *May 29* Amanda is now very comfortable—tho' she does not sit but a few minutes at a time—& has watches now—We don't know what to think of her.
>
> *June 11* I can say nothing encouraging about Amanda, she is comfortably sick—tho' the silent destroyer is busy, her flesh wastes & her countenance for several days past looks very bad—you may depend she is no more to see health.[21]

Amanda lived just long enough to remarry in 1836. Lavinia Norcross (the aunt who, in Boston 11 years later, would take in and console a grief-stricken Emily) had been at Amanda's bedside throughout the final agonizing months. In 1860, when Aunt Lavinia at age 48 lost her own long struggle with pulmonary tuberculosis, Emily was devastated.

Starting in the 1860s, Emily Dickinson established a close bond with Aunt Lavinia's two orphaned daughters, Louisa and Frances, writing to them often, nicknaming them Loo and Fanny, and sometimes "Little Cousins." In 1873 she let them in on this startling piece of family lore: "When I was a baby, Father used to take me to the mill for my health. I was then in consumption!"[22] Alfred Habegger, suspicious of this comment, argues that Edward Dickinson would not have been so cavalier with his toddler's health.[23] Norbert Hirschhorn thinks that Emily's recollection may be accurate: "persons whose occupations exposed them to dust of various kinds (lint, metal, stone, for example) were thought to be more susceptible to tuberculosis," but with a "notable exception of the flour miller. Several eminent authors observed that the 'proverbial miller's cough,' induced by floating particles of flour, did not augur tuberculosis; rather, they thought, it may have had the effect of breaking up tubercular abscesses so that they could drain and heal."[24]

Habegger is sure that Emily Dickinson had "several pulmonary episodes as a girl."[25] At age nine she began her schooling at Amherst academy, was an accomplished student, part of a lively circle of girlfriends, and considered one of the wittiest girls in school, a self-proclaimed free spirit. She missed "a great deal of school for reasons of health," in 1838 and 1844, Habegger calculates, but "her longest forced absence was in 1845–46, when ... she was fully enrolled for only eleven weeks."[26] Hirschhorn notes that her tuberculosis became especially bothersome in 1846. "How is your friend Elizabeth Smith this winter," she asked that year in a letter to Abiah Root, "I hope better, though this season is bad for persons who are consumptive."[27]

Emily seems to imply that it is *others* who are consumptive. She is a bit more forthcoming in a subsequent letter to Abiah: "My health was very poor all through the latter part of spring & continued so through the summer.... I was so unwell as to be obliged to leave school. It cost me many a severe struggle to leave my studies & to be considered an invalid, but my health demanded a release from all care.... I had a severe cough for several weeks attended with a difficulty in my throat & general debility. I left school and did nothing for some time excepting to ride and roam in the fields." But then a comment bordering on denial: "I have now entirely got rid of my cough ... & am quite well and strong."[28] Hirschhorn sees Emily's horseback riding as a clue to her disease,[29] since medical writers at that time advocated exercise in the open air on horseback as a way to free the lungs of inflammation and ulceration.

Did Emily Dickinson, at age 15, envision her own death? She alerts Abiah to the danger of "misspent time and wasted hours," writing that she wants to *give time a tongue*. She has so much to say and, apparently, so little time in which to say it. She lays this piece of wisdom on Abiah: "We take no note of Time, but from its loss. T'were wise in men to give it then a tongue. Pay no moment but in just purchase of its worth & what it's worth, ask death beds. They can tell."[30] Six months later, Emily complained to Abiah of being "quite sick" with "influenza ... my cold settled upon my lungs & I had a hard cough for 3 or 4 weeks."[31]

Emily improved enough to enter Mt. Holyoke Seminary in October. "My cough is almost gone & my spirits have wonderfully lightened,"[32] she wrote to Austin. But the cough returned, and in March of 1848, her father called her home from Mount Holyoke. Edward Dickinson "would have had particular cause for alarm," Hirschhorn writes, "when his own daughter found herself with a cough she couldn't shake and pounds that were melting away."[33] The riding "cure" was reinstated, and Dickinson began to dose his daughter. Emily wrote to Abiah: "Father is quite a hand to give medicine, especially if it is not desirable to the patient, and I was dosed for about a month ... without any mercy, till at last out of mere pity my cough went away."[34]

Emily fails to identify the medicine; Hirschhorn guesses cod liver oil, noting that it "was thought to restore a patient's nutrition and hasten weight gain."[35] He may have been right, since cod liver oil is foul tasting and can bring on nausea, which may have been the unpleasantness alluded to by Emily. Another possibility is that the dose was laudanum, either alone or in addition to cod liver oil. Laudanum was the alcoholic tincture of opium commonly used to quiet coughs and bring on sleep. *New England Popular Medicine* (1846), a leading home remedy handbook, urged its use: "The most effective remedies in the cure of cough are opium and emetics. In all cases, where there is a tickly, dry, hacking cough, the person should take twenty or twenty-five drops of laudanum, or the same quantity of the solution of sulphate of morphia, every night."[36] In *The White Death: A History of Tuberculosis* (1999), Thomas Dormandy writes that opium as a sedative "was supreme, allaying fear and making sufferers tolerant of physical pain, resigned to their fate, even happy.... In the context of the threat of consumption, few worried about the risk of addiction."[37] If laudanum had a drawback, it was its tendency to cause constipation. Constipation (along with doctors eager to purge) may have been, in Emily's words, the side effect "not desirable to the patient."

There was no war on drugs in America in the 1840s. The opposite was true: opium was praised as "God's Own Medicine." George Nixon Briggs, the Governor of Massachusetts from 1845 to 1851, went out of his way to bring narcotics to the home of a needy young consumptive at Pittsfield, where he and his family also lived. When Briggs died, his eulogist applauded this behavior:

> Governor Briggs ... would take time to buy the medicine needed by a poor sick girl in the town where he lived, and would ... carry it, himself, to her sickroom, entering her presence with as much deference and dignity as if she had been the proudest lady in the land.... A distressing cough, and the frequent raising of blood, kept her ill for many years.... McMunn's elixir of opium was the only thing that relieved her from excessive coughing, and enabled her to sleep. Of course, she was obliged constantly to increase the dose; and for a few months before her death she used a vial-full a week. In all these three years, I do not think Governor Briggs once failed to renew her supply ... he was in the habit of buying it for her in Boston, a dozen bottles at a time.[38]

Briggs was *honored* for delivering narcotics! Edward Dickinson most likely knew of these missions of mercy, for he served on the Governor's Council in 1845 and 1846, and Briggs was at several Amherst College's commencements (a 16-year-old Emily Dickinson bragged to her friend, Abiah, that "you don't know Govr Briggs & I do"[39]). Edward Dickinson, like almost all Americans at that time, depended upon opiates as the one effective class of medicines. Cynthia Wolff reports that when he died in 1874, "the family angrily debated the cause of death. Though the attending physician had diagnosed a stroke, the Dickinson children contended that Father had died because of the medicine he had been given, opium or morphine, to which, they claimed, he always had an adverse reaction."[40] Why would Emily's father regularly ingest a drug that brought on physical distress? Was he simply obeying his doctors or, like George Briggs, did he believe in the efficacy of opium?

After a month of home care, Emily returned to school. She was determined to complete the school year. Her recuperation at home in Amherst may have made her fearful that she would, like her mother, become known as an *invalid*. In May, she confided to Abiah: "I could not bear to leave teachers and companions before the close of term and go home and be dosed and receive the physician daily, and take warm drinks and be condoled with on the state of health in general by all the old ladies in town."[41] Was Emily Dickinson, at age 17, already planning to escape public notice of her disease? Ten years later, in one of her earliest poems, she hinted at a need to keep a certain secret from the community. The second stanza implies a deadly disease that announces its presence on the face of its victim:

40

I hav'nt told my garden yet—
Lest that should conquer me.
I hav'nt quite the strength now
To break it to the Bee—

I will not name it in the street
For shops w'd stare at me—
That one so shy—so ignorant
Should have the face to die.

The hillsides must not know it—
Where I have rambled so—
Nor tell the loving forests
The day that I shall go—

Nor lisp it at the table—
Nor heedless by the way
Hint that within the Riddle
One will walk today—[1858]

In August of 1848, Emily left Mount Holyoke for good, having completed half the curriculum. Dickinson scholar Jack L. Capps is straightforward in suggesting the reason why: "It was chronic physical illness that interrupted her studies and finally precipitated her ... departure."[42] Emily's bedroom was to be her base of operations for the next 38 years, first on West Street and, after 1855, on Main. She took walks, a number of them with Ben Newton, and late in 1849, as Ben was about to leave, acquired her "shaggy ally," the Newfoundland dog, Carlo, a gift from her father intended, as Dr. Hirschhorn guesses, "to encourage and accompany her on her long [therapeutic] excursions."[43]

In 1851 Emily's cough worsened, and Father was alarmed at her thinness. Emily likened herself to small summer apples, "skin and bones."[44] Hirschhorn wonders why the examining doctors did not zero in on TB: "Along with the annoying, recurrent cough and loss of weight, Emily also apparently experienced hoarseness, another sign, usually of a more advanced state, of the disease."[45]

Dr. Hirschhorn may be missing the point. Even if they had suspected consumption, the doctors had good reason to be tongue-tied in front of Edward Dickinson, Amherst's leading citizen and a man obsessed with inheritance and honor. First, medical wisdom linked TB to hereditary predisposition, and, second, there was no known cure. To tell Squire Dickinson that his daughter was consumptive would be to announce a tainted family line and a doomed offspring. Furthermore, news of consumption in the Dickinson household would have hurt Austin Dickinson's chances for a good marriage, since parents scrutinized a daughter's suitors for evidence of hereditary disease. (The irony is that the socially prominent Austin may not have been so marriageable after all—in 1856 he wed Susan Gilbert, the orphaned daughter of a consumptive mother, Harriet, who had died when Susan was six, and an alcoholic father, Thomas, a tavern-keeper who died four years later.) Doctors' white lies were a way to avoid unpleasant truths, and served to protect *everyone*, the Dickinsons as well as the doctors.

Although a winter in the South for Emily was out of the question, it became clear that some action was needed and, before the cold weather set in, Squire Dickinson agreed to send Emily and Vinnie off to Boston to consult with doctors. The doctor the Dickinson sisters settled upon was James Jackson, reputedly Boston's leading expert on problems of the lungs. Dr. Jackson's views on consumption were spelled out in his *Letters to a Young Physician*, published in 1855:

> Though almost uniformly fatal, the disease differs much in the rapidity of its course ... from eighteen to thirty-six years of age, men and women are very

subject to it ... some melt away at once ... [others] endure it for ten and twenty years, and perhaps longer.... Next to the diet, and of all things most important, is exercise ... exercise on horseback is commended ... working in a garden would suit some persons ... to patients who can bear it well, opium is invaluable.... The opium is useful in diminishing the cough.[46]

For Dr. Jackson, concealing a diagnosis of consumption was *de rigeur*: "It is often dangerous to acknowledge your fear.... [If] you must deceive the patient, do it thoroughly; do not try to save yourself by equivocal expression."[47]

Back in Amherst, Emily used up Dr. Jackson's medicine and wrote to Austin, then living in Boston, for refills. Hirschhorn feels that these early letters suggest a sense of urgency. For two and a half years, Emily pestered Austin to fill and forward "my prescription":

October 7, 1851: I have tried Dr. Jackson's prescription and find myself better for it. I have used it all up now, and wish you would get me some more ... get three or four times the quantity....[48]

October 10, 1851: I thank you for the vial.[49]

November 20, 1851: Are you willing to get me once more, two or three times this prescription, and bring it when you come?[50]

February 6, 1852: ... get me another bottle, of the same size as the others, namely twice the quantity....[51]

February 16, 1852: The vial and flannel came safely....[52]

March 31, 1852: Are you willing to get the bottle filled up again with my medicine?[53]

April 21, 1852: Austin ... have the vial filled, and send it.... I should be very glad.[54]

May 7, 1853: I hope you do not cough mornings.... If you do, go to that Apothecary who gave you something before, and get something to cure it.[55]

June 26, 1853: Austin—are you wiling to get me another bottle of medicine...?[56]

July 10, 1853: I think I had better have another bottle of medicine, tho' I hav'nt used up the other yet.[57]

November 14, 1853: I send my prescription, Austin, and would be glad to have you attend to it for me.[58]

December 20, 1853: Take care of your lungs, Austin—take just what I told you, and pretty soon you will be well.[59]

December 27, 1853: If it won't bother you too much, are you wiling to get me another bottle of my medicine...?[60]

[Thomas Johnson, editor of these *Letters*, comments that the prescription mentioned in the 12/27/53 letter is "for glycerine and water, one part to three parts (ounces), on which ED has written: 'Mr. Burnett, 33. Tremont row. Please send twice the amount prescribed.'"⁶¹]

January 5, 1854: I should like the vial filled, which you took away with you.⁶²

March 14, 1854: And if the cough troubles you follow my prescription, and it will soon get well.⁶³

Hirschhorn accepts as fact that Dr. Jackson's prescription was *glycerin*, though he wonders why Emily ordered the drug from Boston when Amherst had its own apothecaries.⁶⁴ Habegger is also suspicious; he points out that the first the use of glycerin to soothe coughs did not appear in medical journals until 1855, four years *after* Emily's Boston trip.⁶⁵ In 1851, glycerin was limited to *external* use. Johnson confuses matters by ignoring Emily's references to *coughs* and *lungs*, and to *feeling better*: "ED's 'medicine' is a simple skin lotion, prescribed even today [1957] for rough or chapped hands."⁶⁶

Interestingly, no mention of glycerin appears in *Letters to a Young Physician*, a book published *four years after* Emily Dickinson came under Dr. Jackson's care. On the other hand, Dr. Jackson couldn't say enough about opium. He had long touted the drug. In 1814 one of his colleagues asked him for advice on a patient with consumptive symptoms. Jackson was then in his late thirties, already renowned, co-founder of the Boston Medical Library and a full professor at Harvard Medical School. His advice:

This seems to me a case of phthisis pulmonalis ... cases of this kind [are] very unmanageable, but this patient has been less violently affected.... I propose to you the following mode of treatment. First take from him about six to eight ounces of blood. Then blister him largely on the breast. Give him every night a pill containing ... opium ... one third of a grain.... Above all things he should exercise in the open air, to the fullest extent of his ability, whenever the weather is tolerably good.... I prefer riding on horseback.⁶⁷

Almost half a century later, his belief in opium had *deepened*. In *Another Letter to a Young Doctor* (1861), he wrote that opium "relieves pain; this is its greatest power."⁶⁸ "When sleep has been prevented by a cough, it may often be obtained," he suggested, "by an opiate."⁶⁹ "Without opium, I should hardly be willing to practice medicine."⁷⁰

Years earlier, in 1836, another woman from Amherst had been in Boston, seeking Dr. Jackson's help. In 1836, Deborah Fiske gave up on Dr. Leach, and reported that she had requested a "visit from Dr. Jackson.... He examined my lungs and said his opinion was that they are not diseased.... He said it was very important that I should be taking exercise in the open air every day as much as could be taken without uncomfortable weariness.... As to my diet Dr. Jackson tells me to take some animal food, make much use of friction and take some pills every night such as he thinks will have a tendency to remove the irritations in my throat or somewhere below."[71]

On her way to the grave, Mrs. Fiske held the arm of Dr. Jackson:

> I have ... the best of medical advice, opportunity to ride as much as I please.[72]
>
> I applied a blister between my shoulders yesterday morning and feel much better.[73]
>
> I have been told my difficulty is the chronic bronchitis—some sort of obstruction or inflammation in the passages that lead to the lobes of the lungs—this may be cured.[74]
>
> I ride out, eat oysters and go out in the sitting room when I please.[75]
>
> What I suffer from now is a difficulty in breathing that is apt to seize me in the latter part of the evening and towards morning ... when it has been severe I have been able to remove it by an application of what our physicians call the dry cup, over the spot that seems to hinder me from taking a long breath. This mode of cupping is called dry, because it draws no blood. The way in which it is done, is to dip a little piece of paper in alcohol—put it in the blaze of a lamp, throw it into a wine glass and while the paper is burning, apply it very quick to the place you wish to draw, the air being thus exhausted, the glass clings to your flesh, pulls very hard, and makes the place rather sore.[76]
>
> For two or three days [with an ulcerated tooth] I did not sit up but very little, could get no sleep but by opiates.[77]

Through it all, Deborah Fiske kept up hope, buoyed by occasional remissions: "The first pleasant day I am intending to consult Dr. Jackson respecting my hoarseness, it is no worse, and in all other respects I feel much better than when I left home, but I place confidence in his skill."[78] An optimistic letter from Boston to her husband, Nathan, in Amherst:

> I have consulted Dr. Jackson ... his prescription is a mild tonic which he says cannot increase my cough, washing my neck very thoroughly three times a day in the coldest water, and gargling my throat in very cold water several times a day ... this hoarseness has nothing to do with my lungs, but is a weakness, or disordered state of a certain little spot about the opening of the wind pipe ... it is not immediately dangerous.... As to consumption, he said two thirds of my acquaintances were in as much danger of it as I am; he thinks going to a Warm Climate would be of no service, and says I must accustom myself to a variety of temperature, keep out in the air, no matter how cold.... Dr. J. thinks ... the acute ill turns ... might be occasioned by causes very different, but there could be no objection to my mode of removing them by blisters and tartar sores.... Dr. Jackson calculates to have me live some time longer.[79]

Mrs. Fiske had asked about a warmer climate. Everyone believed cold months were the worst. An 1854 novelist played up that notion:

Her health gradually grew still more delicate each month of the dying year; and when winter finally set in ... and when the days grew shorter, and the nights long and silent, she was but the relic of her former self, shadowy and frail as that former self was. She grew sadder and sadder every day, just as the sun grew fainter and fainter. She watched its shadows on her carpet, and felt that her own life was thus fading away.[80]

The metaphor connecting winter and consumption was compelling but untrue. Think of October to March as New England's "cold" months, and April to September as the "warmer" months. Massachusetts death records for the years 1851–1855 reveal that more men died of TB in the "warmer" months each year than in the "cold" months (755 to 752, on the average), a statistic repeated for women (1,111 to 1,055). Far more interesting is that many more females than males died of consumption in those five years 13,013 to 9,058.[81] The disparity is easily explained: women had close, constant contact with *mycobacterium tuberculosis*: they nursed their consumptive relatives and staffed the death watches. The fact that more men than women "went South" (most often in winter) in desperate search of cures may have tweaked the statistic, as well, since a number of male deaths were recorded in Italy or Cuba or New Orleans rather than in Massachusetts. One was Nathan Welby Fiske who, seeking relief from TB in Jerusalem, died there in 1847, making orphans of Helen (later Helen Hunt Jackson) and Ann Fiske.

Deborah Fiske finally saw through Dr. Jackson. An 1842 letter to her cousin: "We are indeed a complicated piece of mechanism, and I sometimes think physicians might as well prescribe for watches that are out of order by looking at them, feeling of them, and harking to their ticking as to prescribe for us without seeing the parts that are diseased. It is a foolish wish because a vain one, but I do wish I could take a peep into Adeline's wind pipe, Ellen's lungs and mine."[82] She wrote to Nathan: "Give my respect to Dr. Gridley.... I have so much more confidence in him than in anybody else.... Dr. Jackson may understand medicine, but nobody understands me like Dr. Gridley, and he is skillful too, he takes right hold of cases without puddling about them till it is too late."[83]

Emily Dickinson, too, was exasperated by medical advice. Samuel Bowles, a family friend, once implied that matters of sickness and recovery were in the hands of God. Emily disagreed. Like Deborah Vinal Fiske, she wanted to get a good look at what was eating at her body.

202

"Faith" is a fine invention
For Gentlemen who <u>see</u>!
But Microscopes are prudent
In an Emergency! [1861]

2. Dread Disease

What James Jackson kept from his patients, he knew in his heart. The year after Deborah Fiske's death, he advised a medical colleague who had written to him about an advanced case of consumption: "I am aware ... in such cases of long continued hemoptysis [hemorrhaging of blood from the lungs], remedies often fail entirely." But physicians cannot admit to being in the dark. Dr. Jackson suggested that a perpetual blister "no larger than a half dollar" be placed upon the breast.[84]

We know Dr. Jackson gave opiates to Mrs. Fiske. Whether he did the same for Emily Dickinson may never be known. Deborah Fiske wrote to others, giving explicit details of her symptoms and treatment and documenting the progression of her pulmonary tuberculosis. In stark contrast, Emily Dickinson's published letters reveal little about her own health, or the health of her mother and other family members. The word *consumption* appears only a few times. Yet she, too, wrote extensively about consumptive illness, *but in slant*, and in her poems.

In 1862, as Dickinson was regaining her strength after a prolonged health crisis, she wrote a telling poem. She had been in bed, ill, for months, perhaps wondering if this siege was the one that would end in death. The poem alludes to the hectic circle on the cheek, compensation for a fading complexion. *Brazilian threads* can, of course, refer to spectacular fall foliage, but the phrase might also signify red streaks of blood in the sputum. At the poem's end, Dickinson shares a dazzling insight: life-threatening illness has its positive side, in that it opens a path to a deeper awareness of self, and to the joys of living on earth.

288

My first well Day—since many ill—
I asked to go abroad,
And take the Sunshine in my hands
And see the things in Pod—

A'blossom just—when I went in
To take my Chance with pain—
Uncertain if myself, or He,
Should prove the strongest One.

The Summer deepened, while we strove—
She put some flowers away—
And Redder cheeked Ones—in their stead—
A fond—illusive way—

To Cheat Herself, it seemed she tried—
As if before a Child
To fade—Tomorrow—Rainbows held
The Sepulchre, could hide.

"So has a Daisy vanished"

She dealt a fashion to the Nut—
She tied the Hoods to Seeds—
She dropped bright scraps of Tint, about—
And left Brazilian Threads

On every shoulder that she met—
Then both her Hands of Haze
Put up—to hide her parting Grace
From our unfitted eyes—

My loss, by sickness—Was it Loss?
Or that Etherial Gain
One earns by measuring the Grave—
Then—measuring the Sun—[1862]

> ... oh! what a triumph it is to die the Christian's death, as did the good Aurelia Lanier! It is a victory, greater, by far, than has ever been achieved upon bloody battle-fields ... the Christian dying in the firm faith of a Saviour's love ... is a victory the like of which cannot be found in all the pomp and glitter of earthly magnificence.
> —Philip Goodwyn, *Lily White*, 1858

3. Impenitence

In *Lily White*, Aurelia Lanier and her daughter, Lily, resolve an emotional stalemate by talking one evening, lovingly, of Christ and redemption. One cannot picture such a scene in the Dickinson household, where the practice was to let sleeping dogs lie. It's unlikely that Emily and her mother were ever really open to one another, especially in the 1850s and early 1860s, when Emily was caught up in disease and death. The poet was dismissive in her 1862 letter to Thomas Wentworth Higginson: "My mother does not care for thought."[1] When Dickinson first met with Higginson, she was disparaging: "Could you tell me what home is? I never had a mother. I suppose a mother is someone to whom you hurry when you are troubled."[2]

It seems that no one in the family hurried with their concerns to Emily Norcross Dickinson. They saw her as *different*. Father had set the rules: Mother was *frail*—no one was to bother her. Edward, too, seems to have followed his own rule, especially in bed. After birthing three children in five years of marriage, Emily Norcross Dickinson never had another. "The reasons for thus abruptly limiting the family," Cynthia Wolff contends, "must have been of life-threatening seriousness, for at that time the only really effective method of birth control available to Edward and his wife was abstinence."[3]

For years, Mother was the sole professing Christian in the Dickinson household. In 1831 she had joined Amherst's First Church, testifying to her obedience to Christ. It would be nineteen years before the next family member took that step—Emily grew to adulthood knowing that Austin, Vinnie and her father were, like herself, unsaved. How *awkward* it must have been whenever Mother's unnamed illness took a turn for the worse. What was there to say? How does an impenitent reach out to one fully prepared to meet her Savior?

Emily Norcross Dickinson had accepted Christ at the persistent urging of her younger sister, Lavinia Norcross. There were advantages to professing Christ; those who refused to be saved were stigmatized as self-centered, pleasure-seeking, bull-headed candidates for eternal damnation. Charles Grandison Finney, President of Oberlin College, preached the subject in 1846:

> I now wish to show what constitutes impenitence.... It is that state of self-seeking into which men not influenced by the Spirit of God, always fall.... It never depends on God—always and only on self ... it is a spirit of self-righteousness. It everywhere and always rejects Christ's righteousness, and goes about to establish its own ... impenitence begins in the selfish preference of its own little interests, to the greater interests of God.... And as ray after ray of light breaks in ... setting forth the claims of God right over against the demands of its own self-gratification, guilt is every moment increasing ... as light increases, the obstinacy of the sinner's mind increases, or he cannot remain in a state of impenitent resistance. He must gird himself up to resist, or he could not withstand the force of this light. How much I have seen of this in revivals of religion. Light pours in—the sense of obligation is quickened—conscience lifts her voice; but the sinner girds himself for desperate resistance, as he never did before.... Often, for a time, sinners almost believe their own lies.... O what guilt this sinner must incur who will fight his way down to hell against such influences put forth by God to save his soul![4]

Religious revivals swept into Amherst in the early 1840s. Emily, twelve years old, wobbled. In a letter to Abiah Root three years later, she described a *mini-conversion*, the "few short moments in which I loved my Saviour ... I determined to devote my whole life to his service.... But the world allured me & and in an unguarded moment I listened to her syren voice. From that moment I seemed to lose my interest in heavenly things by degrees.... I feel that I am sailing upon the brink of an awful precipice, from which I cannot escape."[5] In another letter to Abiah at about the same time, Emily Dickinson again unburdened herself:

> I continually hear Christ calling to me Daughter give me thine heart.... I am continually putting off becoming a Christian. Evil voices lisp in my ear—There is yet time enough.... How ungrateful I am to live along day by day upon Christ's beauty and still be in a state of enmity with him & his cause. Does not Eternity appear dreadful to you. I often get thinking of it and it seems so dark to me that I almost wish there was no Eternity. To think that we must live forever and never cease to be. It seems that Death which all so dread because it launches us upon an unknown world would be a relief to so endless a state of existence.[6]

In September of 1846, Emily confided to Abiah: "I feel I have not yet made my peace with God.... I have perfect confidence in God and his promises & yet I know not why, I feel the world holds a predominant place in my affections. I do not feel that I could give up all for Christ, were I called to die."[7] Seventeen years later, in 1863, she was still holding back, but by then she seemed to know why. In the poem that begins "I reckon—When I count at all—" (Fr533), she ranks her values:

> First—Poets—Then the Sun—
> Then Summer—Then the Heaven of God—
> And then—the List is done—

On second thought, she realizes that poets serve "To Comprehend the Whole— / The Others look a needless Show—." And she explains her reluctance to profess Christ: "It is too difficult a Grace— / To justify the Dream—."

Just how "difficult a Grace" was the process of conversion? Why did Emily resist?

> Conversion [one historian of New England religion explains] consisted of a sequence of clearly mapped-out steps, each of which was accompanied by a powerful emotion that led the penitent from the terror of eternal damnation through redemption to the promise of heavenly salvation. The process of conversion characteristically began in a state of "concern" about the state of one's soul and "inquiry" into what were called the doctrines of salvation propelled by the question "what can I do to be saved?"
>
> This led to a state of acute spiritual "anxiety," marked by deep fear over the prospect of eternal damnation, which in turn grew into an unmistakable sense of "conviction," the heartfelt realization that one stood justly condemned for one's sins and deserved eternal damnation.
>
> Conviction was the terrifying point of recognition that no matter how much one might desire it, there was absolutely nothing one could do to earn salvation. But there was something the penitent could do, indeed, was bound to do. That was to fully repent and surrender unconditionally to God's will to do with as he saw fit and to serve him fully. It was this act of repentance, surrender, and dedication to serving his will that ... was the moment of conversion.[8]

Late in September of 1847, just prior to entering Mount Holyoke Female Seminary, Emily received a letter from her favorite cousin and dear friend, Eliza Coleman. Eliza and her older sister Olivia had been considered the most strikingly beautiful girls in Amherst. They were also consumptive. Their parents had moved the family to Princeton, New Jersey, anticipating a healthier climate. Riding out in her carriage, Olivia had died, quite suddenly. At age nineteen, she was one more Norcross snatched by consumption. A few weeks later, Emily wrote from Mount Holyoke to Abiah Root: "You probably have heard of the death of O. Coleman. How Melancholy!! Eliza. had written me a long letter giving me an account of the death, which is beautiful and affecting."[9]

Mount Holyoke was not an easy fit for Emily Dickinson. Mary Lyon ran the seminary with the goal of maximizing religious conversion. Students were sorted into Christians, "Hopers," and "No-Hopers." Emily attended Miss Lyon's daily devotionals and evangelical lectures and, as a "No-Hoper," endured countless extra meetings. Much has been made of Emily's "no" vote at a meeting to outlaw the "pagan" celebration of Christmas, of the intense on-campus revivals, and of the *snitching* on Emily by her cousin, Emily Lavinia Norcross. Wolff characterizes the religious leveraging at Mount Holyoke as "unremitting and inescapable."[10] Clara Newman Turner reported this item, supposedly told to her by cousin Emily:

> To illustrate the independence and honesty of her convictions,—Miss Lyon, during a time of religious interest in the school, asked all those who wanted to be Christians to rise. The wording of the request was not such as Emily could honestly accede to and she remained seated—the only one who did not rise. In relating the incident to me, she said, "They thought it queer I didn't rise"— adding with a twinkle in the eye, "I thought a lie would be queerer."[11]

Refusing to profess Christ, Emily Dickinson remained an immovable object. The irresistible force was Mary Lyon, equipped with an iron will and a sophisticated array of tactics. The *New England and Yale Review* published this glowing tribute to Lyon after her death in 1849:

> Women who have been trained on the principles which Miss Lyon possessed ... will know their own duty.... The millennium must begin in, and spread from, the nursery.... It is not men of science and letters, nor merchant-princes whose ships are in every sea, nor all the authors of great and valuable improvements in the arts and conveniences of life ... it is the noiseless but effectual care of mothers alone ... sleeping even with the eyes open, nipping vice in the early bud ... commending the right by their own bright example, and shaming the wrong, maintaining God's cause and their own....
>
> One such woman as Miss Lyon is worth a world full of men, to train young ladies for that retired, if you please, but all-important sphere to which the God of Nature and of the Bible has appointed them.... It required her laws, and God's law, to be written on the hearts of the controlling majority of the school. She took care to write them on her pupils' hearts.... They obeyed her, and thought they were governing themselves. With pupils, stiff-necked and rebellious, such a system must, of course, be a failure.[12]

Emily Dickinson, of course, was one of the "stiff-necked." After her health-related "Spring break" in 1848, she resumed her studies, determined

3. Impenitence

to complete what she knew would be her final term. But the pressure began to mount, beginning with the death of her friend Jacob Holt in Amherst. Holt, a professing Christian, had discussed God and salvation with Emily, and she had copied one of his poems into her Bible. On the day after Holt died of consumption, William Fowler (son-in-law of Noah Webster, father of Emily Fowler, widower of Harriet Fowler) preached at Mount Holyoke, aiming his message at the "No-Hopers." Emily was there, and immediately wrote to Abiah Root: "I regret that last term, when the golden opportunity was mine, that I did not give up and become a Christian. It is not now too late, so my friends tell me, so my offended conscience whispers, but it is hard for me to give up the world."[13]

The climax to the story of Emily Dickinson's standoff with Mary Lyon has never been told in detail. On May 18, Emma Washburn, a student in Emily's junior class, took ill at school. The *Mount Holyoke Journal* called it a "difficult case of Lung Fever,"[14] a gentle way to announce that Emma had *quick*, or *galloping* consumption. The deathwatch, taking up one week, served as a perfect teaching moment for Mary Lyon and her staff. The *Mt. Holyoke Journal* stayed with the story:

> [Miss Lyon] commended Miss W. to our prayers, adding that she thought we had occasion to mingle gratitude with our petitions inasmuch, as the dear one thus prostrated, was not selected from those who had no hope.[15]
>
> Our sick one still lingers with us.... To our great surprise, she revived this morning so as to be able to speak considerably. Her words were for a time addressed to her Heavenly Father, asking him to glorify Himself in her death; to sustain her parents; and with the greatest tenderness and earnestness, she sought a blessing on those of our family who are out of Christ.[16]
>
> Our sick one still lingers with us.... Her greatest desire this morning is, to persuade her impenitent friends to flee to Christ.... Miss Lyon read to the weeping family [students and staff] 2. Cor. 5 Chap—and exhorted each to listen to the voice, in which God is now addressing us—Especially would she entreat the impenitent to heed this call.[17]

Emma Washburn was perfect in her tragic role. She was compassionate, highly intelligent and, like Emily Dickinson, musically gifted. Professing Christ at age twelve, she had for the next five years exhorted all others to follow suit. Emma was a model student, but never boastful or competitive. Her needs were secondary to those of her Mt. Holyoke friends and classmates, and she carefully obeyed all the seminary rules, even those she found a bit silly. She adored both her mother and her father, a congregational minister in Suffield, Connecticut, and actively sought their advice. Her last teacher at Holyoke wrote to the grieving parents: "My first impressions were never disappointed. That amiable docility which shone so clearly in her countenance, and was expressed so sweetly in all her deportment, endeared her to us all day by day."[18]

Near the end, Emma told Miss Scott, her teacher, "*I should be perfectly willing to die if my friends were only Christians*, but how can I leave them out of the ark of safety?"[19] Miss Scott quoted Emma: "I must see those of my friends here now, who have not given their hearts to God. Oh, send for them, quick, do send for them now—for if you do not, it may be too late. I want to speak to them, now I am able."[20] An offer Miss Scott could not resist: "Soon, about ten of them came into the room, and stood around her bed. She was much exhausted, and spoke with great difficulty.... Her voice was sweet and peculiar, almost unearthly. She said to them, 'I thought I could say something, but there are so many, too many to be without hope. My companions, I have been with you a little while—now I am going to the mansion prepared for me before the foundation of the world. I don't weep; if I did it would be for joy, I am so happy. I have been very wicked, I am very wicked now; but His mercy endureth forever, *forever, forever*. Do you think how long *forever* is? I know I shall be saved, because his mercy endureth *forever*. Dear girls, you must be where I am—you must come to this; what would you do, if called, with only *four days* for preparation? Jesus loves you—he calls you—will you come to him?'"[21]

Seven days after she first fell ill, Emma was dead.

> After our silent meal ... We sung the verse, "Jesus can make a dying bed." ... In the course of the morning opportunity was given, for all to look at the corpse.[22]
>
> Miss Lyon's theme this morning was the great salvation.... A division has been made, so that Miss Whitman has a meeting with those who have indulged a hope this year, and Miss Scott with all the impenitent.[23]

The Mount Holyoke staff and student body gathered and sang the hymn noted for the line, "Jesus can make a dying bed." It's not likely that Emily joined in:

> Why should we start, and fear to die!
> What tim'rous worms we mortals are!
> Death is the gate of endless joy,
> And yet we dread to enter there.
>
> The pains, the groans, the dying strife
> Fright our approaching souls away;
> Still we shrink back again to life,
> Fond of our prison and our clay.
>
> Oh! if my Lord would come and meet,
> My soul should stretch her wings in haste,
> Fly fearless through death's iron gate,
> Nor feel the terrours as she pass'd.

> Jesus can make a dying bed
> Feel soft as downy pillows are;
> While on his breast I lean my head,
> And breathe my life out sweetly there.[24]

Emily Dickinson, squeezed into this tableau, refused to answer Christ's call. Emma's message was indistinguishable from the one Emily had heard throughout the years: man and woman's loss of free will, and their inborn sinful nature, beginning with the fall of Adam; God's decision to save a select portion of humanity, *the elect*, irrespective of their merits or their faith; Christ's willingness on the cross to bear the full punishment of the elect; the insignificance of life on earth, of human strivings and ambitions, when compared to eternal life in Heaven; the need to profess Christ, to openly and completely take on God's grace.

The problem for Emily at age 17 was not Christ, but God. She identified with Christ, although she never expressed the conviction that he was divine and supreme. Christ was palpable; he had spoken out against injustices, had suffered on the cross, and had sacrificed his life for others. In contrast to Christ, God was unknowable, an abstraction. Christ was wont to hold, to love; God seemed indifferent to human despair. Christ called on those in pain; God was The Lord on High. Emily could not see how the two could be one in the same, and years later, in one of her cleverest poems (Fr615) she morphs God ("a distant—stately Lover who Woos, as He states us—by His Son") into Miles Standish, and Jesus into John Alden, who advances Standish's cause before the fair Priscilla Alden. "Verily, a Vicarious Courtship," Dickinson calls it, and she wonders why Priscilla wouldn't be tempted to "Choose the Envoy—and spurn the 'Groom."

The body of Emma Washburn, double-coffined, was taken home to Suffield. The Washburns, vacationing in Vermont, rushed home, too late to see their daughter alive. Concerned for their feelings (and for Mount Holyoke's reputation), Mary Lyon had Emma's coffin placed in a larger ice-filled one. Miss Scott described the effect: "the precious dust was so perfectly preserved that not the least change had taken place when the parents arrived the following Friday. The countenance was lovely even in death, and a sweet smile was distinctly marked upon the features, so that the appearance was like Emma in a pleasant sleep."[25] Emma's parents were at peace with the outcome. When the Reverend Asahel Cornwell Washburn published a 100-page memorial to his daughter in 1849, he chose to title it *The Young Christian's Victory*.

Imagine Emily's distress. Mount Holyoke was *celebrating* the unexpected and horrific death of an intelligent, caring and talented young woman, and furthermore, using that death to deepen the commitment of professing

Christians and to attract others to the fold. Emma, as much a vibrant personality as Olivia Coleman or Jacob Holt, had been turned (quite willingly, to be sure) into a *function*. The significance of this episode to Emily may be that it served as an early and unforgettable reminder of her *otherness*. She could not have escaped the realization that she was distanced from the larger community. We can speculate on what she found troubling. How could all the others be so certain that pulmonary consumption was central to God's plan? Parents were burying their children, all the while thanking God for watching over the flock. Emily Dickinson had her doubts:

91

Some, too fragile for winter winds
The thoughtful grave encloses—
Tenderly tucking them in from frost
Before their feet are cold—

Never the treasures in her nest
The cautious grave exposes,
Building where schoolboy dare not look,
And sportsman is not bold.

This covert have all the children
Early aged, and often cold,
Sparrows, unnoticed by the Father—
Lambs for whom time had not a fold. [1859]

By August, Emily was home in Amherst, and starting off on her first walks with Ben Newton. Her religious instruction began in earnest, and the next sixteen months with Ben changed her life; Habegger calls the experience a "seismic lurch in her sense of things, a shift from Calvinist depravity and discipline to the immanent dignity of life and the validity of human intuition."[26] Dickinson paid homage to Newton when she wrote to Thomas Higginson in 1862 of "a friend, who taught me Immortality—but venturing too near, himself— he never returned."[27] Was Emily angry with a God who either would not or could not spare someone as decent and valorous as Ben Newton?

245

God permits industrious Angels—
Afternoons—to play—
I met one—forgot my schoolmates—
All—for Him—straightway—

God calls home—the Angels—promptly—
At the Setting Sun—
I missed mine—how <u>dreary</u>—<u>Marbles</u>—
After playing <u>Crown!</u> [1861]

Surprisingly, no Dickinson scholar has seen fit to explore the underpinnings of Ben Newton's religious views. A Unitarian, he attended the Church of the Unity in Worcester,[28] whose first minister was Edward Everett Hale. Hale was a graduate of Harvard, only 24 years old (one year *younger* than Newton) when he was called to the pulpit in Worcester. Hale boasted that the "first time I ever preached in that church, namely May 3, 1846, there was but one person in it who had gray hair ... we were a set of young people, starting on a new church, which had, I assure you, no dust in the pulpit-cushions."[29] Hale led the Church of the Unity for ten years before going to Boston as pastor at the South Congregational (Unitarian) Church for the next 45 years. He wrote dozens of magazine stories, some well-received science fiction, and the classic short novel, "The Man Without a Country." In 1903 he became chaplain of the U. S. Senate, serving in that post until his death in 1909.

In Worcester, Hale stretched Christianity to its humanistic limits. No formal church was ever organized, no creed or covenant adopted. His Sunday school (at the start, 36 children, most under age 9) could not have been more progressive. Hale recalled that "we started out without a library ... in the corner of my study Jo Matthews and I put up some three-cornered shelves, on which I kept about a hundred books such as children like ... and then, as I sat reading, writing, or stood fussing over my fuchsias or labeling the mineralogical specimens, there would come in one or another nice girl or boy, to borrow a "Rollo" or a "Franconia," or to see if Ellen Liston had returned "Amy Herbert." And so we got very good chances to find each other out. It is not a bad plan for a young minister, if he really wants to know what the young folk of his parish are."[30] Each child was there, not to absorb a creed, but to discover and grow into his or her unique character. Child development trumped theology. Hale found validation for his approach in Charlotte Brontë's *Jane Eyre*. He wrote to his mother in 1848: "the event of the week has been 'Jane Eyre.' We talk in this house of nothing else.... I read and re-read it again and again."[31]

Perhaps Ben Newton was at the Church of the Unity on June 28, 1847, when Hale delivered his 154th sermon, "Let Life Teach the Value of Life." By then, the young minister had found his voice. He called on his congregants to review the week that had just passed:

> In that review we compel life to be its own preacher. We turn to that great Gospel of Life which tells us the Good Tidings of a Constant Providence ... which tells us in voices of experience what futures we are to meet.... It teaches of God as he has been—and will be. More simply, it teaches us of ourselves. What we are—where our spirits have come in their training.

We can learn from the faithful study of past life—and from that alone. What do we do? How do we do it? These are the questions that show us what we are—and why ... the exact springs of motive, separate impulses and waves of thought, more engrossing than any romance, more improving than any philosophy ... Let Sunday then—as a day of retrospection—not attempt distant flights, but pass backward only on a few days of our changing, crowded lives ... the Matchless Value of Life—not from Scripture ... but as life itself proclaims it. As Spring herself trumpets it. She shows change upon change—the meanest weed advancing, propagating itself, enlarging.... This Season, though really not more full of life than any Season, is the banner Season of the year to display the life which is in us all. It compels us—as what incident, what change of life does not compel us—to see the absolute value of each instant of our lives! Eternity of course is all valuable. But passing time does not lower, thence, its lessons of life's value. It is the value of life in time, the value of every instant as an advanced signal of Eternity that these passing hours proclaim to us—the value of those hours themselves.

... Ask yourselves—answer to yourselves—of the sweeping value of each incident which you are now looking back upon

Meeting
Parting
Travel
Sickness
Reading
Letters
Accidents
History

—each fraught with results that are eternal.[32]

When Edward Everett Hale listed "Sickness" as a life motif, he was well aware that death by consumption had impacted, in some way, each member of the Church of the Unity. Now he was offering each man and woman there quiet time in which to inventory their feelings. One would expect, in any gathering of Unitarians, little certainty and a range of concerns: sickness as God's punishment ... intentions of marrying someone who was phthisical ... deathbed professions of Christ ... God's choice to let one sicken but not another ... the need to hide the onset of hemorrhage from the lungs ... deaths of innocent children.

Each congregant at the Church of the Unity was invited to work out his or her own theology of sickness and death. That Ben spoke to Emily of Hale's church is plausible, given the fact that they talked often of religion. Emily's family attended the First Church of Christ, Amherst, only forty miles to the west of Worcester, but it might as well have been on the other side of the moon! Calvinists in Amherst followed a fixed theology, even when confronting the morbidity of young children. A religious verse popular at the time exalted the deaths of the very young:

> God took thee in his mercy
> The lamb untouched, untried
> He fought the fight for thee
> He won the victory
> And thou are sanctified.

Mercy was not a term Dickinson would have used to explain the deaths of infants and children, the smallest of the daisies, designated by the tiniest headstones in the cemeteries. Her "assurance of God's love was deeply troubled," Elizabeth Petrino wrote in 1998, "by the deaths of children. Ravaged by tuberculosis and childhood diseases, most children born in the nineteenth century died before reaching adolescence; of these, more than half died before they reached the age of five."[33] Dickinson questioned a belief system whereby babies were brought into the world *sinful*, and she rejected those doctrines of baptism and penitence that doomed some of the little victims to eternal hell. In fact, the very idea of heaven and hell did not sit well with Dickinson. An 1863 poem (Fr1609) begins "Who has not found the Heaven—below— / Will fail of it above." And in an undated prose fragment, she gave thought to this irony: "Paradise is no journey because it is within— but for that very cause though—it is the most Arduous of Journeys...."[34]

In a 2006 article, "Wrestling with silence: Emily Dickinson's Calvinist God," Magdalena Zapedowska writes of Dickinson's quarrel with God, and of

> the ferocity of much of her religious verse, whose sarcasm and resentment are pointed not only at the Calvinist system of belief but also at the Deity himself.... Dickinson defies the Calvinist image of God in poems ... protesting against Jehovah's possessiveness and jealousy, greed and indifference, cruelty and readiness to inflict suffering and death, and, perhaps most fiercely, his sovereign detachment and disrespect for human dignity.... Undermining the dogma of God's benevolence, Dickinson contemplates the terrifying possibility that the metaphysical order is different from Calvinist teaching and that the human individual is left wholly to him/herself, unable to rely on the hostile Deity against the chaos of the universe ... anyone she loved could be taken away by God's whim ... she envisions the hidden, silent God of Calvinism as a cruel experimenter with humanity who refuses to reach out to people with his saving grace but leaves them to grope for faith, testing the limits of their belief and endurance.... As a woman poet privileged by her family's social and financial status but disenfranchised by the patriarchal systems of society and religion, it was in the private realm of poetry that Dickinson could freely stage her combat with God, envisaged variously as the wrestling of equals or a confrontation of human vulnerability with God's indifferent omnipotence.[35]

1752
God is indeed a jealous God—
He cannot bear to see
That we had rather not with Him
But with each other play. [undated]

Her religious views were again put to the test in the early 1850s. Unlike Vinnie, she had not been baptized. She and Austin had not qualified for infant baptism because Calvinists in Amherst insisted that one parent be a full Christian, and Mother's conversion had not occurred until 1831. Edward Dickinson's status as a non-convert was another matter. It's not that he resented his religion. His father, Samuel Fowler Dickinson, had led the movement to create Amherst College as a Western Massachusetts counterweight to religiously liberal Harvard, and Edward continued that family tradition, serving as the college's treasurer for many years. He prayed with his family every day, took them to church on Sunday. He was the pre-eminent member of the community, and beyond reproach. No one dared to challenge his simple assertion that he had yet to feel Christ's call.

Soon after Newton left, a revival swept Amherst. From Ipswich Academy, Vinnie wrote to Austin and Emily: "Oh! Austin, if the Spirit of God has awakened *you*, I entreat you not to grieve it away. Do become a Christian *now*. How beautiful, if *we three* could all believe in Christ.... Does Emily think of these things at all? Oh! that she might!"[36] Emily Fowler sent this warning: "Just now God is reminding us of our duty.... I feel sure that there will be nothing of bravado or sneer about you, or of affectation or indifference—you would be above such miserable pretence. No one can be utterly thoughtless, if they are a spark raised above the brute, and the higher and clearer and more powerful the mind, the more eagerly they will seize wondrous truths—Christ died for sinners, and we are all sinners."[37]

Dozens of Amherst College students converted. Emily Dickinson wrote to Jane Humphrey: "How lonely the world is growing, something so desolate creeps over the spirit and we dont know its name, and it wont go away.... Christ is calling everyone here, all my companions have answered, even my darling Vinnie believes she loves, and trusts him, and I am standing alone in rebellion."[38]

Edward Dickinson was the first to convert, Vinnie was second. Conversion came hard for Austin. He had debunked religion as "a delusion, the bible a fable, life an enigma."[39] Sue Gilbert used their engagement to urge a change in his position. Austin finally caved in, professing Christ in 1856, and going so far as to explicitly annul his earlier statement—he now asserted that the Bible was "*no* fable, that the law of love it commands could have originated in no human breast," and that Christianity was "the happiest brightest, most joyous thing" available to humankind.[40] He and Susan married soon after, and moved into the newly-built Evergreens. Emily was now the family's sole impenitent.

> 1260
>
> Is Heaven a Physician?
> They say that He can heal—
> But Medicine Posthumous
> Is unavailable—
> Is Heaven an Exchequer?
> They speak of what we owe—
> But that negotiation
> I'm not a Party to—[1872]

Richard Chase realized that Dickinson's poetry originates "in the most urgent personal dilemmas," and its "purpose is to relieve suffering, to make pain bearable, and at most to suggest to the suffering soul the final purpose of its travail."[41] Chase never connected Dickinson to chronic illness, and yet he was able to recognize that her poems express "the terrible helplessness and dependence of the child who fears the sky may tumble down on her..."[42] She confesses that 'I live on dread....' The permanent cumulative harm of small injuries, the 'processes' of 'dilapidation,' the small 'leech on the vitals,' one 'anguish in a crowd,' the unrelenting whips that finally slay the heart— these are the substances of life. Yet she thought it still possible, barely so, to endure life and to make it meaningful."[43] Chase imagines the poet's idea of God: "God is the unmoved mover; He wills that we should die; He sends the imperial afflictions which gradually call us to his bosom."[44] Dickinson's world prefigures the world of Franz Kafka, writes Chase, a world of "comic or tragic incongruities,"[45] one in which she is forbidden to know the secrets of God, but in which God easily understands hers.

Kafka was 33 years old when he first coughed up blood, and he suspected that his death would not be far off. "For healthy people," he told a friend, "life is only an unconscious and unavowed flight from the consciousness that one day one must die. Illness is always a warning and a trial of strength. And so illness, pain, suffering are the most important sources of religious feeling."[46] It was only after he was diagnosed with pulmonary tuberculosis that Kafka came to the realization that the healthy and the chronically ill are anchored in places widely separated.

The year before Kafka died, tuberculosis claimed the life of another European writer, Edith Södergran, now recognized as one of Finland's foremost poets. TB took Södergran's father when Edith was 14, and after she, too, developed the disease, she abandoned rhyme and meter and the use of the German, and instead began writing poetry in Swedish in a modernistic style. Some years later, she wrote to a friend: "Surrender yourself to my will, to the sun, to the force of life ... Let life fight to the utmost ... I want to pour over you my living reserves of strength. I am life, the joyous life."[47] In one of her poems (translated into English), she draws a picture of her most intimate companion, *pain*. Södergran explains the gifts that pain bestows "upon her chosen ones":

> She offers us pearls and flowers, she gives us
>   songs and dreams, she gives us a thousand
>   empty kisses, she gives us the one kiss that
>   is real.
> She gives us strange souls and our odd thoughts,
> She gives us all of life's highest winnings:
>   love, solitude, and the face of death.[48]

Stina Katchadourian, who translated Södergran into English, likened her to Dickinson: "Edith had a sister in American literature.... Emily Dickinson wrote: 'I find ecstasy in living: the mere sense of living is joy enough.'"[49] Dickinson and Södergran each threw open their senses to the world about them, conscious of the fact that their days on earth were short. They placed a premium on the value of life, and the need for compassion. Dickinson withdrew from the prevailing religion in Amherst, recoiling from its drumbeat of sin and repentance. Near the end of her life, she shared her feelings in writing with a neighbor: "When Jesus tells us about his Father, we distrust him. When he shows us his Home, we turn away, but when he confides to us that he is 'acquainted with Grief,' we listen, for that also is an Acquaintance of our own."[50] Emily once told cousins Loo and Fanny that "seeing pain one can't relieve makes a demon of one.... Heaven is so cold! It will never look kind to me that God, who causes all, denies such little wishes. It could not hurt His glory, unless it were a lonesome kind. I 'most conclude it is."[51]

In *An Emily Dickinson Encyclopedia*, Beth Maclay Doriani discusses Dickinson's concept of God:

> Most often, she portrayed him as distant, uncaring, even punishing and vindictive, as opposed to her softer, more accessible image of Jesus. In one poem ... God is a coldhearted murderer who sends the frost to assassinate an unwitting flower.... God seems to be a terrifying presence with the power to give and take away.... Overall, Dickinson seemed less able to trust God's power to save than the divine power of human love.[52]

3. Impenitence

There were times when Emily Dickinson wished she had never been born.

>   581
> Of Course—I prayed—
> And did God Care?
> He cared as much as on the Air
> A Bird—had stamped her foot—
> And cried "Give Me"—
> My Reason—Life—
> I had not had—but for Yourself—
> 'Twere better Charity
> To leave me in the Atom's Tomb—
> Merry, and naught, and gay, and numb—
> Than this smart Misery. [1863]

> "Can you now forgive me, dear Juliette?" he faintly asked. "Do you not read the fatal secret that dashed the cup of joy from our lips? Was this wretched body a fit mate for thine?" "Oh, speak not thus to me, George. It was not the body I loved—thy spirit mated mine. See, upon this hand I have ever worn the ring; am I not thy spirit-bride?"
>
> —Edward H. Dixon, *Scenes in the Practice of a New York Surgeon*, 1855

4. Ben Newton

A man and a woman, drawn to one another, but forced to separate by a difficult disease. The man, noble, self-sacrificing, fights to the end to stay alive. The woman knows she will never be his, but cherishes their relationship. It is only at the time of his death that she realizes the depth of her love for him, and she vows to carry on for the two of them, as his "spirit-bride." The story of George and Juliette, yes, but also something of the story of Ben Newton and Emily Dickinson.

Critics have no problem spotting Dickinson's spirit-bride persona. Richard Chase senses the lover to be "rather ghostly. Very little appears to happen to him; she possesses him and the experience he brings her, and she makes the 'marriage' an integral part of her life."[1] Jerome Loving writes of a lover who "had to be embalmed in the memory of her songs in order for her to keep him."[2] Dickinson's sense of immortality, Judith Farr argues, is "full of elation, rapture and self-forgiveness ... it is love, and the painful longing issuing from it, that give Dickinson her vision of eternity."[3] That vision, Farr adds, is a "profound love between two people, the terrible loss of one, and permanent reunion of both in heaven."[4] Cynthia Wolff finds the speaker in Dickinson's poems needing "neither the Divinity nor His Heaven; the lovers can make their own paradise because the beloved is, himself, a sufficient redeemer."[5]

Chase, Loving, Farr and Wolff all stop short of *naming* Dickinson's love interest. As a candidate for that honor, Ben Newton is at a disadvantage: we have no way to know what he looked like. Thousands of visitors to the Dickinson Homestead in Amherst have entered the upstairs front room that, until recently, served as a picture gallery, and have seen likenesses of

Charles Wadsworth, frail, somber and spiritual, and Samuel Bowles, intense, brooding and darkly handsome (images that are routinely included in Dickinson biographies). Docents at the Homestead sometimes inform visitors that one of these two men is Dickinson's love interest, the "Master" to whom she addressed one cryptic letter in 1858 and two more in 1861.

Charles Wadsworth was the happily married Presbyterian minister who stopped by in Amherst to visit Emily Dickinson in 1860 and again, twenty years later, in 1880. Emily is said to have met Wadsworth in 1855, and to have heard him preach, during her two-week stay with Eliza Coleman and the Coleman family in Philadelphia. Evidence that Wadsworth became Dickinson's love interest is thin. Wolff traces this notion back to a tale spun by Vinnie and by Susan Dickinson's daughter, Martha Bianchi, a tale that "became an unsubstantiated staple of the Emily Dickinson legend."[6] In fact, Wolff seems to think that the real significance of the Philadelphia visit was not Emily's brief encounter with Reverend Wadsworth, but her close and prolonged contact with Eliza Coleman:

> When Emily looked into the void just behind life's veil, she apprehended a terrible force of desertion, destruction, and death. It had been thus from the beginning of her life: as an infant, she had encountered death walking the corridors of the Norcross farm; later she had looked upon death in the face of Sophia Holland; eventually, she had seen death's triumph in the contagion that had ravaged the face of her cousin Emily Lavinia Norcross. Even now she could see death lurking in Eliza Coleman's febrile beauty, and Mother's persistent, nameless infirmity merely confirmed this vision of life as a condition always haunted by the presence of death.[7]

Eliza and Emily were very much alike; Richard Sewall characterizes Eliza as "Emily's special friend and admirer."[8] After Eliza departed Amherst following an August, 1854 visit, Emily wrote to their cousin John Graves, a frequent visitor to the Dickinson home when a student at Amherst College: "Quite sad it is when friends go.... Eliza went yesterday morning. I miss her thoughtful eyes."[9] Back home in Philadelphia, Eliza also wrote to Graves:

> In my room is a little place which I call my "poet's corner,"—here I have my desk, & favorite books, & upon the wall I have hung a few faded flowers, & some gems of poetry—From the [August] Harper you sent, I carefully cut "The Long Ago," & this is now ever before me.... Emilie, too, sends me beautiful letters & each one makes me love her more. I know you appreciate her & I think few of her Amherst friends do. They wholly misinterpret her, I believe—[10]

A woman who in 1854 met the Coleman family for the first time wrote to her husband, describing Eliza: "Miss Coleman is a beautiful and accomplished girl but is I fear destined to an early death. Her only sister died at twenty of consumption and their remarkable beauty seems only a symptom of decay."[11] Like Emily, Eliza was caught up in a life-in-death mindset, and this helps to explain why she was so taken by the poem, "The Long Ago." The "Editor's Corner" of *Harper's* did not identify the poem's author, but did supply an introduction: "It requires not especially 'sentiment' to appreciate the lines which ensue. Feeling, deep, true feeling, is their characteristic; and they who look upon the loved and lost who have gone before, will feel them in their 'heart of hearts.'"[12] Eliza may have given thought to her sister, Olivia, when she read the following stanzas in "The Long Ago":

> "There is a magical Isle up the river Time,
> Where the softest of airs are playing;
> There's a cloudless sky and a tropical clime,
> And a song as sweet as a vesper chime,
> And the Junes with the roses are staying.
>
> "And the name of this isle is the Long Ago,
> And we bury our treasures there:
> There are brows of beauty and bosoms of snow—
> There are heaps of dust, but we loved them so!
> There are trinkets and tresses of hair.
>
> "There are fragments of song that nobody sings,
> And a part of an infant's prayer;
> There's a lute unswept, and a harp without strings,
> There are broken vows, and pieces of rings,
> And the garments that she used to wear.
>
> "There are hands that are waved when the fairy shore
> By the mirage is lifted in air;
> And we sometimes hear, through the turbulent roar,
> Sweet voices we heard in the days gone before,
> When the wind down the river is fair."[13]

Emily and Eliza had a lot of catching up to do during Emily's two-week stay with the Colemans in March, 1855. One suspects that, among other things, they compared notes on matters of health and sickness, on good and useless doctors, on what was stocked in their medicine cabinets, and on the condition of their mothers (Eliza's mother was consumptive). And if they attended Arch Street Church that first Sunday, they had another topic to discuss: Charles Wadsworth, Philadelphia's most celebrated preacher. Eliza Coleman was positioned to catch any chatter or gossip about the celebrated and mysterious minister, since her father, Lyman, had been in charge of the Presbyterian Academy in Philadelphia since 1848, mixing with the families at Wadsworth's church. And Wadsworth was the kind of public figure people love to talk about: charismatic in the performance of his duties, but reclusive at all other times. George Whicher sized him up as "ordinarily diffident and reserved. At the Arch Street Church his pulpit was so arranged that he could enter and leave it through the basement and thus avoid greeting his congregation. He would cross the street to escape an encounter that might lead to a casual chat."[14]

Wadsworth's health was problematic; the Philadelphia press reported on his "feeble" physical presence in the pulpit. In 1852 a colleague asked him to write something for publication. Wadsworth's reply mentions a serious health problem: "...nothing could afford me greater pleasure.... But my poor sermons are all in so imperfect a state, and my own health is just now so much impaired that it is altogether out of my power to prepare one for publication."[15]

How much did Eliza know of Charles Wadsworth's health profile, and of the terrible losses he had endured in recent years? His father, Henry Wadsworth, sickened and died at age 48 in 1830; the widow (Charles's mother) remarried in 1834 and relocated to the interior of New York State, leaving the children destitute and homeless. Charles wound up in Union College in Schenectady in 1834 and soon after, at age 20, professed Christ in a Dutch Reformed church. Later that year his sister Mary Ann, age 22, married Rev. William Pitcher. Both Pitcher and Wadsworth had studied at the Princeton Theological Seminary in the 1830s, and both would go on to long careers in Protestant churches. At the start, each was called to preach in the Troy (NY) area, Pitcher (1840–54) at the Reformed Church of the Boght in Cohoes, and Wadsworth (1840–50) at the Second Presbyterian church in Troy, a few miles away on the other side of the Hudson River. Charles must have visited regularly with his sister and brother-in-law, and he probably joined them in special joy at the birth and baptism of Henry Wadsworth Pitcher, his first nephew. Then came the time of trouble, beginning with the death on November 29, 1841 of his sister, Mary Ann Pitcher, at the age of 29. He saw her buried at Crescent Union Cemetery in Halfmoon, just north of where Route 9 now crosses the Mohawk River. Ten days later he returned, this time for the burial of his only nephew, little Henry Wadsworth Pitcher.

Reverend Pitcher remarried, this time to Jane Elizabeth Wadsworth, Charles' only remaining sister. (More than likely, Jane Elizabeth had come to the Troy area to be of assistance to her failing sister and to care for a newborn nephew and, of course, to renew her ties with her brother, Charles.) Jane and William Pitcher's first-born, William, died two weeks after he was born, on March 25, 1845, and he too was buried at Crescent Union. In poor health (there is nothing on record to indicate the disease[s] that took the lives of the Wadsworth sisters), Jane nonetheless gave birth to Evalina, Charles Wadsworth, and her namesake Jane Elizabeth, and began to mother them. The children were only six, four and one years old when Jane Elizabeth Wadsworth Pitcher died at in 1853. Her remains were placed alongside those of her sister, nephew, and infant son.

The *Christian Intelligencer*, a Dutch Reformed publication, ran a memorial to Jane Elizabeth Wadsworth Pitcher in which she was described as "a lady of extraordinary qualities of intellect and heart." It seems that she was much like Emily Dickinson, minus the impenitence and rage:

> Died March 28, at the parsonage, Watervliet, Jane Elizabeth Wadsworth, wife of Rev. William Pitcher, in the 36th year of her age. She was endowed with poetic fancy and fervor ... and had not superior duties forbidden the cultivation of this talent, she might have been distinguished among the bards of the age. But the peculiar grace of her spirit was a warm and devoted piety. Though highly imaginative, she did not yield herself to spiritual vagaries, but strongly affected the practical and beneficent things of religion. The fear of death was entirely taken away.
>
> In life she was favored at different times with remarkable manifestations of the Saviour to the soul. Some of these, enjoyed during her sickness, she declared suspended the sense of suffering, or made it quite tolerable. She ... affirmed that "no consideration except God's right to give her further work to do, would reconcile her to the idea of being restored to health. She was an ardent lover of nature, and delighted to roam amidst its beauties; but she never suffered this taste to interfere with the most diligent performance of her duties as a housekeeper, mother, and a minister's helper. Though uncommonly diffident and retiring, she has left the impress of her character on the church of her love ... [and] in her triumphant death and glorious prospects beyond the grave. May God give the church many such daughters, and to every minister such a wife![16]

Was Wadsworth drawn to Dickinson, in large measure, because she reminded him of Jane Elizabeth? When he stopped in Amherst to see Emily in 1860, was he en route to the Troy area to kneel at the gravesites of his sisters and their babies?

Several months after Wadsworth's death in 1882, his friend James D. Clark wrote to Emily Dickinson, filling her in on details of Wadsworth's earlier life. Emily responded:

> The Griefs of which you speak were unknown to me, though I knew him as a "Man of Sorrow," and once when he seemed almost overpowered by a spasm

of gloom, I said "You are troubled." Shivering as he spoke, "My Life is full of dark secrets," he said. He never spoke of himself, and encroachment I knew would have slain him.[17]

Wadsworth and Dickinson offered each other consolation, for he was another of her *daisies*, one of "those born pure and made perfect through suffering," to use Joseph Lyman's phrase.

The same might be said for Samuel Bowles. The spirited editor of the *Springfield Republican* first visited the Dickinsons in the summer of 1858, and returned for several fun-filled evenings at Evergreens, a fashionable Italianate house commissioned by Edward Dickinson as a wedding gift for Austin and Susan Gilbert Dickinson. Evergreens was only steps from the Dickinson Homestead, and Emily Dickinson came over when Bowles visited. Bowles was a Unitarian; he spoke out for women's rights; his favorite novelist was Charlotte Brontë; he gave *Jane Eyre* as a gift to Sue. Emily found him stimulating, and over the years wrote dozens of letter to him, and to his wife, Mary. Emily tossed the word "Daisy" into these letters, and "Daisy" became one of the nicknames pinned on Emily by Bowles.

Wolff rejects Samuel Bowles as a candidate for Dickinson's "unrequited passion," arguing that "Dickinson sent him at least thirty-seven of her poems, but none was a love poem," and that "her relationship with him is remarkable for the kind of emotional distance that she consistently maintained."[18] Alfred Habegger is in agreement with Wolff, noting that "Bowles entered the poet's life after the generally received date of her first "Master" draft, spring 1858," proving that "he could not have been Master."[19]

If Emily was not in love with Bowles, then why did he crowd her mind? Was it because, like her, he felt death at hand? In 1986, biographer Stephen Weisner indexed Bowles's "chronic poor health": "dyspepsia, bowel difficulties, sciatica, severe headaches (probably migraine), frequent lung problems."[20] The "lung problems" were not only "frequent;" they were almost certainly signs of pulmonary tuberculosis. There are many clues that point in this direction. An earlier biographer (1885), George Merriam, records that Bowles, in his youth, was sent to Louisiana in the winter of 1844–45 because "a weakness of the bowels became severe and chronic, and it was feared that his lungs were in danger."[21] At 18, Bowles was indispensable at the *Springfield Republican*, working alongside his father to put out a daily issue, and yet he was sent off for months to what was thought to be a more salubrious climate. "Going South" in search of better air would seem to be more an issue of lungs than of bowels.

Bowles was always on the lookout for cures. "Against the assaults of disease," Merriam writes, "his chief resources were a careful regimen, horseback exercise, and occasional absences from Springfield."[22] "I am going through a 'crisis,' Bowles wrote to a friend in 1860, when he was 34, "not even twenty-three miles of saddle on Saturday drove it off."[23] Was it indigestion or the fear of a headache or weak bowels or sciatica that drove Bowles to such a frenzy of equine activity? Probably not; more likely, the "crisis" was connected to signs of worsening consumption. The next year, he traveled up the Connecticut River valley to Northampton, where for a month or two he tried the water cure at E. E. Denniston's home for invalids.[24]

Alerting his loyal *Republican* readers in 1862 that he was on a "tour for health,"[25] and that they should expect no dispatches from him, he sailed off to Europe. After short stops in England, France, the Netherlands and Germany, he stayed for two months in the Swiss Alps, a good part of the time in Vevey, a gathering place for well-to-do European and American consumptives. A few years later, when Colorado began to hype its healthful climate, Bowles traveled there, and afterwards wrote that, for those with lung problems, the Denver area was the place to be. He called it the "Switzerland of America."

Refusing to give in to chronic disease, Samuel Bowles made the Springfield *Republican* into one of America's leading newspapers, and earned a national reputation as a social reformer. He would make two more trips to the West, and another trip to Europe, but the pulmonary problem that threatened him in his teenage years was also named as the major cause of the illness that led to his death in 1878, an illness described in the *Republican* as "complications of disorders, arising from congestion of the lungs."[26]

In 1864, Emily Dickinson wrote to Bowles, expressing a deep concern for his health:

> ... Austin told—Saturday morning—that you were not so well. 'Twas Sundown—all day—Saturday—and Sunday.... Teach us to miss you *less*—because the fear to miss you *more*—haunts us—all the time ... We pray for you—every night—a homely shrine—our knee.... Dear friend—don't discourage![27]

Samuel Bowles made his way through a life of pain and disease, the final 20 years under the very watchful eye of Emily Dickinson.

Long before the literary critics opted for Wadsworth or Bowles as Dickinson's love interest, the rumor mill in Amherst had been busy. One legend circulating the village for years was retold by George Whicher in *This Was a Poet*:

> [It] has to do with an early attachment to an eligible young man, whose attentions were forbidden by Emily's father on the ground that the suitor's prospects were not sufficiently hopeful. Gossip specifies a lovers' meeting in

the garden interrupted by lantern light, a stern father ordering the young man off the premises, a defiant Emily promising never to leave her home until her lover could claim her and to wear nothing but white for his sake, and a broken-hearted lover dying after a few years of agonized separation.... [The legend] refers to Emily's friendship with a law student in her father's office during and immediately after her year stay at Mount Holyoke.[28]

Whicher names Ben Newton as that "eligible young man."

Legends aside, we know Newton left Amherst for Worcester in the winter of 1849–50. He and Emily exchanged letters over the next three years, and it seems likely that Emily saved every letter, reading them over and over down through the years. One of Ben's earliest letters delighted Emily, the one enclosed with the book of Emerson's poems. After receiving it, Emily wrote to Jane Humphrey on January 23, 1850: "I can write him in about three weeks, and I *shall*."[29]

Biographers puzzle over her delay in responding. With emotions brimming over, why would she wait *three weeks* before writing back? There is no evidence for the surmise by some critics that Edward Dickinson was then monitoring the correspondence of his nineteen year old. A simpler explanation is that Emily was entertaining romantic notions. *Three weeks from January 23 is Valentine's Day*! Emily was famous among her friends for penning lengthy and high-spirited valentines, and her 1850 "Valentine's Eve" piece could very well have been sent to Newton. There is no addressee. Thomas Johnson, who edited over a thousand Dickinson's letters, guesses the valentine was sent to George Gould, since it appeared in *The Indicator*, an Amherst College publication. Gould, a friend of Emily's brother, Austin, was in the group of students then publishing *The Indicator*.

"Valentine's Eve" opens with a bit of nonsense ("Magnum bonum, 'harum scarum,' zounds et zounds, et war alarum, man reformam, life perfectum, mundum changum, all things flarum?"), then quickly becomes flirtatious:

> Sir, I desire an interview; meet me at sunrise, or sunset, or the new moon— the place is immaterial. In gold, or in purple, or sackcloth—I look not upon the raiment.... In coach, or in wagon, or walking, the equipage far from the man.... I propose, sir, to see you. And not to see merely, but a chat, sir, or a tete-a-tete, a confab, a mingling of opposite minds is what I propose to have. I feel sir that we shall agree.... We will talk over what we have learned in our geographies, and listened to from the pulpit, the press and the Sabbath School....
>
> Our friendship, sir, shall endure till sun and moon shall wane no more.... We'll ... cherish, soothe, watch, wait, doubt, reform, elevate, instruct.... Don't be afraid of it, sir, it wont bite. If it was my Carlo now! The Dog is the noblest work of Art, sir.

But the world is sleeping in ignorance and error, sir, and we must be crowing cocks, and singing larks, and a rising sun to wake her.... We'll build Alms-houses, and transcendental state prisons, and scaffolds—we will blow out the sun, and the moon, and encourage invention. Alpha shall kiss Omega—we will ride up the hill of glory—Hallelujah, all hail![30]

Four factors make it likely that this valentine was enclosed in the letter earmarked for Ben "in about three weeks." First, the mention of *Carlo* certifies that the author is in fact Emily Dickinson, and narrows the field of recipients to male friends aware of the dog. Edward Dickinson presented the Newfoundland to Emily around the time Newton left Amherst, and she named it soon afterward. Perhaps the dog joined them on their final walks; if not, Emily surely mentioned Carlo in her early letters. Second, the mention of a *wagon* or *coach*. Any traveler who required such transportation to reach Amherst must have lived at a considerable distance. Third, the call to social activism, involving *Alms-houses and transcendental state prisons*, raises issues associated with Edward Everett Hale, matters that Emily knew would stir Ben Newton. And fourth, an allusion to the very activity that Emily and Ben had lovingly engaged in—*a chat, sir, or a tete-a-tete, or confab*."

There is no record of Ben returning for that *confab* with Emily (or, for that matter, of Edward Dickinson confronting the couple in the garden). What *is* on record is the wedding on June 4, 1851 of Benjamin F. Newton and Sarah W. Rugg.[31] The newspaper item apparently caught Emily off guard. Writing to Austin, she added a postscript in a larger hand: "*B F N is married*."[32] The Worcester-Amherst correspondence survived this bump in the road, and letters were exchanged for another 20 months. Emily received Ben's final letter only days before his death. When "Newton died with the best of his life before him," Whicher writes, "she felt that death was rioting over helpless mortality."[33] Emily wrote to her brother: "Oh Austin, Newton is dead. The first of my own friends. Pace."[34] Whicher argues that she fell apart: "Her loneliness and depression are discernible in her letters."[35]

Two months after Newton's death, Emily wrote to Austin: "Somehow I am lonely lately—I feel very old every day, and when morning comes and the birds sing, they don't seem to make me as happy as they used to."[36] One senses a dark subtext in this letter. It was years before Emily would find a way to cope with her loss:

719

If He were living—dare I ask—
And how if He be dead—
And so around the Words I went—
Of meeting them—afraid—

> I hinted Changes—Lapse of Time—
> The Surfaces of Years—
> I touched with Caution—lest they crack—
> And show me to my fears—
>
> Reverted to adjoining Lives—
> Adroitly turning out
> Wherever I suspected Graves—
> 'Twas prudenter—I thought—
>
> And He—I pushed—with sudden force—
> In face of the Suspense—
> "Was buried"—"Buried"! "He!"
> My Life just holds the Trench—[1863]

Dickinson critic Paula Bennett is convinced that, after 1853, "Dickinson's letters travel a steady downward path toward suicidal depression.... The letters she wrote to friends and family alike in this period are filled with major and minor complaints. Many are morbid and reeking of nostalgia for a lost, better past.... She avoids old friends, refusing invitations. She recalls and dwells on those who passed away years before, particularly Ben Newton.... She develops a 'box of Phantoms' in which she places the lost ghosts of the past, 'blossoms' she 'will ... gather in Paradise.'"[37]

If Bennett had known of Dickinson's tuberculosis, would she have gone this far? Dealing with a chronic and potentially lethal disease, one that had taken "adjoining Lives," Dickinson had reason to suspect the end was near. The "box of Phantoms" alluded to by Bennett may have included dozens of letters from Newton. What Bennett takes to be suicidal behavior may simply have been Dickinson's willingness to surrender to consumption, in the hope that she might meet up again with Ben.

Forty miles to the east, in Worcester, there were others who felt the loss. The Worcester *Daily Transcript* announced Newton's death:

> We are called upon this morning to record the decease of Benjamin F. Newton, the Government Attorney for this District. He died at his residence in this city yesterday afternoon at 4 o'clock, victim to that unsparing destroyer, consumption, which had long preyed upon his life.... Kind and affable in his intercourse with others, amiable and upright in his character, devoted and faithful in his profession, he had won the confidence and esteem of a large circle of friends in whose affection his memory will be long and tenderly cherished.
>
> Mr. Newton was 32 years of age. For some days past he had been slowly failing, though not so as to excite any new fears on the part of his friends, for his decease had long been anticipated ... only three quarters of an hour before he died, he was sitting up and conversing with a friend, apparently in very much the same state of health in which he had been for many months past.[38]

Three days later, the newspaper supplied more details:

> FUNERAL SOLEMNITIES OF THE LATE B. F. NEWTON—These services were attended at Rev. Mr. Hale's Church, yesterday morning. A large audience was present, including the members of the Worcester County Bar ... the coffin containing the remains of the deceased, accompanied by its train of mourners and friends, was borne into the church ... the prayer by E. E. Hale, together with the funeral melodies of the orchestra, were exceedingly solemn and impressive. We understand the coffin was removed to Northboro for interment.[39]

Why was the burial in Northborough, and not in Worcester? Every Dickinson biographer from Whicher to Habegger has pegged Newton the son of Benjamin Franklin Newton Jr. and Sabra Newton, and the grandson of Benjamin Franklin Newton and Molly Newton, all of Worcester. And, all these years, they've had it wrong! In the Howard Street Cemetery in Northborough is the headstone of *Benjamin Franklin Newton* (d. March 24, 1853), adjacent to headstones with the names *David Newton* and *Beulah J. Newton*. In the space for "Parents" on his 1851 marriage certificate, Ben entered *David* and *Beulah*.[40] Ben Newton was *not* "third generation Worcester." He was from Berlin, a village bordering Northborough, 15 miles to the east of Worcester.

Why does this matter? Newton is paid less and less attention as time passes, in part because he is so undefined. Scholars tend to be quiet or tentative on matters involving him, and understandably so. While accurate vital statistics—parentage, place of birth, age at marriage, children, residence, occupation, income, death, probate—are not the sum of Ben Newton's life, they are a baseline for any serious investigation into his place in Dickinson's life.

At the turn of the 20th century, genealogists Franklin Rice and Ermina Newton Leonard each assumed, incorrectly, that the Benjamin Franklin Newton *born* in the town of Worcester on March 19, 1821 was also the one who *died* there.[41] He wasn't: the Newton born in Worcester lived on to the age of 65, and died in Rhode Island. Somehow, Rice and Leonard lost sight of a *second* Benjamin F. Newton born in 1821, not on March 24 but on September 30, and 15 miles to the east, in the village of Berlin. This is the one who clerked at the Dickinson law firm, who bonded with Emily Dickinson, who married Sarah Rugg, who became state attorney, and who died of consumption on March 24, 1853 at the age of 31 (not 32).

The two B.F. Newtons were fifth cousins. Worcester Newton's great-great-great-great-grandfather was John Newton (b. 1641), brother to Moses Newton (b. 1645), the great-great-great-grandfather of Emily's tutor. John and Moses were sons of Richard Newton, who left England for Massachusetts in 1638, where he helped found the towns of Marlborough and Southborough. *Founders* in those days were also *occupiers*, and Moses Newton became caught up in the Native American insurgency known as King Philip's War. For 60 years, Moses repeated the story of how he was shot in the arm rescuing an elderly woman from attacking savages. He lived to age 90, an unremarkable achievement within his family, for the Newtons were a long-lived clan. Richard Newton died in his 100th year. David Newton, Ben's father, died at age 84, Beulah Johnson Newton, Ben's mother, at 77, and Ben's older siblings, John Flavel and Susan Amelia, at 79 and 74.

But a long life span was not in the cards for Ben. The young man who arrived at the Amherst law office of Edward Dickinson in the autumn of 1847 was, one suspects, already a dying man.

It's time to separate the two Benjamin Franklin Newtons:

Vital Statistic	Benjamin Franklin Newton (1821–86) "Worcester Newton"	Benjamin Franklin Newton (1821–1853) "Emily's Newton"
Date of Birth	March 19, 1821	September 30, 1821
Place of Birth	Worcester, Mass.	Berlin, Mass.
Mother	Sabra (Titus) Newton	Beulah (Johnson) Newton
Father	Benjamin Franklin Newton, Jr.	David Newton
Siblings	Sillistina, b.1809; Fanny, b.1811; Mahala, b.1817; Ann, b.1819; Fayette, b.1823	John Flavel, b. 1809; Susan Amelia, b. 1815
Spouse	Sarah M. Newton of West Boylston, Mass. (1825–1886)	Sarah Warner Rugg of Lancaster, Mass. (1809–1899)
Wedding Date	November 2, 1841	June 4, 1851
Wedding Place	Shrewsbury, Mass.	Fitchburg, Mass.
Children	Gusty, b.1845; Mandana, b.1847; Lafayette, b.1851; Frank, b.1853; Ann, b.1857	None
Occupation	Blacksmith	Lawyer, District Attorney
Residence	Worcester, Mass. Pawtucket, R.I.	Berlin / Northborough, Mass. Worcester, Mass.
Date of Death	April 20, 1886	March 24, 1853
Place of Death	Pawtucket, Rhode Island	Worcester, Massachusetts
Burial Site	Not Discovered	Northborough, Mass.

"Worcester Newton" has no place in the story of Emily Dickinson. He was the fifth of six children, and the oldest son. His grandfather was named Benjamin

Franklin Newton, his father Benjamin Franklin Newton, Jr. Records of the Worcester tax assessor show that Benjamin Newton Jr.'s taxes for 1819 were $4.14, placing him in the bottom third of all taxpayers in town.[42] In 1820, Newton reported a personal income of $1500 and paid even less in taxes, $3.31. In the year Worcester Newton was born, 1821, the family's income dropped by half, to $750. The assessor in 1822 inventoried the family's wealth: 42 acres (16 acres woodland, 26 improved), a house, a barn, and a shop[43] (Data below leads one to think that it was a blacksmith shop).

After 1825, Benjamin Newton, Jr. disappears from the assessor's report. Was it then that he and his family, including a tot named Benjamin Franklin, moved to Rhode Island? Thousands of small farmers abandoned Massachusetts at the time; the opening of the Erie Canal had brought in agricultural products from the fertile areas to the west, depressing food prices. Worcester was hit especially hard, since it was now cheaper to float goods downstream to New York City than to trans-ship them by horse-drawn wagon to Boston. A farmer/blacksmith would suffer income loss in both occupations.

It doesn't pay to guess why the four girls in this relocated family leave no statistical trace, aside from their births. However, one can picture their younger brothers, Benjamin Franklin and Lafayette ("Fayette"), becoming skilled blacksmiths over the next twenty years in Pawtucket, Providence, R.I., as they worked alongside their father. Vital statistics point in this direction. The 1860 federal census for Pawtucket shows a Benjamin F. Newton, age 39, born in Massachusetts, working as a blacksmith. His wife is listed as "Sarah M., age 35," also born in Massachusetts.[44]

We know that "Worcester Newton" lived in Rhode Island from at least 1841, since marriage records in Shrewsbury, Massachusetts show a "Benjamin F. [Newton] of Providence, R.I., and Sarah M. Newton of West Boylston, Nov. 2, 1841."[45] When Whicher ran into this fact, he simply wished it away: "Leonard ... refers to a marriage of Benjamin F. Newton 'of Providence, R.I.' and Sarah M. Newton ... this might conceivably be a first marriage, but is more probably a confusion."[46] The confusion was Whicher's— Worcester Newton's children were all born in Rhode Island. The 1860 census lists Augusta,15, Mandana,13, Lafayette, 9, Frank, 7, and Emily, 4.[47] Worcester Newton died in Pawtucket on April 20, 1886. *Rhode Island Death Records, 1885-1888* lists him as a blacksmith, married, born in Worcester, Massachusetts. Newton's exact age at death: "65 yrs., 1 month & 1 day."[48] The math adds up—his birth date was, indeed, March 19, 1821. Sarah Maria Newton survived her husband by only four months. The two had been married for 44 years.

Center stage now belongs to Emily's "dying tutor." Ben Newton was born in his mother's town, Berlin, next door to Northborough. *Vital Records of Berlin* enters his birth as September 30, 1821.[49] His father, David, was a farmer; the 1850 Federal Census for the town of Berlin shows him in possession of 100 acres, 80 improved, mostly in corn and oats. The property is valued at $4000, farm implements at $50, 5 cows and 3 hogs at $150.[50] These are the assets of a hard-working farm family, one with little cash on hand. We know that Ben Newton was a self-made man, a lawyer who never went to college. Where did he get the money to board in Amherst during his two years of studying and clerking law under Edward Dickinson, and for another year or so in Worcester before he was licensed? In the years prior to his arrival in Amherst, did Newton work to save up a little money, perhaps as a teacher?

We know almost nothing of Ben Newton's life before he showed up in Amherst, but by turning to vital statistics, we can start filling in the blanks. The 1850 Census shows David and Beulah Newton living with a third person, Susan A. Lincoln, age 34, Ben's older sister.[51] Susan Amelia Newton (1815–1889) had been in a childless marriage to Levi Lincoln, a carpenter. Levi, suffering from tuberculosis, died on April 16, 1849,[52] only months before Ben and Emily entered into their final walks and talks, a time when love and commitment may have hung in the air, unstated. If Ben had been thinking of a future with Emily, he may have backed off upon learning of the death, at age 34, of his consumptive brother-in-law. We have no way to know if Ben shared his feelings on any of this with Emily or whether, in fact, he even gave her the news of Levi Lincoln's death. Dickinson's love poems hint at complexities, ambiguities. For the record, Ben left that winter for Worcester, returning to a bereft and grieving sister.

We know at least one event Ben did *not* divulge to Emily—his decision to marry. She read of the June 4, 1851 wedding in the newspaper. The ceremony took place in Fitchburg, miles away from Worcester, and from the families of both bride and groom. Sarah Warner Rugg listed her age as 31, subtracting ten years from her real age.[53] Newton was surely in on this subterfuge. After all, a first marriage involving a bride a decade older than her husband was then almost unheard-of.

Why such a discreet (and suspect) ceremony? Had Ben Newton struck a bargain? George Whicher was the first to suggest that the bride may have been "more nurse than wife."[54] Habegger, building on Whicher's hunch, wonders if Newton's "life insurance may have been her promised remuneration" for Sarah's nursing services.[55] Rugg certainly had the credentials. Living at home in Lancaster, she had cared for a widowed mother, Betsey Warner Rugg, who died in 1846 after a long battle with consumption.[56]

Sarah then joined her younger brother, Asa Warner Rugg, who was in Worcester learning his trade as pianoforte maker. Asa's wife, Margaret Walker, died in 1849 at age 26, leaving behind an infant son, Frank. A likely scenario is that Sarah arrived in Worcester in time to nurse her dying sister-in-law, and stayed on to tend to little Frank.

Only months later, Sarah, Asa and little Frank were in Boston. Here, Sarah first experimented with taking 10 years off her age, perhaps to suggest to landlords a conventional family unit. On September 17, 1850, a census taker in Boston listed Asa W. Rugg, age 34, pianoforte maker, Sarah Rugg, *age* 30, and Francis Rugg, age 2.[57]

A scant 35 weeks after that census entry—a *whirlwind courtship* seems out of the question—Sarah married Ben Newton. A marriage of convenience can sometimes grow into something more. This hardly seems the case for Ben and Sarah. They shared a little place in the center of Worcester, and Ben left each morning to walk the few blocks to his law office or to the county courthouse. After working for a year with Benjamin Franklin Thomas's law firm, he opened his own practice, and a year later, when the state created the Middle District (Worcester County), he became that district's first State Attorney. The *Massachusetts Spy* announced the news on May 26, 1852:

A GOOD APPOINTMENT

Mr. Newton has been, for most of his life, a resident of Worcester County, and probably no man of his years enjoys the respect of a larger circle of friends. In spite of every disadvantage of circumstance, and despite of feeble health, he has conquered obstacles which would have crushed the energies of most men, and made himself, by his own unassisted efforts, a good advocate, and a thorough lawyer.[58]

Throughout his stay in Worcester, Newton corresponded regularly with Emily Dickinson, and his last words to her—"If I live, I will go to Amherst—if I die, I certainly will"—were charged with emotion. It seems that Ben Newton's dying thoughts centered, not on his wife, but on a certain young lady in Amherst. In fact, it looks like he cared about everyone *except* Sarah. He had enjoyed camaraderie with his fellow lawyers, and had become widely admired for his personal integrity and love of life. Two days after Newton's burial in Northborough, the *Daily Transcript* granted a "Friend" his say:

When I looked up, all was still. Before the altar rested a plain, neat coffin which contained the remains of him, who, for thirty-two years, had struggled bravely on, had surmounted obstacles manfully, had marched forward with the dignity of noble worth, and had shared the sweet intercourse of love and friendship among friends who now do grateful homage to his memory.

4. Ben Newton

I felt sad for my farewell look; for his hopes were big, his aims high, truthful and sincere; he was firm in purpose, refined in his tastes, social, and apt in conversation, a worker in his profession, enjoying the well-earned fruits of his toil, with the prospect of "the splendor of honest wealth" and station as his own. He enjoyed life in its truest, simplest and loveliest forms, and to relinquish all and say of his earthly career, "'tis finished," must have been hard indeed. Still it was done without a murmur; the calm and peaceful spirit of a truly good and virtuous man was traced in his every feature.[59]

It's obvious that Ben Newton was a very special kind of person. And yet, knowing he was likely to die at any time, this "truly good and virtuous man" did not provide for his wife's future well being. Habegger was in error in thinking that Newton's life insurance was part of a marriage bargain. Newton's policy did not include any amount for Sarah; the *Daily Transcript*, correcting their earlier story (the one used by Habegger), explained that the $500 policy, obtained "some years since," was "for the benefit of a brother-in-law, Mr. [Levi] Lincoln, now deceased. The insurance now falls to the widow of Mr. Lincoln."[60] That widow was Ben's sister, Susan Amelia. A small fortune to the sibling, and not a penny to the wife. Whether this was an uncaring act on Newton's part depends on the understanding that he and Sarah Rugg had entered into in 1851.

Which raises another question: Why didn't Newton prepare a will? He must have known the ordeal awaiting the survivors of those who died intestate. In the months following Newton's death, Sarah Rugg Newton was put through the legal wringer. As the widow, she was appointed administrator of the estate, and ordered to draw up a complete list of Newton's personal estate (he had no real estate), and to have the list appraised. She completed the task in a week:

1 Sofa	15.00		1 Silver Watch	5.00
3 Chairs	9.00		1 Case Drawers	1.00
1 Cntr. Table	7.00		1 Round Table	.75
1 Mirror	8.00		1 Cherry Table	1.25
1 Parlour Carpet	20.00		1 Pine Table	1.00
1 Candelabra	3.00		1 Clock	1.00
4 Curtains	3.00		1 Clothes Frame	.50
1 Bedstead	3.00		3 Kitchen Chairs	1.00
1 Hair Mattress	8.00		1 Refrigerator	5.00
1 Feather Bed	20.00		1 Cooking Pan	2.00
1 Stool Chair	1.00		3 Stone Pots	1.00
1 Looking Glass	.75		Baskets, Brooms, Etc.	1.50
1 Air-Tight Stove	1.50		1 Silver Tea Set	5.00
1 Washstand/Ewer	2.00		Plated Spoons	3.00

1 Trunk	1.50	Table Cutlery	5.00
1 Extension Table	7.50	Glass Ware	5.00
1 Lounge	5.00	Crockery Ware	15.00
1 Glass	2.50	1 Tea Pot	1.50
6 Cane-Seat Chairs	4.50	Tin Ware	2.00
1 Easy Chair	5.00	8 Demijohns	2.00
1 Stove	4.00	Cans, Pails, Baskets	1.00
1 Easy Chair	1.50	Articles in Store Room	1.50
1 Carpet/Oil Cloth	10.00	Iron Ware	1.00
3 Curtains/Fixtures	1.50	Law Books	20.00
1 Work Stand	1.50	1 Office Desk	5.00
1 Portable Desk	2.00	Wearing Apparel	50.00
1 Mattress/Bedding	10.00	Money	50.00[61]

That was it. A modest rental on Southbridge Street, near the courthouse. Functional, bare-bones. Perhaps three rooms in all. Dying men do not invest in real estate. Newton was pulling in a good salary for about a year as District Attorney, and apparently was spending much of it on clothing (to accommodate his weight loss?) and perhaps on evenings out with his comrades.

It's difficult to know what to make of the two mattresses and sets of bedding.

The Worcester County Probate Court accepted the list, valued at about $400, and decided to grant Sarah $200, "a reasonable allowance out of the personal estate."[62] The court now asked creditors to step forward, and eventually certified their claims. Claims, of course, that came at the expense of Sarah Rugg Newton, the widow. The creditors showed no mercy. Benjamin Franklin Thomas, the Worcester lawyer who first hired Newton, was owed $40.87; Dwight Foster, a lawyer who assisted Sarah through the legal thicket, wanted $122.74; attorneys Henry Dwight Stone and Charles Hartshorn asked for $54.22 and $20.50 respectively; a hatter, James S. Kettell, demanded $17.82; the clothing firm of Macullar & Williams was owed $64.10; a tailor, Joseph Partridge, was apparently willing to cut back a dying man's suits, but not his bill for services, which came to $60.50. The probate took many months, and realtor Lovell Baker asked for 70.74, probably for back rent. *Even Newton's mother got into the act!* Beulah Newton hit up her daughter-in-law for debts of $36.90 and $11.40.[63] What does *that* say about the nature of the marriage!

Sereno D. Hunt put in the largest claim, $400.01, and another for $43.00.[64] Of all the probate entries, these items catch the eye and stir the imagination. Sereno Dwight Hunt was 15 months younger than Ben Newton, and seems to have been, like Newton, an intellectual, and dedicated to his profession. He was a life-long educator, and the principal of Concord High School from 1847 to 1855. His annual salary for the school year 1850–51 was $590, by far the most paid to any of the town's educators,[65] but not the sort of income that would encourage a loan of $443.

In 1854 Hunt married Sarah Stacy, 23, the daughter of John Stacy,[66] who for many years was in the mix with Ralph Waldo Emerson and Henry David Thoreau. Stacy was owner of the bookstore in the Milldam section of Concord, and for three decades he ran the day-to-day activities of the members-only Concord Social Library. Emerson served the library in a number of capacities, and for one year was its president. As librarian, John Stacy bought most of the Social Library books and in the 1840s was also the library's treasurer. He was in frequent direct contact with Ralph Waldo Emerson, and he apparently hired Thoreau to survey a plot of land he had given to his daughter, Sarah, who at the time was about to wed Hunt.

Hunt ended his domain at Concord High School on a sad note. The April 1855 report by the School Committee of the Town of Concord announced that Hunt would not return to run the high school in the fall. The report also included this testimonial to Hunt's talents and depth of character:

HIGH SCHOOL
Mr. S. D. Hunt, Teacher

The year just closed completes the eighth of Mr. Hunt's connection with this School. During this period he has established a high reputation as an able, faithful and successful teacher ... and we are persuaded that it is owing, in a great degree, to his fidelity and perseverance, and the excellent moral influence which he has exercised over his pupils, that the school has attained its present high rank. But both the scholars and the studies have become so numerous that, for a long time, Mr. Hunt had felt he could do justice neither to himself of to the School without the aid of an assistant ... [and] that, unless this evil could be remedied, he should not be willing to take the school again....

We cannot refrain from expressing our sincere regret at the result. We believe that, in not being able to retain the services of so valuable a teacher, the town will sustain a great, and we feel, irreparable loss.... The sincere respect and strong attachment of his former pupils to him ... are among the gratifying tokens of the high esteem in which he is held ... he will carry with him the best wishes of the entire community.[67]

Sereno Hunt did not really need the $104.20 he ultimately received from Newton's estate in October, 1854—by then he was married for two months to Sarah, and (perhaps with financial help from John Stacy) pursuing an exciting new venture. He opened North Bridgewater Academy, spending $2000 for a vacant building and another $3000 for renovations to make it a modern and well-equipped school. The Academy operated four terms a year for nine years, averaging 75 students per term.[68] When it closed in 1864, Hunt was 41 years old. He would teach and administrate in area schools for the next three decades.

We may never know how Newton met Hunt, or why he owed Hunt so much money. A logical guess is that Hunt helped to bankroll Newton's law studies. Sudbury, Hunt's hometown, was only twelve miles from Newton's home in Berlin, and Concord a few miles beyond. Newton may have been referred to Hunt by members of the Puffer Family. Reverend Reuben Puffer, a Harvard graduate, came from Sudbury to Berlin in 1781, where he was an ordained minister at Berlin's Congregational church, and continued as pastor there until his death in 1829. Reverend Puffer's firstborn, Sophia Puffer (1780–1857), married a man in neighboring Northborough. Perhaps she was the go-between, since her cousin in Sudbury, also named Sophia Puffer (1794–1874), was the mother of Sereno Dwight Hunt.

Both Sereno Hunt and Ben Newton were born into families of hard-working farmers, and both had to make their own careers. In the 1840s, many would-be lawyers and doctors from low-income families dabbled in teaching to help finance their professional studies. Sereno Hunt took up teaching, loved it, and made it his life's work. The likelihood is that he helped Newton obtain a teaching position somewhere in the area, at the very time (1843–47) when Thoreau and Emerson were coming into prominence. Thoreau was setting up his cabin on Walden Pond, lecturing at the Concord Lyceum ("John Carlyle" in 1846, "History of Myself" in 1847), getting arrested and jailed after failing to pay taxes in protest against the Mexican War. Emerson, who had already known as an essayist and lecturer, was the author of a new book of poems, one copy of which Ben, not long after, gave as a parting gift to Emily. We know from her own words that Ben tutored her in Immortality. Did he also share with her an enthusiasm for Thoreau and Emerson?

Whatever the depth and circumstances of their relationship, Hunt's claim for $443.01 raised the Newton estate's liability to $1031.29. Even though Sarah Rugg received the balance of the salary owed to Newton and some fees from cases he had settled privately, the estate was ultimately valued at only $263.50. The Court declared that Newton had died insolvent, and therefore reduced all the creditor's claims by 80 percent. On October 3, 1854, a year and a half after her husband's death, and after she had dutifully prepared for and attended the prolonged probate, the widow Newton was left with $200.⁶⁹ The community that so adored her husband had not rallied to her side.

In fact, Sarah was now homeless. Her parents and sister were dead, a second brother lived outside the area, and Asa Warner Rugg was in Boston's South End, the thriving center of the American piano industry, where he boarded close to piano-making factories. *The Boston, Massachusetts City Record and Business Directory for 1860* placed him at 753 Tremont Street in Brookline,⁷⁰ a few doors from the celebrated firm of Chickering & Sons, a building complex that covered five acres (only the Capitol in D.C. was larger) employing 400 men and producing 60 pianos a week. Asa, gainfully employed, did not extend a welcoming hand to his sister. He married again in 1858, to Mary E. Lynde, and two years later they had a child. Asa Rugg built an estate worth $5000. The 1870 Federal Census places him as a manufacturer of piano reeds, living with wife Mary and son Edward in Worcester.⁷¹ He died there in 1876.

Sarah Rugg Newton's life took a different turn. Following Newton's death, she returned to Lancaster. In 1860 she was living with her paternal aunt, Polly Rugg Warner, 78. Nathaniel Warner, 75, Polly's husband, worked a farm worth only $2000. Living with the elderly Warners were Oliver Warner Carter, 24, and Sarah Frances Carter, 21, two grandchildren who had been deserted by their father after their mother died. All four were listed by the census as "farm laborers." Also listed (with her correct age) was "Sarah Newton, 50," no occupation.⁷² It cannot have been a happy quintet. Twenty years later, in 1880, the household had dwindled to three people: O. W. Carter, a "farmer" age 44, his sister, Sarah S. Carter, 41, "keeping house," and a Sarah W. Newton, age 70 (again, correct), "no occupation."⁷³ Sarah became, in essence, a ward of the Carter family for over a quarter century. She lived on to age 90, dying in 1899.

Newton lived with Sarah Rugg for 21 months. He knew Emily Dickinson three times as long, and over that time he had become, as Whicher puts it, "particularly dear to her."⁷⁴ It would take her years to come to terms with his death. In a number of her poems, she seems to revisit their relationship:

712

I could suffice for Him, I knew—
He—could suffice for Me—
Yet Hesitating Fractions—Both
Surveyed Infinity—

"Would I be Whole" He sudden broached—
My Syllable rebelled—
'Twas face to face with Nature—forced—
'Twas face to face with God—

> Withdrew the Sun—to other Wests—
> Withdrew the furthest Star
> Before Decision—stooped to speech—
> And then—be audibler
>
> The Answer of the Sea unto
> The Motion of the Moon—
> Herself adjust Her Tides—unto—
> Could I—do else—with Mine? [1863]

Ten months after Ben's death, Emily felt the need to send a letter off to Edward Everett Hale at the Church of the Unity in Worcester. Apparently, she knew that Ben had gone to church there:

> Rev. Mr Hale—
> Pardon the liberty, Sir, which a stranger takes in addressing you.... I think, Sir, you were the Pastor of Mr B. F. Newton, who died sometime since in Worcester, and I often have hoped to know if his last hours were cheerful, and if he was willing to die.... You may think my desire strange, Sir, but the Dead was dear to me, and I would love to know that he sleeps peacefully.
> Mr. Newton was with my Father two years, before going to Worcester—in pursuing his studies, and was much in our family.... Mr. Newton became to me a gentle, yet grave Preceptor, teaching me what to read, what authors to admire, what was most grand or beautiful in nature, and that sublimer lesson, a faith in things unseen ... he taught me of them all, earnestly, tenderly, and when he went from us, it was as an elder brother, loved indeed very much, and mourned, and remembered. During his life in Worcester he often wrote to me, and I replied to his letters—I always asked for his health, and he answered so cheerfully, that while I knew he was ill, his death indeed surprised me. He often talked of God, but I do not know certainly if he was his Father in Heaven—Please, Sir, to tell me if he was willing to die, and if you think him at Home, I should love so much to know certainly, that he was today in Heaven....
>
> Yours very respectfully,
> Emily E. Dickinson[75]

"This is no perfunctory letter of pious inquiry," Whicher observes, "Emily's words throb with a scarcely restrained emotion. They leave no doubt of Newton's importance to her at the most impressionable period of her life."[76] Emily Dickinson grieved for half a decade before settling upon a means to honor and sustain her relationship with Ben Newton. It seems she took on the role of *spirit*-bride, and that many of her early poems (1858–1863) can be read as attempts to keep in touch with Ben. Emily hinted at this posthumous relationship, not entirely strange in her day, in a letter to Louise and Frances Norcross. After noting that Robert Browning had "made another poem" (so soon after the 1861 death of his beloved wife, Elizabeth Barrett Browning), she told her cousins she was "astonished—till I remembered that I, myself, in my smaller way, sang off charnel steps."[77] This analogy only makes sense in the context of Newton's death. As curious as it may seem, Newton's importance to Emily *intensified* in the years following his death.

Her ongoing grief shows up in the poems. Almost a decade after her letter petitioning Reverend Hale for details on Ben's death, Emily wrote "To know just how he suffered—would be dear." Despite striking similarities between that poem and the earlier letter to Hale, Dickinson scholars have never linked the two pieces of writing.

688

To know just how He suffered—would be dear—
To know if any Human eyes were near
To whom He could entrust His wavering gaze—
Until it settled broad—on Paradise—

To know if He was patient—part content—
Was Dying as He thought—or different—
Was it a pleasant Day to die—
And did the Sunshine face His way—

What was His furthest mind—of Home—or God—
Or What the Distant say—
At News that He ceased Human Nature
Such a Day—

And Wishes—Had He any—
Just His Sigh—accented—
Had been legible—to Me—
And was He Confident until
Ill fluttered out—in Everlasting Well—

And if He spoke—What name was Best—
What last
What one broke off with
At the Drowsiest—

Was he afraid—or tranquil—
Might He know
How Conscious Consciousness—could grow—
Till Love that was—and Love too best to be—
Meet—and the Junction be Eternity [1863]

"My dying Tutor told me he would like to live till I Had been a poet," she wrote to Higginson in 1862, "but Death was much of Mob as I could master—then—and when far afterward—a sudden light on the Orchard, or a new fashion in the wind troubled my attention—I felt a palsy, here—the Verses just relieve."[78] Judith Farr finds this comment significant:

> Dickinson's tutor was Benjamin Franklin Newton ... the loss of one who so believed in her delayed her growth as a poet. She had to grieve before she could continue to develop (and the grief was itself a means of developing) ... she connects her anguish over Newton with the Palsy she feels in seeing a "sudden light in Orchards" or "a new fashion in the wind." His passing, like the experience of seeing light or feeling wind, was apocalyptic.[79]

Emily's reference to *palsy* is in line with a maxim of the mid-1800s: love troubles lead to crises of health, and worse. *Palsy* is rooted in the French word for *paralysis*. Today, it might be called *depression* (the fourth of five stages in the cycle of grief). Dickinson's Mount Holyoke anatomy textbook saw it more like a *broken heart*: "If the brain be depressed by grief, tormented by anxiety, or absorbed in abstract thought ... the lungs are not so fully inflated ... [this is] followed by the deposition of tuberculous matter in different parts of the system and the individual dies of scrofula or consumption."[80] Emily's generation was awash in stories of doomed romances and consumptive deaths.

In fact, one doomed romance involved her friend, Emily Fowler, about at the time Dickinson was writing to Reverend Hale. Emily Fowler had often visited with Vinnie and Emily in the early 1850s, and the sisters were well aware of the crisis in her life. William Fowler had not approved of his daughter's fiancé, Francis Andrew March, but Emily Fowler was holding fast. Then March started to hemorrhage from the lungs. He left his job and, in an act of chivalry, released Emily Fowler from the engagement. Like many consumptives with money, he set sail for the South. Emily Dickinson expected her friend to stand by Francis March in his time of trouble. Instead, Emily Fowler entered into a swift courtship with Gordon Ford, her ex-fiancé's wealthy Wall Street partner. The newly engaged couple stopped by to visit the Dickinson sisters, much to Emily's distress. Her heart went out to Francis March, who was in a desperate fight for his life in Cuba.

Emily ridiculed Ford in a letter to Austin written three months after Newton's death, calling him a "popinjay."[81] A *popinjay*, of course, is a parrot, but Noah Webster (Emily Fowler's grandfather and Emily Dickinson's lexicographer) had come up with the definition Dickinson must have had in mind: "A gay, trifling young man; a fop or coxcomb."[82] And *coxcomb*? Webster: "A fop; a vain showy fellow; a superficial pretender to knowledge or accomplishments."[83]

When Emily Fowler and Gordon Ford married, one Mount Holyoke graduate promptly wrote to her sister: "I hear that Emily Fowler is married but not to Mr. March—It seems cruel that she should desert him so—It is true that he broke off the engagement but he felt he had no right to bind her to him any longer—sick and disheartened as he is and so he released her—How sad and forlorn he must be!"[84]

Consumption is a disease of endless surprises. Francis March hemorrhaged from the lungs at age twenty-six.[85] Slated to die, he lived on for another sixty years, earning national acclaim as a distinguished Shakespearean scholar.

As much as Emily Dickinson was rooting for Francis March, she must have understood the complexity of the situation facing March and Emily Fowler. It was not unlike her experience with Ben, and she may have been uncertain as to whether it was herself or Ben who had pushed the other away. Perhaps she felt that it was not too late to make amends. Was her goal to keep his spirit alive, and near, until they could be joined? Did she idealize Ben as an advance scout, journeying on, preparing to be her mentor in the next life as he had been in this one? Picture, if you will, Emily, alone in an upstairs bedroom, coughing her dry cough, reading and rereading Ben's letters, wondering at why she had been caught by surprise at the news of his death, then picking up pencil and paper and responding with the beginnings of still another poem of love, loss, and dreams of reunion. The human spirit is elevated by love, even to the point where love, and not God, can become the focus of one's religion. Was Emily thinking of Ben when she wrote this little poem?

> 951
>
> Unable are the Loved to die
> For Love is Immortality,
> Nay, it is Deity—
>
> Unable they that love—to die
> For Love reforms Vitality
> Into Divinity. [1865]

> ...that childless wife clinging to you... That wife, over whom your love broods, is fading.... What anxiety! ... How you struggle to fancy—there is no danger.... Your eye follows the physician as he leaves your house: is he wise, you ask yourself; is he prudent? is he the best?
>
> —Ik Marvel [Donald Grant Mitchell],
> *Reveries of a Bachelor*, 1850

5. First Love

More than likely, Emily in Amherst and Ben in Worcester exchanged thoughts on a new book that Emily had snapped up, read and loved, *Reveries of a Bachelor* (1850). In a letter to Austin, Emily called the book "great," and praised its "exquisite writing."[1] Her copy, available at Harvard, shows her penciled markings throughout. For years afterward, she talked up this sentimental fantasy and its author, Ik Marvel (Donald Grant Mitchell).

From the start, Dickinson biographers have sensed the importance to Emily of *Reveries*. Whicher: "Like Charlotte Brontë and Mrs. Browning, Ik Marvel fostered her interest in the workings of the human heart, particularly in its unsatisfied yearnings and tender regrets."[2] Chase: "Mitchell's 'reveries,' we cannot doubt, stirred the imagination of a poet who was to speak of the superiority of heart over head, of the transport of religious joy, of the anatomy of death, of achieving immortality through love."[3] Habegger: "The most immediately inspiring book Dickinson read in her early twenties was *Reveries of a Bachelor*."[4]

What did Emily find so compelling? Richard Sewall suggests it was the "meditative passages" on "life and death, time and eternity, love frustrated or fulfilled; marriage versus the solitary life; silence; hiding one's feelings; home; Past and Present; dreams; letter writing; or the plight of a woman without religion."[5] It must have amused Emily and Ben that the Bachelor's dog had the same name as Emily's shaggy pet, Carlo (perhaps both dogs were named after the one owned by St. John Rivers in *Jane Eyre*). The Bachelor looks into the fireplace, smokes his cigars, and dreams of what lies ahead—he envisions a first love, someone who will become his soul mate. But, at the same time, he anticipates heartbreak. Dickinson marked the following passage:

Love only, unlocks the door.... Affection is the stepping stone to God. The heart is our only measure of infinitude. The mind tires with greatness; the heart—never. Thought is worried and weakened in its flight through the immensity of space; but Love soars around the throne of the Highest, with added blessing and strength.[6]

Dickinson and Mitchell were members of the same species—the chronically ill. What Sewall and others do not notice in *Reveries* is the presence and impact of disease. The Bachelor's dreams of homestead, marriage and parenthood go up in smoke; he loses an only daughter, an only son and, soon after, a lovely wife. The word *consumption* is never mentioned, yet it leaps out at the knowing reader. Emily Dickinson could not have missed it. And tragedy involving her father's sister, Emily's Aunt Mary, drove the story home. In 1852 Mary Dickinson Newman and her husband Mark Newman, both still relatively young, died of pulmonary tuberculosis. As guardian, Edward brought the four orphaned Newman nieces from New York City to Amherst. The girls lived for years nearby the Dickinsons, and the younger two, Clara, 14, and Anna, 12, moved in next door with Austin and Sue Gilbert Dickinson, where they stayed until Clara's marriage in 1869. Her Newman cousins arrived just as the news of Newton's death reached Emily, and she seemed unnerved by their presence. "They are not *like us*,"[7] she wrote to Austin.

Reveries was a different sort of sentimental novel. There are no Calvinist deathwatches; the Bachelor derides mourning rituals as intrusive and impersonal. Sin, redemption, grace, and an all-knowing God are conspicuously absent. Physicians are mentioned disparagingly, clergyman not at all. The Bachelor refuses to sugarcoat disease and death; there are no consolatory passages to indicate that God works in mysterious ways, or that the dead and those that grieve them are somehow in a better place. Donald Grant Mitchell had, writes one of his biographers, "a permanent distaste for institutional religion."[8]

Reveries combined fiction, essay, and autobiography. When he wrote the story, Mitchell, like his narrator, was a bachelor contemplating marriage. Born into a consumptive family in 1822, he also developed the disease.[9] His father died in 1831. In the winter of 1836–37, his mother, older brother and a younger sister—all three deeply consumptive—traveled to St. Croix in the Caribbean in search of a cure. His brother died first, in 1838, his mother next, in 1839, and his sister in 1841. An older sister lasted until 1845, when she also died of TB.[10] Donald Grant Mitchell graduated Yale in 1841 as the valedictorian of his class, but his plans to study law were interrupted by his worsening tuberculosis. Is it any wonder that the Bachelor in *Reveries* feared the onset of marriage and children?

The first reviewers of *Reveries* commented on its similarity, in content, tone and style, to the stories of Washington Irving. Mitchell was quick to agree; in fact, he prefaced his next work, *Dream Life*, with a "Dedicatory Letter" to Irving, in which he detailed what he had learned from "one who has been so long my teacher":

> MY DEAR SIR: ... It is true, that until six months ago, I had never had the honor of meeting with you, but ... I know not to what writer of the English language, I am more indebted, than to you.... I have tried to show a truthfulness of feeling, that is not lighted by any counterfeit of passion, but rather by a cordial sympathy with human suffering—I know not to what man's heart, that truthfulness will come home sooner, than to yours.[11]

Both Irving and Mitchell were survivors, having lost loved ones to consumption and having themselves lived through the disease. It's unlikely that either of them knew of the other's blighted past; one can't imagine them exchanging such confidences at their first meeting. The facts of Irving's inconsolable grief were made available to the public only after his death.

Irving's story is the archetype of first love, doomed by consumption. In January of 1802, at age 19, he began clerking in the Manhattan law office of Josiah Hoffman, whose youngest child was Matilda, 12 years old. Writing to his parents while on a trip up the Hudson River that summer, Irving revealed chest pain and a persistent night cough. Concerned about their younger brother's incipient consumption, William and Peter Irving met the expense of sending him off to Europe as a restorative measure. For two years Irving moved through Italy, Sicily, France, and England, delaying long at Rome, Genoa, and Paris.

Upon his return to New York in 1806, he fell helplessly in love with Matilda Hoffman, and after a period of courtship, the two became engaged. Matilda was noted for her ethereal beauty, her sweet nature, and cultured mind. When she suddenly died ("added to the ravages of that relentless and invincible enemy to earthly happiness, the *consumption*,"[12] her obituary explained), Irving was shattered. He visited her grave nightly for months, kept and cherished her cameo picture and a lock of her hair, slept with her small Bible under his pillow.

Irving was at Matilda's bedside throughout her last days, and held her hand when she died. Emily Dickinson was not with Newton when he died, nor is there any record that she visited his gravesite. Each of us needs some kind of *closure* when we lose a person we love. Was Emily seeking out Ben when she wrote the following poem?

442

I see thee better—in the Dark—
I do not need a Light—
The Love of Thee—a Prism be—
Excelling Violet—

I see thee better for the Years
That hunch themselves between—
The Miner's Lamp—sufficient be—
To nullify the Mine—

And in the Grave—I see Thee best—
It's little Panels be
A'glow—All ruddy—with the Light
I held so high, for Thee—

What need of Day—
To Those whose Dark—hath so—surpassing Sun—
It deem it be—Continually—
At the Meridian? [1862]

Washington Irving remained a bachelor for half a century, devoted to Matilda, yet not once mentioning her name or allowing others to do so in his presence.[13] He died in 1859 at the age of 76. Grieving relatives found a locked box containing a cameo of Matilda, her Bible, a lock of her hair, and a slip of paper with two words written in Irving's hand: "Matilda Hoffman."[14] The box also contained 16 pages written by Irving *fifteen years after* his sweetheart's death. Some excerpts:

> We saw each other every day, and I became excessively attached to her. Her shyness wore off by degrees. The more I saw of her, the more I had reason to admire her. Her mind seemed to unfold itself leaf by leaf and every time to discover new sweetness.... I idolized her ... she was taken ill with a cold. Nothing was thought of it at first; but she grew rapidly worse, and fell into a consumption.
>
> I cannot tell you what I suffered.... I saw her fade rapidly away; beautiful, and more beautiful, and more angelical to the very last. I was often by her bedside; and in her wandering state of mind she would talk to me with a sweet, natural, and affecting eloquence that was overpowering.... Her dying struggles were painful and protracted. For three days and nights I did not leave the house, and scarcely slept. I was by her when she died.... I was the last one she looked upon.... She was but about seventeen years old when she died.
>
> I cannot tell you what a horrid state of mind I was in for a long time. I seemed to care for nothing; the world was a blank to me.... Months elapsed before my mind would resume any tone; but the despondency I had suffered ... seemed to give a turn to my whole character, and throw some clouds into my disposition, which have ever since hung about it.... For years I could not talk

on the subject of this hopeless regret; I could not even mention her name; but her image was continually before me, and I dreamt of her incessantly.[15]

Irving released his grief by writing stories of love sundered by mysterious wasting diseases, stories discussed by Emily Dickinson and her book club friends in Amherst. His stories are filled with spirit-brides and spirit-grooms. In one, Irving has the narrator confess that "I believe in broken hearts, and the possibility of dying of disappointed love. I do not, however, consider it a malady often fatal to my own sex; but I firmly believe that it withers down many a lovely woman into an early grave."[16] In Irving's "Pride of the Village," the narrator comes upon a funeral in a rural English village, and is told the sorrowful tale of a beautiful maiden of "natural grace and delicacy of character."[17] She had fallen in love with a young officer in a regiment quartered nearby.

> There was nothing in his advances to startle or alarm. He never even talked of love: but there are modes of making it more eloquent than language, and which convey it subtly and irresistibly to the heart. The beam of the eye, the tone of voice, the thousand tendernesses which emanate from every word, and look, and action—these form the true eloquence of love, and can always be felt and understood, but never described. Can we wonder that they should readily win a heart, young, guileless, and susceptible?
>
> As to her, she loved almost unconsciously; she scarcely inquired what was the growing passion that was absorbing every thought and feeling, or what were to be its consequences. She, indeed, looked not to the future. When present, his looks and words occupied her whole attention; when absent, she thought but of what had passed at their recent interview. She would wander with him through the green lanes and rural scenes of the vicinity. He taught her to see new beauties in nature; he talked in the language of polite and cultivated life, and breathed into her ear the witcheries of romance and poetry.[18]

Her swain, who had been so attentive, had left her behind. Both Irving and his readers could anticipate the story's ending:

> It was, like other tales of love, melancholy. She avoided society, and wandered out alone in the walks she had most frequented with her lover. She sought, like the stricken deer, to weep in silence and loneliness, and brood over the barbed sorrow that rankled in her soul.... She felt a conviction that she was hastening to the tomb, but looked forward to it as a place of rest.... By degrees her strength declined, that she could no longer leave the cottage. She could only totter to the window, where, propped up in her chair, it was her enjoyment to sit all day and look out upon the landscape. Still she uttered no complaint, nor imparted to any one the malady that was preying on her heart. She never even mentioned her lover's name.... Her poor parents hung, in mute

anxiety, over this fading blossom [hoping] that the bright unearthly bloom which sometimes flushed her cheek might be the promise of returning health....[19]

In "Rural Funerals" (1820), Irving wrote:

The sorrow for the dead is the only sorrow from which we refuse to be divorced. Every other wound we seek to heal—every other affliction to forget; but this wound we consider it a duty to keep open—this affliction we cherish and brood over in solitude.... Who, even when the tomb is closing upon the remains of her he most loved; when he feels his heart, as it were, crushed in the closing of its portal; would accept of consolation that must be bought by forgetfulness?—No, the love which survives the tomb is one of the noblest attributes of the soul. If it has its woes, it has likewise its delights.... Though it may sometimes throw a passing cloud over the bright hour of gayety, or spread a deeper sadness over the hour of gloom, yet who would exchange it even for the song of pleasure, or the burst of revelry? No, there is a voice from the tomb sweeter than song.[20]

Irving and Matilda. The meeting of a talented young man and a spirited younger lady, both showing signs of consumption; a romantic courtship, the rapid decline and death of the man's beloved and, then, his consecration of their love for years afterward.

This is also the story of Ralph Waldo Emerson. Emerson was only two when his father died of TB in 1811. *Mycobacterium tuberculosis* was active in Waldo and in his three brothers, Edward, Charles and William. When Emerson found his symptoms worsening in 1826, he closed the school he was operating and traveled to Florida, hoping to find a climate more favorable to his lungs.[21] Feeling somewhat better upon his return to the Boston area, he proposed marriage to Ellen Louisa Tucker. They wrote letters to one another (sometimes in French), and invented pet names—Emerson was "Grampa" and "King," Ellen was "Ellenelli," "ma belle reine."[22] She was 17; he was eight years older. They were engaged for only a month when Emerson wrote to his brother William: "My beautiful friend has ... that dangerous complaint which often attacks the fairest in our stern climate. She has raised blood."[23] Emerson was frightened, telling his brother, Charles, "she is too lovely to live long."[24]

Emerson put Ellen under the care of Dr. James Jackson (the *same* Dr. Jackson who ministered to Deborah Fiske a dozen years later and to Emily Dickinson another dozen years after that!). In 1828 Dr. Jackson, 51 years old, was already a legend, as founder of Massachusetts General Hospital and several times president of the Massachusetts Medical Society. He ordered vigorous outdoor exercise for Ellen, gave opiates, and assured her, repeatedly, that she was getting better. Nothing indicates that he used the word *consumption*. Waldo was convinced that Ellen would respond to "medicine & care so entirely, that she shall not be exposed to attacks ... in the future."[25] Ellen had some misgivings about Dr. Jackson, calling him "*Betty* Jackson (forgive)"[26] in a letter to Emerson. She improved for a time, suffered a setback in June, but then seemed healthier than ever afterwards. That summer she wrote to Emerson: "I have ridden 9 miles this day—and the rain did its best to drive me home—but I have not taken a bit of cold and am stronger today than I have been ever."[27] The optimistic twosome married in September, 1829.

Ellen had begun to write poems in her early teens. She continued to do so during her illness and decline. These poems are the focus of Janet Anderson's 1999 article, "Ellen Emerson and the Tubercular Muse." Tuberculosis is pictured as the creative catalyst and the dominant metaphor of the poems.[28] Anderson likens Ellen Emerson's "To the South Wind" to the poems of Dickinson. It seems that Ellen, like most consumptives, was more than a bit wary about the coming of Spring.

> O come not now to lure
> Me back to earth again
> That moment I was sure
> I felt the latest pain.
>
> And yet ye're heaven's messenger
> And bear soft words to me:
> But breathe not yet, but wait until
> My spirit is set free.
>
> Then whisper round my grave
> The tale of my release—[29]

Reading this poem, Anderson thought of Dickinson: "The relationship between respiration, spirit, and inspiration is manifest here in Dickinsonian brevity. The wind as heaven's messenger becomes a muse, ironic in its form, which kills as it inspires. Ellen pleads with the air she can scarcely breathe any longer not to send her back to her tortured existence."[30]

According to Anderson, the poem below was Ellen's final creation:

> And Hope, sweet bird & kind, at last has flown
> And of her beauty scarce a trace is found
> Save a slight tinge where her last splendour shone
> And there a golden feather quivering on the ground—
> Just bright enough to cheat the eager eye
> Just strong enough temptation for a lie.[31]

The poem, for Anderson, is "reminiscent of Dickinson ... [Ellen's] references to flight—'sweet bird,' 'flown,' 'golden feather'—plummet with her hopes, which she would not have rise fruitlessly again."[32] Anderson admires Ellen Emerson: "Her writings helped her to understand and endure her fate, to befriend the invading disease and turn it into art; to wrench meaning from her abbreviated life; to console herself and her family; to impose order; to rage, in her gentle way, against the night; to create alternatives to the unutterable; and to connect with her human community."[33]

Nowhere does Anderson link Dickinson and TB (she and Norbert Hirschhorn were writing their articles at about the same time), and yet Anderson's comments on Ellen Emerson seem almost tailor-made for Dickinson:

> It was between the poles of tubercular destruction and creation that Ellen Emerson created poetry.... Her prose is punctuated by exclamation points, dashes, underlines, emphatics....[34]
>
> Ellen's imagery and metaphoric word play ... [are a] response to her physical condition. For example, fluctuation from cold to excessive warmth is among the physical symptoms of TB.... The sun often represents her husband, while the moon is classically chaste, cold and unfeeling ... her noon is health, her midnight a time for death....[35]
>
> Tubercular themes intrude ... death; leave-taking; relationship with God; and, of course, love heightened by imminent leave-taking. Far from being mere sentimentality, these themes reflect both her disease and the process of working toward the acceptance of her fate ... creating beauty out of devastation is mythic, primal....[36]
>
> By personifying fearsome objects such as the grave, Ellen grounds the intangibles of her world in real things, giving them personality and robbing them of their ability to terrify and disorder ... she rejects death's victory and insists on her own. She will transcend in spirit.[37]

In August, 1830, Ellen again spat up blood, and asked if she might not go South for the winter. Emerson consulted with his three brothers and with Dr. Jackson, to whom he gave the deciding vote. On October 1, Charles wrote to William that Dr. Jackson was of "a decided opinion that it was needless to go away, [better] to spend the winter quietly keeping house like good & sensible people."[38] The good doctor felt that Ellen should not migrate to Cuba or anywhere else unless she was prepared to stay for ten years.[39] The fact that Ralph Waldo Emerson had been called to the pulpit of the prestigious Second Church in Boston may have contributed to the decision. Dr. Jackson's medical advice was gender-specific. Eleven years earlier, when William Cullen Bryant sought a remedy for his hemorrhaging father, Dr. Jackson had strongly urged a long voyage to Italy, the Indies or New Orleans.[40] And soon after saying "no" to Ellen, he said "yes" to Edward

Emerson, her brother-in-law. Showing symptoms much like Ellen's, Edward was dispatched on Dr. Jackson's advice to St. Croix. He was recuperating there when Ellen wrote to him:

> Pray ... pick out a pretty spot for Waldo & wife to live—for such golden dreams ... do I indulge.... Cold winds and changes here—scorpions & debilities there—The latter, I urge not so soul annoying as the former—One is a slow, uncertain death or an ill-spent life, the other a quick and sure remedy or a certain and not agreeable but more preferable death.[41]

Ellen continued to go outside, despite the December winds. In mid-January, she bled again from the lungs. Dr. Jackson came daily. At his advice, she went out to ride each day. The time came when everyone understood there would not be another remission, that Ellen was dying. Charles Emerson: "she has been in less pain—sometimes torpid under the influence of her opiates, but at others serene and fully conscious."[42] On February 8, 1831—eight weeks after Emily Dickinson was born—Ellen Emerson died. She had not lived to be twenty.

Two hours after Ellen's death, Emerson wrote: "My angel is gone to heaven this morning & I am alone in the world and strangely happy. Her lungs shall no more be torn nor her head scalded by her blood."[43] Although he was glad that Ellen was no longer in pain, he was also terrified at the possibility of losing all contact with someone that he loved so completely. He entered this poem into his journal:

> Dost thou not hear me Ellen
> Is thy ear deaf to me
> Is thy radiant eye
> Dark that it cannot see
>
> In yonder ground thy limbs are laid
> Under the snow
> And earth has no spot so dear above
> As that below
>
> And there I know the heart is still
> And the eye is shut and the ear is dull
>
> But the spirit that dwelt in mine,
> The spirit wherein mine dwelt
> The soul of Ellen, the thought divine
> From God that came—for all that felt
>
> Does it not know me now
> Does it not share my thought?
> Is it prisoned from Waldo's prayer
> Is its glowing love forgot?[44]

He records his torment. April: "The days go by, griefs, & simpers, & sloth, & disappointments. The dead do not return, & sometimes we are negligent of their image. Not of yours, Ellen—I know too well who is gone from me."[45] July: "...the awful solitude in which here a soul lives.... Here I sit alone from month to month filled with a deep desire to exchange thoughts with a friend who does not appear ... shall I find or refind that friend? ... was this glorious fabric made for nothing? Will not its day & means & Object come? Will not Heaven's Matches be made or restored? ... Count it not strange if the fool should say there is no God.... When I think of you sweet friend, wife, angel, Ellen on whom the spirit of knowledge & the spirit of hope were poured in equal fullness—when I think of you I am sure we have not said everlasting farewells."[46]

In September, seven months after Ellen's death, Emerson was beside himself. How could it be possible for two perfectly matched souls to sever contact with one another? It would almost seem that Emerson was going out of his mind:

> She never comes to me
> She promised me a thousand times
> That she would dearly dearly love me
> That in sickness & in health
> Others present others absent
> Whilst air was round & heaven above me
> She would be present in my life
> My holy gentle tender wife
> She promised in my secret ear
> When none but God & I could hear
> That she would cleave to me forever
> There was one will between us
> There was one heart within us
> And God upon his children smiled
> As we with love the hours beguiled
>
> And now I am alone
> Unheard I moan
> She never comes to me
> Sits never by my side
> I never hear her voice
> She comes not even to my dreams
> O Ellen[47]

Emerson walked each morning to Ellen's grave. A year after her death, he made this astonishing journal entry: "I visited Ellen's tomb and opened the coffin."[48] This sounds more like something right out of Poe! Emerson was slow to learn that dead soul mates are unresponsive to valentines. His grief process might seem more than a bit desperate to us today, but his behavior was not atypical in the nineteenth century. Emily Dickinson reacted similarly, reaching out to a lover in the grave, and begging that lover for any sign that the two of them were still in contact:

461

We Cover Thee—Sweet Face—
Not that We tire of Thee—
But that Thyself fatigue of Us—
Remember—as Thou go—
We follow Thee until
Thou notice Us—no more—
And then—reluctant—turn away
To Con Thee o'er and o'er—

And blame the scanty love
We were Content to show—
Augmented—Sweet—a Hundred fold—
If Thou would'st take it—now—[1862]

It wasn't long before consumption robbed Emerson of others. Margaret, Ellen's sister, was the first, followed by her mother, Margaret Tucker Kent, and then by Emerson's brothers Edward (in the West Indies) and Charles. Dr. Jackson, true to form, sugarcoated his reports on Charles's condition. Ralph Waldo Emerson, who would come to be celebrated as The Sage of Concord, was easily taken in:

> *April, 1836*—I fear I shall not feel any love ... until Charles's cough is relieved.... He is not seriously ill otherwise.... Dr. Jackson says he cannot find any thing is the matter with him.
>
> *May 3, 1836*—[to William Emerson, his brother]—You ought to tell Dr. Perkins what Dr. Jackson so carefully repeats, that he must not judge Charles by the first appearance.... As carefully as Dr. J. was able to examine, he did not find the lungs diseased.
>
> *May 11, 1836*—We arrived too late. Charles died Monday afternoon.[49]

Emerson waded through sorrow, fearful of the day when his desire to cherish Ellen's memory would lessen in intensity. He lived on for a half century. A practical man, he made adjustments, remarrying, becoming a proud father in 1836 (a boy, Waldo), and then naming his first daughter Ellen Tucker Emerson, after his first love. Though his second marriage brought him an intelligent and loving companion, he held to his conviction that "there is one birth & one baptism & one first love."[50] And then he bumped up against further tragedy: little Waldo contracted scarlet fever and died in 1842. Devastated, Emerson penned "Threnody," a poem included in the gift volume sent by Ben Newton to Emily Dickinson.

In "Threnody," Emerson describes a "wondrous child," a flower cut off from the "Day's eye." The poem opens with these lines:

> The south-wind brings
> Life, sunshine, and desire,
> And on every mount and meadow
> Breathes aromatic fire,
> But over the dead he has no power,
> The lost, the lost he cannot restore,
> And, looking over the hills, I mourn
> The darling who shall not return.
>
> I see my empty house,
> I see my trees repair their boughs,
> And he,—the wondrous child,
> Whose silver warble wild
> Outvalued every pulsing sound
> Within the air's cerulean round,
> The hyacinthine boy, for whom
> Morn well might break, and April bloom,
> The gracious boy, who did adorn
> The world whereinto he was born,
> And by his countenance repay
> The favor of the loving Day,
> Has disappeared from the Day's eye.[51]

Dickinson had this poem in hand. Ben's gift of Emerson's poems was, for Emily, a precious keepsake, and a source of poetic images. Did she come to see Newton as *her* daisy, *her* sun? Marietta Messmer is unhappy with certain critics who tend to read the word "daisy" in the context of acceptable Victorian feminine qualities of dependency and weakness. She feels that these critics picture Dickinson as someone "who completely abandons her own independent identity and becomes invisible to anyone but her 'master' in order to please him," and she calls for a larger reading, noting that in Old and Middle English, "daegesege" and "dayesye" both signify the sun itself. "In this way, 'Daisy' can stand for both the demurely insignificant little flower and the most powerful ruler of the sky itself," Messmer concludes.[52]

In the passage from "Threnody," quoted above, Emerson expresses misgivings about the coming of summer and, given the carnage that has visited his family over the winter, he doubts the restorative powers of the south wind. For reasons much the same, Emily Dickinson offers up a similar point of view:

363

I know a place where Summer strives
With such a practised Frost—
She—each year—leads her Daisies back—
Recording briefly—"Lost"—

But when the South Wind stirs the Pools
And struggles in the lanes—
Her Heart misgives Her, for Her Vow—
And she pours soft Refrains

Into the lap of Adamant—
And spices—and the Dew—
That stiffens quietly to Quartz—
Opon her Amber Shoe—[1862]

Irving and Matilda. Emerson and Ellen. One more story needs to be told. No first love was as true or as tragic as that of James Russell Lowell and Maria White. Emily Dickinson knew little of them until she talked to Higginson for the first time in 1870. What was it in Dickinson's appearance, speech, demeanor or poetry that prompted Higginson to bring up the name of Maria White Lowell? Did he tell Dickinson of Maria's early death from consumption? In two letters to Higginson, Dickinson asked for additional details about Lowell and her poems.

We know Higginson cherished the memory of Maria. In *Cheerful Yesterdays* he wrote of being with Lowell and Maria White shortly after the two became engaged, in 1840: "Lowell's first volume [of poems] had just been published ... he and his betrothed were to me, as they seemed to be for those in their circle, a modernized Petrarch and Laura, or even Dante and Beatrice, and I watched them with unselfish reverence. Their love-letters about which they were extremely frank, were passed from hand to hand, and sometimes reached me.... I have some of Maria White's ballads in her own handwriting, and still know by heart a letter she wrote.... I was fortunate enough to hear Maria White sing or 'say' ballads in moonlight evenings—it seemed as if I were in Boccaccio's Florentine gardens."[53]

At the time, Maria White was 19, a vibrant and accomplished woman, a seminary graduate, a fighter for abolitionism and temperance, a translator of German poetry, a poet herself, and an exquisite singer. She was also strikingly beautiful. James Russell Lowell, 22, possessed a brilliant mind, a Harvard law degree, and was soon to gain considerable notice as a poet and critic. It was all too perfect, and Lowell fell into the kind of reveries Ik

Marvel would make famous a few years later. Premonitions of Maria's death began to haunt him: "I dreamed that I went to see M. W., that I saw her walking before me, and that when I strove to overtake her, she vanished."[54]

Married six months, they became wealthy when her father died in 1845, leaving them $20,000. They talked of Italy, where Maria might build up her health, but pregnancies and motherhood intervened. Higginson noted her declining health: "The angel is thinner and paler and is destined to be wholly an angel ere long, I fear."[55] The Swedish novelist Fredrika Bremer recorded her impressions of Maria: "There is a trace of beauty and taste in everything she touches, whether of mind or body; and above all, she beautifies life.... Pity it is that this much-loved young wife seems to have delicate lungs. Her low, weak voice tells of this."[56]

The Lowells had four children in quick succession; but two, Blanche and Rose, died in infancy. The couple, with their remaining children, Mabel and Walter, and a nurse and a milch goat (goat's milk was thought to ward off consumption) sailed to Europe in 1851. In Italy, they learned that James's father was gravely ill, and Maria wrote to the Lowell family in Boston. The letter was tactful, because Maria knew of the sensitivities involved. Anna Cabot Jackson Lowell, Maria's sister-in-law, was the niece of Dr. James Jackson (*again, he's on the scene!*). Anna adored her famous uncle, and often urged his medical services on the large Lowell clan. It's likely that Dr. Jackson treated Maria and perhaps James and the children. Maria had strong views about Dr. Jackson's inadequacies, views likely to infuriate Anna. Maria was always direct in her communications, but this time she was also diplomatic:

> Let us know everything in regard to this attack.... Now our anxiety is intense. Frank & Sarah Shaw, who are with us ... are exceedingly anxious that you should see Dr. Elliott. They say he has a wonderful success in cases of this nature, both in the way of prevention & cure. Do see him and talk with him. His perceptions are so acute and his notions so clear, that even if you did not follow his prescriptions, you might find comfort & relief from what he said and advised in regard to the best mode of avoiding any future attack of the same kind. He will come to see you as a friend and need not interfere in any way with other physicians.
>
> It would be best if my letter or that this part of it should not be seen for Anna might feel hurt and think we underrated her Uncle, Dr. Jackson's skill, but I must say that I think Dr. Elliott's diagnosis of a disease is most remarkably clear, and that his chemistry enables him to do more in the way of a cure, than those who follow in a beaten track can ever attain to.[57]

Death struck six months later. Not in Boston, but in Rome. Not at Maria's father-in-law, who would die ten years later at age 79, but at little Walter Lowell, her only son, 18 months old. Maria wrote afterwards to Sarah

Shaw: "The baby was remarkably well and running round all day in the garden, but that very night he was taken ill, and after nearly a month's intense solicitude and anxiety all was over. He was just unfolding a rare and lovely nature but it [is] useless and terrible to think of it. I am tired of broken promises, and dare not think of a future for Mabel."[58] On the way home to Boston, Maria was examined (and lied to) by a French physician—she wrote to Shaw that he found "no tubercular disease although there was a good deal of irritation in the bronchial tubes."[59] James Lowell may have intuited that contagion, and not heredity, caused little Walter's death, for he wrote to a friend: "It is a terrible thing to have only one child. It seems as if the air were full of invisible bullets flying in every direction, so that not a step can be taken in safety."[60]

Now seriously ill, Maria continued to write. Hope Jillson Vernon designates two poems—"An Opium Fantasy" and "The Sick-Room"—as "doubtless inspired by frail health,"[61] and Katharine Rodier suggests that "An Opium Fantasy" explores an "altered consciousness, a state between drugged waking and dreaming ... undeniably a part of her own convalescent experience."[62] Rodier implies that the "intentionally hallucinatory" Lowell was more candid than Dickinson, that "An Opium Fantasy" "remains very literally told, clearly grounded in two worlds by explanatory clues of the sort the enigmatic Dickinson elected not to give."[63] The first three stanzas:

> Soft hangs the opiate in the brain,
>   And lulling soothes the edge of pain,
> Till harshest sound, far off or near,
>   Sings floating in its mellow sphere.
>
> What wakes me from my heavy dream?
>   Or am I still asleep?
> Those long and soft vibrations seem
>   A slumberous charm to keep.
>
> The graceful play, a moment stopped,
>   Distance again unrolls,
> Like silver balls, that, softly dropped,
>   Ring into golden bowls.[64]

Certain images in "An Opium Fantasy" are remarkably similar to a poem written in 1864 by Dickinson:

867

> I felt a Cleaving in my Mind—
> As if my Brain had split—
> I tried to match it—Seam by Seam—
> But could not make them fit—

> The thought behind, I strove to join
> Unto the thought before—
> But Sequence ravelled out of Sound—
> Like Balls—opon a Floor—[1864]

Cheryl Walker sees a "convergence" in the poems: "Lowell recounts a dream or at least a vision. Many critically ill patients used opium in the nineteenth century, so one does not wonder that Maria White Lowell knew something of its effects. Other women poets wrote about drug experiences too, but Lowell's account is the most Dickinsonian ... there is no exact match here, and yet Lowell's silver balls and golden bowls stanza and this poem [F867] sound as though they might have been written by the same poet."[65] Like Rodier, Walker stops just short of imputing opium use to Dickinson: "it is well to take note of the space-time conflation in Lowell's line 'Distance again unrolls.' It is, in fact, reminiscent of similar surprises in Dickinson's work, where she too assigns materiality to abstractions such as space and time (see 'Behind Me—dips Eternity') or conflates the one with the other ... something similar is going on in the strategies employed by the two poets to suggest forms of disorientation."[66]

"The Sick Room," to Walker, sounds "surprisingly Dickinsonian."[67] Walker points to the word "punctual" used by Lowell as "no other nineteenth-century poet to my knowledge did except for Emily herself. Lowell's poem contrasts the burgeoning springtime outside the window with the ominous shadows inside the sick room."[68] The poem begins:

> A spirit treading the earth,
>   As wind treads the vibrating string;
> I know thy feet so beautiful,
>   Thy punctual feet, O Spring![69]

Dickinson had parallel phrasing, as we see in "New feet within my garden go—" (Fr79):

> New Children play opon the green—
> New Weary sleep below—
> And still the pensive Spring returns—
> And still the punctual snow! [1859]

Both poems "use the word 'punctual' to drive home the timely untimeliness of illness and death,"[70] Walker states. She is the latest critic to notice the close connection between Lowell and Dickinson. S. Foster Damon, Professor of English at Brown University in the 1930s, was the first, styling "The Sick-Room" as "Dickinson before Dickinson: it is a cry of despair from an invalid, who senses the spring flooding the world outside her chill bedroom, while her life wastes away like the wood on her hearth—wood that also once responded to the coming of spring."[71]

Maria Lowell, at age 32, was near death in 1853. James Lowell wrote to a friend: "she is very dangerously ill—growing weaker and weaker.... It is only within the last week that I have realized the danger. She has been so often ill and rallied from it that I supposed she would soon begin to grow better. But there seems no force left now."[72] When Maria died, James felt the anguish that had seized Helen Fiske and Emily Fowler in 1844, at the funerals of their mothers. Like them, he rejected the balm of religious solace. Fiske and Fowler, in their early teens, let loose their grief, railing at death. That course of action was closed to Lowell, a mature man in the public eye (although at Maria's funeral he did lean against a tree a long while, weeping.) Privately, to a friend, he poured out his feelings:

> O, I do abhor sentimentality from the bottom of my soul, and cannot wear my grief upon my sleeves, but yet I look forward with agony to the time when she may become a memory instead of a constant presence. She promised to be with me if that were possible, but it demands all the energy of the soul to believe without sight, and all the unmetaphysical simplicity of faith to distinguish between fact and fancy. I know that the little transparent film which covers the pupil of my eye is the only wall between her world and mine, but that hair-breadth is as effectual as the space between us and the sun.
>
> I cannot feel when I come home that she comes to the door to welcome me as she always did. I can only hope that when I go through the last door that opens for all of us I may hear her step upon the other side. That her death was so beautiful and calm and full of faith as it was gives me no consolation, for it was only that rare texture of her life continuing to the very end, and makes me feel all the more what I had and what I have not.[73]

Lowell felt that something had broken his life in two, and that he could not piece it together. It was one cruelty too many. When his first born, Blanche, died at fifteen months, he had hung the baby's shoes in his study, where he could see them. Now, after Maria's death, he completed a commemorative poem, entitled "After the Burial." The opening stanza:

> Yes, Faith is a goodly anchor;
> When skies are sweet as a psalm,
> At the bows it lolls so stalwart
> In bluff broad-shouldered calm.

But then the tempest, with its deadly outcome. Lowell was grieving three children, and now his beloved Maria was also gone. Blanche's little booties were always within sight, a constant reminder to Lowell of all he had lost—and God nowhere to be found.

> But, after the shipwreck, tell me
>   What help in its iron thews,
> Still true to the broken hawser,
>   Deep down among sea-weed and ooze?

Lowell ended the poem with these thoughts:

> Your logic, my friend, is perfect,
>   Your morals most drearily true,
> But the earth that stops my darling's ears
>   Makes mine insensate too.
>
> Console, if you will; I can bear it;
>   'T is a well-meant alms of breath
> But not all the preaching since Adam
>   Has made Death other than Death.
>
> Communion in spirit! Forgive me,
>   But I, who am earthy and weak,
> Would give all my incomes from dreamland
>   For her rose-leaf palm on my cheek!
>
> That little shoe in the corner,
>   So worn and wrinkled and brown,—
> Its motionless hollow confutes you,
>   And argues your wisdom down.[74]

Emily Dickinson later praised Lowell's "After the Burial" for its "sweet despair,"[75] and in her late forties she penned this empathetic follow-up to his "After the Burial":

1516

> One thing of thee I covet—
> The power to forget—
> The pathos of the Avarice
> Defrays the Dross of it—
>
> One thing of thee I borrow
> And promise to return—
> The Booty and the Sorrow
> Thy sweetness to have known—[1879]

Irving and Matilda. Emerson and Ellen. Lowell and Maria. First loves, cut short by pulmonary tuberculosis. Irving, Emerson and Lowell were consumed by grief, and each behaved for a time in ways that might seem almost bizarre. But why judge them? Nothing is more devastating than the loss of a loved one.

And they weren't alone. The Great White Plague triggered storms of grief and despair. Calvinist pitchmen responded to the spike in emotional intensity; as TB mortality rates soared, religious revivals popped up again and again in the Connecticut River valley. Evangelical Christianity reached out to the terrorized and the despondent; Sheila Rothman notes that the "intense religious fervor" of revivalism had "a particular appeal for invalids."[76]

Irving, Emerson and Lowell, like Emily Dickinson, rejected revivalist religion. Their grief was piercing, private. And yet, as they became embedded in long and rewarding literary careers, their first loves became, not constant presences, but somber memories. Letting go was more of a problem for Emily Dickinson. Hidden from the public, sealed within her privacy, she held tight to her daisies, and especially to Ben Newton:

> 1781
>
> The distance that the dead have gone
> Does not at first appear;
> Their coming back seems possible
> For many an ardent year.
>
> And then, that we have followed them,
> We more than half suspect,
> So intimate have we become
> With their dear retrospect. [undated]

The sense of despair began to lift in 1858, when Dickinson turned to writing poems, including one (Fr6) that opens:

> Adrift! A little boat adrift!
> And night is coming down!
> Will <u>no</u> one guide a little boat
> Unto the nearest town?

The writing of poems became Dickinson's passion, and the means by which, adrift, she gained the courage to guide her little boat on her own.

One might think of it as a flip of the coin. Emily Dickinson lived on, while others with parallel talents, infected by the same disease, did not. Had Dickinson been snatched away in her early twenties, in the midst of her grief, we would have no reason to remember her today. The coin, of course, has another side: if Matilda Hoffman and Ellen Tucker Emerson and Maria White Lowell had all lived on to age 55, it's conceivable that at least one of them would be remembered today as an important American poet.

And what kind of life unfolded for the author of *Reveries of a Bachelor*? Unexpectedly, one with a happy ending! Donald Grant Mitchell gave up his doleful bachelorhood in 1853, marrying Mary Pringle, a wealthy young woman from Charleston, South Carolina. First love, for Mitchell and Pringle, continued on for half a century, until Mary's death in 1901. Mary gave birth to eleven children. The first died at age seven, but the next ten lived to maturity. Six lived past age seventy, and one, Walter Louis Mitchell, lived on to 1955, the year in which Marilyn Monroe starred in "The Seven Year Itch." *Walter's father, Donald Grant Mitchell, had been born in 1822!*

Mitchell, the consumptive youth who lost his mother, brother, and two sisters to TB, the bachelor who, in 1850, dreaded the vision of what first love would bring, was 86 when he died in 1908.

> Many said that my sister [Emma] was too beautiful for this world. They frequently made this remark after the red began to deepen and burn on her cheek, and she at first coughed a little, and then more and more.... Our parents were alarmed, and sent for the family physician. He took a little blood, and gave some medicine, which my father said was mostly opium....
> —Mary Sargeant Gove Nichols, *Mary Lyndon, or Revelations of a Life.* 1855

6. Spirit-Bride

Emma Lyndon was no Emily Dickinson. Mary Lyndon summed up her gorgeous but self-absorbed sister: "She sang like a nightingale; she danced like a sylph; her taste in dress was exquisite ... but she never cared for books. She used to say, 'Pore over your books, Mary, and frighten all the men.... I am pretty enough to get a beau without taking a book for bait.'"[1] Picture Ben Newton out on a walk and talk, not with Emily Dickinson, but with someone like Emma Lyndon. Don't look for a spark, or a meeting of minds, or a bonding of spirits.

We know Emily Dickinson as the sensitive and fiercely independent poet we now read. In early adolescence, however, before her long encounter with illness and pain, Emily was a bit like Emma Lyndon. At age 14, she wrote to Abiah Root: "I am growing handsome very fast indeed! I expect I shall be the belle of Amherst when I reach my 17th year. I don't doubt that I shall have perfect crowds of admirers at that age."[2] And several months later, she told Abiah she wore her "golden tresses done up in a net-cap. Modesty, you know, forbids me to mention whether my personal appearance has altered. I leave that for others to judge."[3]

When did Emily stop trying to make herself look pretty? Was it in the years following Ben Newton's death?

> 471
> To make One's Toilette—after Death
> Has made the Toilette cool
> Of only Taste we cared to please
> Is difficult, and still—
>
> That's easier—than Braid the Hair—
> And make the Boddice gay—

> When Eyes that fondled it are wrenched
> By Decalogues—away—[1862]

Early death denied Emma Lyndon the chance at a deeper sense of self. The deathwatch that unfolded in *Mary Lyndon* was typical for the times. The ritual was both consolatory and more than a bit unsettling: assurances that Christ would be waiting in heaven were undercut by inquiries into the dying person's state of grace. Reverend Barker not only serenaded Emma with religious hymns, he also held her feet to the fire. He asked her to account for her sins, to declare true repentance, and to profess Christ. Emma's father, a skeptic, chafed at the process. He knew that Emma, up to the time of her serious illness, had given little thought to death or immortality. Now she *and he* were being exhorted to confess sins and accept Christ. Mr. Lyndon stood his ground, armed with conscience and with his version of common sense. But his doubts about God and immortality were brushed aside, and even derided, by the fervent townsfolk who had joined the deathwatch. For Emma's sake, there was nothing he could do but swallow hard and look on.

Emily Dickinson would have sympathized with Emma's father. A minority within her own family, and an anomaly in Amherst, Emily expected to die *unsaved*, and on her own terms. The odds were against her. Father and Vinnie, and even Austin, had joined Mother as professing Christians. Amherst had its contingent of Christian ladies of uncertain age, veteran death-watchers, eager to step in. Critic Caroline Hogue: "What we know of Emily Dickinson gives us assurance that ... she would abhor the deathbed scene." And why? Amherst's way of meeting death, Hogue stated, "was affected with a public interest and concern, and was witnessed by family and friends. They crowded the death chamber to await expectantly a burst of dying energy to bring on the grand act of passing. Commonly it began with last minute bequests, the wayward were called to repentance, the backslider to reform, gospel hymns were sung, and finally as climax the dying one gave witness in words to the Redeemer's presence in the room, how He hovered, transplendent in the upper air, with open arms outstretched to receive the departing soul. This was death's great moment."[4]

None of this suited Emily. Instead, she set up *solitary* deathwatches, one for Ben and one for herself. It was all so *gothic*. Albert Gelpi recognized Dickinson's "necrophilic preoccupation."[5] "The poet dies again and again," Gelpi writes, "she is laid out in the coffin; she bends over to catch her lover's dying breath; she looks forward to fondling his corpse and preparing him for burial; she anticipates love in a shared grave."[6] Dickinson's deathwatch poems are among her most famous, recognizable by their first lines: "As by the dead we love to sit ; Safe in their Alabaster Chambers ; Dying! Dying in the night! ; To die—takes just a little while ; I like a look of Agony ; I felt a Funeral, in my Brain ; It was not Death, for I stood up ; Because I could not stop for Death ; I heard a Fly buzz—when I died." As David Baker put it in 2005, "Emily Dickinson is gloriously at home with death, her weirdly familiar afterlife, and the language of that other world. How often does she sink through floorboards or grass into the grave.... How many times does she speak, as a corpse, to corpses?"[7]

It's only natural that consumptive poets would write often, and searchingly, about death. Unlike those in robust health, they find it impossible to sublimate the idea of death. A Dickinson contemporary, the consumptive English poet George Heath (1844–1869), was known in the Staffordshire area as "the Moorland Poet" and "the Invalid Poet." He published two slim volumes of verse, his major themes being death and the frustration of unfulfilled ambition. Not knowing that George Heath wrote the following piece, one might easily attribute it to Emily Dickinson:

> I looked Death firmly in the face, and ceased
> To start and tremble at the thought of him.
> I reasoned with my coward faculties,
> And quivered at the name, and conjured up
> Before in array the figure Death,
> In every possible shape, and drew a line
> Round all his terrors and his properties,
> And analysed, and pondered deep, and viewed
> Them o'er in every aspect, till my mind,
> Accustomed to their seeming, ceased to fear.
> I chose the fearfullest of shapes, and reasoned thus:
> "The worst, if it should come, is only so.
> I'll steel my soul to meet the most severe.
> A thousand things may hap to soothe the blow,
> Or may be change the current for a time.
> There are full many chances in the lap
> Of Providence: 'tis probable that I
> Shall draw a blank; and yet 'tis possible
> That I may draw a prize; I cannot tell:
> I know not, but at least Death will but be
> A visitor once; why should I die and die
> A hundred deaths a week? I thought, I'll work,
> And do the little I may do while I can.[8]

One half of Dickinson's deathwatch—monitoring her own precarious health—was deceptively simple. Everyone knew consumptives who had died. The *Encyclopædia Americana* (Boston, 1851) article on "PULMONARY CONSUMPTION" was standard stuff:

It begins with a short, dry cough, that at length becomes habitual, but from which nothing is spit up for some time, except a frothy mucus.... The breathing at the same time is somewhat impeded ... oppression at the chest is experienced; the body becomes gradually leaner, and great languor, with indolence, dejection of spirits, and loss of appetite.... In this state the patient frequently continues a considerable length of time....

By degrees the matter which is expectorated becomes ... streaked with blood. In some cases, a more severe degree of hemoptysis attends, and the patient spits up a considerable amount of florid, frothy blood. The breathing at length becomes more difficult, and the emaciation and weakness go on increasing. With these the person begins to be sensible of pain in some part of the thorax ... particularly on coughing.... A pain is felt on one side, and at times prevails in so high a degree, as to prevent the person from lying easily on that side ... at the same time the face flushes, particularly after eating ... the respiration is difficult and laborious ... and by degrees the disease assumes the hectic form ... a florid circumscribed redness appears on each cheek ... at other times the face is pale....

In the last stage of the disease, the emaciation is so great, that the patient has the appearance of a walking skeleton; his countenance is altered, his cheeks are prominent, his eyes look hollow and languid, his hair falls off, his nails are of a livid color, and much incurvated....[9]

The progress of the disease, however, was not always so clear-cut. The problem for Emily, as for all consumptives, was the impossibility of knowing how close she was to the end. Consumption ran on erratic timetables. One might seem be in the first stage of the disease and be dead within the week. This was *quick* or *galloping* consumption, the kind that took Olivia Coleman and Emma Washburn. There was also an *intermittent* form of the disease, the consumptive shuttling between the first two stages of the disease. Consumptives might live for years or even decades, exhibiting symptoms when the immune system was weak, rallying as the immune system improved—Ben Newton held on to age 31; Eliza Coleman Dudley managed 25 years before dying at the age of 39; Francis March survived hemoptysis by 60 years. This chronic form of the disease was on Robert Louis Stevenson's mind when, six years before his death, he remarked: "I am really an invalid, but of a mysterious order. I might be a *malade imaginaire*, but for one tangible symptom, my tendency to bleed from the lungs."[10] Near the end of his life, living in Samoa in hopes of overcoming his disease, he observed that he hadn't had a fair chance, and that he'd spent all his life in expectation of death. Stevenson died in 1894 at the age of 44.

Like Stevenson, Emily Dickinson lived much of her life anticipating death. She experienced an ominous recurrent cough during the years 1846 to 1852, and those around her repeatedly expressed concerns over how *thin* she was.

The 1850s were hard on her. She punned about her loss of weight in a letter to Austin written one week after she learned of Ben Newton's marriage: "For our sakes, Austin wont you try to be careful? I know *my* sake an't much, but Vinnie's is considerable—it weighs a good many pounds—when *skin and bones* may plead, I will become a *persuasion*."[11] Emily and Vinnie were examined and treated by the family physician in Amherst. "We are satisfied that he doesn't know what ails us, and we are tired and wearied of being under his care," Emily wrote to Austin, adding that "sometimes we think to ourselves that we shant ever get well."[12] *Uncertainty* was the most troublesome part of being chronically ill. There is nothing on record to indicate that Emily was diagnosed a consumptive; she had no way to predict the future course of her ailment; she was ignorant of the stage of her disease; she lacked reliable information on treatment and alternate systems of care. A deathwatch can be a tricky thing.

775

Suspense—is Hostiler than Death—
Death—tho'soever Broad,
Is just Death, and cannot increase—
Suspense—does not conclude—

But perishes—to live anew—
But just anew to die—
Annihilation—plated fresh
With Immortality—[1863]

Late in 1855 the Dickinsons were about to move back to the house in which Emily had been born, the Dickinson Homestead on Main Street. It was an exciting moment, but Emily's mind seemed focused on the state of her health, and on the possibility that she might soon die. In a letter to her friend Jane Humphrey, she confided: "We shall be in our new house soon; they are papering now, and—Jennie, we have *another* home—'house not made with hands.' Which first will we occupy?"[13] Five months later Emily wrote to her cousin, John Graves, complaining that she was not emotionally ready for the warm months:

> Much that is gay ... upon this April grass—then there are sadder features—here and there, wings half gone to dust ... a mouldering plume, an empty house, in which a bird resided. Where last year's flies, their errand ran, and last year's crickets fell! We, too, are flying—fading, John—and the song "here lies," soon upon lips that love us now—will have hummed and ended. To live, and die, and mount again in triumphant body, and next time, try the upper air—is no schoolboy's theme! It is a jolly thought to think that we can be Eternal—when air and earth are full of lives that are gone—and done—and a conceited thing indeed, this promised Resurrection![14]

In the summer of 1858, Emily sent this somber comment to Joseph Sweetser: "Much has occurred, dear Uncle, since my writing you—so much—that I stagger as I write, in sharp remembrance.... God gives us many cups. Perhaps you will come to Amherst, before the wassail's done. Our man has mown today, and as he plied his scythe, I thought of *other* mowings, and garners far from here. I wonder how long we shall wonder; how early we shall *know*."[15] Two months later, fixating on the Grim Reaper, she asked Samuel Bowles if he, his wife and two daughters were *still alive*: "In such a porcelain life, one likes to be *sure* that all is well, lest one stumble upon one's hopes in a pile of broken crockery."[16] *Death*, and its imminence, permeates Dickinson's letters and early poems.

Emily's second deathwatch—looking out for Ben—was something of the norm for the times; Barton Levi St. Armand has dubbed this practice the Sentimental Love Religion.

> The image of the mourning maiden had archetypal resonances for the popular culture of Dickinson's time.... The loved dead would be seen again in a domesticated heaven, and sometimes their angelic voices even whispered warnings in the ears of those who were left below.... To Dickinson ... the loved dead were astral guides and spiritual mediums to a better world.[17]

Dickinson, St. Armand adds, "reacted selectively to the popular gospel of consolation. Sometimes she accepted its formulas without question; sometimes she subverted them through exaggeration, burlesque, and distortion; sometimes she used them only as pretexts for outright skepticism and satire."[18] And these keen insights:

> [She] was raised with a respect for facts, and as the one rebel against orthodoxy in a family all of whom eventually became church members ... she could not entirely swallow the candied placebo of a family reunion in heaven or the idea that afflictions were an inevitable means to sanctifying grace.
>
> Caught between the stern rock of Calvinist upbringing and the hard place created by her own uncompromising conscience, Dickinson was forced to wonder if her childlike impudence would be any more welcome in heaven than it was in Amherst.... Dickinson solved this problem by imagining a purely conjugal heaven built not for the restoration of old family ties but for the fulfillment of new personal relationships that had been thwarted on earth.... Dickinson wrote of the loved dead, though gradually she trimmed her honors list ... to only two candidates: herself and her lover.[19]

St. Armand's message is clear: *the loved one addressed in Dickinson's poems is dead and buried.*

75

Sexton! My Master's sleeping here.
Pray lead me to his bed!
I came to build the Bird's nest—
And sow the early seed—

That when the snow creeps slowly
From off his chamber door—
Daisies point the way there—
And the Troubadour. [1859]

Dickinson's spirit-bride poems are remindful of "Annabel Lee." Poe visits his lover, the wife taken by tuberculosis: "...the wind came out of the cloud by night, / Chilling and killing my Annabel Lee. / But our love it was stronger by far than the love / Of those who are older than we ... And neither the angels in heaven above, / Nor the demons down under the sea, / Can ever dissever my soul from the soul / of the beautiful Annabel Lee ... And so, all the night-tide, I lie down by the side / Of my darling—my darling—my life and my bride...."[20]

Like Poe, Dickinson was not ready to separate from a lost love. With paper, needle and string, she began in 1858 to arrange her poems into booklets (later called *fascicles*), storing them in a drawer in her bedroom dresser. A dying Ben Newton had promised to be on hand to celebrate her emergence as a poet. If she took his last words to be a troth, were the poems her response?

In *Emily Dickinson's Gothic: Goblin with a Gauge*, Daneen Wardrop advances the idea that Dickinson's poems constitute a dowry, one that empowered the poet:

> One of the major activities of the gothic bride entails the maintenance of a dowry.... Dickinson's bride ... is no exception. The dowers ... assure her prospects as an eligible, lovable, 'legitimate' wife-to-be; they validate her waiting....
>
> Waiting takes on its quality of desire.... The dowry gives the waiting its backing, its promise and hope, without which there remains no reason for gothic hesitation, no suspense.... The dowry affords the heroine's identity, the waiting her quandary....
>
> Because the family's fear of flawed heritage underlies every gothic love union, what the future wife and husband bring to the union deserves close attention....
>
> The bride, then, gathers many items into dowerment, including easily her self, spirit and body, and opulent feminine symbols of her poetry. Indeed, the most important item in Dickinson's dowry is her art....
>
> Dickinson's bride stands suspended in readiness before the bridal threshold by dint of her powerful and invaluable bolts of melody. She legitimizes

herself to her groom-to-be through the word. Poetry is the bride's most persuasive come-on.[21]

Although Wardrop sees the poems as a "hope chest," she isn't sure *why* Dickinson decided to sew her verse into booklets. Perhaps that *why* is Ben Newton. In 1858 and for the next six years, Dickinson took the trouble to sew *eight hundred* poems into forty fascicles, hiding them away in the dresser. Of all the possibilities for organizing and storing poems, why did she choose this one? A *labor of love* is the cliché that springs to mind. As she threaded in each new set of poems, did Emily feel she was keeping faith with Ben?

200

The Rose did caper on her cheek—
Her Boddice rose and fell—
Her pretty speech—like drunken men—
Did stagger pitiful—

Her fingers fumbled at her work—
Her needle would not go—
What ailed so smart a little maid—
It puzzled me to know—

Till opposite—I spied a cheek
That bore <u>another</u> Rose—
<u>Just</u> opposite—another speech
That like the Drunkard goes—

A Vest that like her Boddice, danced—
To the immortal tune—
Till those two troubled—little Clocks
Ticked softly into one. [1861]

George Whicher was certain that two of the fascicle poems were written with Newton in mind. The first (Fr418) opens with "Your Riches—taught me—Poverty," and ends seven stanzas later in a tribute to "the Pearl— / That slipped my simple fingers through / While just a Girl at school." "Some years later, " Whicher observed, Emily "sent this poem to her sister-in-law with the words: 'You see I remember.' Sue would know what."[22]

The Pearl that slipped through the poet's fingers was Ben Newton, Whicher concluded. And he had no doubt that *The Gem* in a second poem was also Newton:

261

I held a jewel in my fingers—
And went to sleep—
The day was warm, and winds were prosy—
I said "'Twill keep"—

> I woke—and chid my honest fingers,
> The Gem was gone—
> And now, an Amethyst remembrance
> Is all I own—[1861]

"Her dying tutor had wished to see her a poet," Whicher wrote. "Very well, her last and best tribute to his memory would be to show that she had become one."[23] A number of fascicle poems seem to cast Ben Newton in the role of advance scout, making celestial arrangements and smoothing the way for the time when the two of them would be together once more.

Dickinson's need to commemorate Ben and her other daisies paid unexpectedly dividends. The *need to write poems* took over her life, and the intricacies of that task absorbed all her energies in the years immediately ahead. Her poems—reaching a total of 1789, according to R. W. Franklin—would be the only redemption of which she would ever be certain. In her anxiety to locate Ben Newton and to keep him close, she discovered, in full, her extraordinary capabilities and talents.

In 1862, Emily was not yet ready to give up her role as Ben's spirit-bride. It had been nine years since Newton's death in Worcester, and four years into her routine of churning out verse. At the time she penned the poem below, she had already created 25 percent of her final output of poetry.

Emily Dickinson was now white hot.

In 1863 Dickinson crafted 295 poems—many quite lengthy, by her standards—almost one poem a day! And it would seem that Ben Newton was, if not her muse, still central in her thoughts:

> 454
>
> I rose—because He sank—
> I thought it would be opposite—
> But when his power dropped—
> My Soul grew straight.
>
> I cheered my fainting Prince—
> I sang firm—even—Chants—
> I helped his Film—with Hymn—
>
> And when the Dews drew off
> That held his Forehead stiff—
> I met him—
> Balm to Balm—
>
> I told him Best—must pass
> Through this low Arch of Flesh—
> No Casque so brave
> It spurn the Grave—

6. Spirit-Bride

I told him Worlds I knew
Where Emperors grew—
Who recollected us
If we were true—

And so with Thews of Hymn—
And Sinew from within—
And ways I knew not that I knew—till then—
I lifted Him—[1862]

> I have noticed that persons with consumptive diseases are ashamed of them.... A consumption is called a "cough," ... a "bronchial difficulty," ... a "weakness of the lungs...." The victim of consumption carries around with him into society for a long time, often, his pale, wan, or unnaturally flushed face, and holds out his card of health to everybody.
> —Samuel H. Elliot, *Dreams and Realities in the Life of a Pastor and Teacher.* 1856

7. Queen Recluse

Samuel Bowles, owner-editor of the *Springfield Republican,* dropped by the Dickinson Homestead late in November, 1862, after a five-month stay in Europe for reasons of health. Austin, Sue and Vinnie were glad to see him, but Emily refused to meet Bowles face to face. Instead, she sent this message downstairs: "I cannot see you. You will not less believe me. That you return alive, is better than a Summer. And more to hear your voice below, than News of any bird."[1] After Bowles left the house, Austin and Vinnie upbraided their sister for her incivility.

What kept Emily from walking downstairs to see Bowles? Only months before, she had written to Italy, and seemed to *pine* for him: "Would you please come home? ... I grope fast, with my fingers, for all out of my sight I own—to get it nearer—"[2] For Bowles, it didn't add up; bristling over Emily's snub, he sent a note to Austin Dickinson: "To the [Newman] girls & all hearty thought—Vinnie ditto—& to the Queen Recluse my especial sympathy—that she has 'overcome the world.'"[3]

The label "Queen Recluse" would not have startled Austin or Sue or Vinnie; they already knew Emily to be a deep-seated homebody. A number of Dickinson's biographers describe her withdrawal from society as neither abrupt nor abnormal, but voluntary, little more than a preference for company of her own choosing, not a phobia but rather a lifestyle arrived at by temperament and by choice, a consolidation of creative forces, an act of power. Emerson once explained the need writers have for solitude: "They are lonely; the spirit of their conversation and writing is lonely; they repel influences; they shun general society; they incline to shut themselves in their chamber in the house."[4] In Dickinson's case, there was also the presence, decade after decade, of a sickly, and possibly tubercular, mother—Emily tended to Mother, while Vinnie took on the bulk of the household chores. Ten years after Emily's death, Vinnie tried to set the record straight: "Our mother had a period of invalidism, and one of her daughters must be constantly at home; Emily chose this part and, finding the life with her books and nature so congenial, continued to live it."[5]

According to Vinnie, her sister's withdrawal was "only a happen."[6] The problem with this *lifestyle* explanation is that it does not account for Dickinson's over-the-top avoidance tactics. Her refusal to see Samuel Bowles was not an isolated incident; one critic offers a list of eye-catching behaviors:

> her occasional refusal to come downstairs even to meet even close friends; her flurried flights from the room or from the garden at the approach of outsiders; her listening to music from the next room; her appointments to meet people "at the foot of the back stairs by moonlight alone"; her conversations from behind a door that stood ajar to screen her; ... her ghostly appearances at social gatherings in the house (infrequent as such appearances were, until finally discontinued) when, having awaited "a moment when conversation lagged a little, she would sweep in, clad in immaculate white, pass through the rooms, silently curtseying and saluting right and left, and sweep out again"; her insistence even in her last illness that the only examination permitted the doctor was to observe her as she walked by an open door while he remained seated in the next room.[7]

Recent explanations for Dickinson's reclusion focus on dysfunction: a social anxiety disorder, where Dickinson was easily frightened, as when she recoiled from a knock at the door; anorexia, a reference to her weight loss; seasonal affective disorder (SAD), where in winter she fell into hopelessness and self-doubt; agoraphobia, with its depersonalization and psychic terror. This psychopathology gives Dickinson little credit for inner direction, for autonomy. Fright, even fright bordering on panic, is not necessarily "abnormal," as veterans of war or survivors of terror know only too well. Ben Newton and her many daisies were gone, and Dickinson could not have been sure of what was in store for her. She may have felt that to stroll the streets of Amherst was to hold out her card of health to one and all. The result would be predictable: gossip, then inquiries into the state of her health, then visiting delegations of the pious and, finally, the beginnings of a deathwatch. Emily "had the choisest friendships among the rarest men and women all her life," Vinnie stated in 1895, adding that her sister had been "cut to the heart when death robbed her again and again."[8] Dickinson was a *wounded deer*.

181

> A <u>wounded</u> Deer—leaps highest—
> I've heard the Hunter tell—
> 'Tis but the extasy of <u>death</u>—
> And then the Brake is still!
>
> The <u>smitten</u> Rock that gushes!
> The <u>trampled</u> Steel that springs!
> A Cheek is always redder
> Just where the Hectic stings!
>
> Mirth is the mail of Anguish—
> In which it cautious Arm,
> Lest Anybody spy the blood
> And "you're hurt" exclaim! [1860]

The meaning of this enigmatic poem hinges on the possibility that someone will spy the deer's blood. Not to damage the deer further, but to commiserate. The *leaps* of the deer can be seen as upsurges of frenetic post-hemorrhagic activity. "So much were the Greek physicians impressed with the peculiar nervous force displayed at times by consumptive patients," Rene and Jean Dubos wrote in *The White Plague*, "that they invented a word for it. They characterized *spes phthisica* by a perpetual hope of recovery even in the face of devastating disease, and by a feverish urge for accomplishment, as if the patient were anxious to achieve all of which he was potentially capable in an exciting race with death."[9]

Cynthia Wolff found the poem's key in the word *hectic*, which she defined as "the 'habitual fever' of consumption."[10] In the 1850s, *hectic* as an adjective was used interchangeably with the word *consumptive*. Hectic as a noun referred to the fevered red spot on the cheek of a consumptive. In "A wounded Deer," *hectic* is used as a noun. Emily's was mirthful at occasions such as the Amherst College commencement party, held each year at the Dickinson home. That way, no one would suspect her pain. (Kafka employed the same ruse: "I simulate gaiety, in order to vanish behind it. My laughter is a concrete wall."[11]) Except for cameo appearances at these events, Emily all but dropped from sight. Did she fear a community deathwatch, one that would infringe upon her commitment to Ben Newton?

Dickinson and Kafka weren't the only ones to know that a consumptive might choose *mirth* as a shield against detection. In 1854, an American novelist inserted this behavior pattern into his plot:

> Mary was dying of consumption. It was the marks of hectic fever which first fastened my attention upon her. How the flashing light of her eye, the crimson glow on her cheek, and the merry ring of her childish glee, seemed to mock

the malady that was preying upon her life. To a thoughtless observer her mirth was faulty in its exuberance, and her manner too childishly free for one of her age. Poor Mary! Society was a festival to her ... and something of the mirthfulness she showed was owing to the opium she took to suppress her cough while in the room.[12]

By the end of the 1850s, Dickinson had become a confirmed recluse. Her letters to Higginson hint at the extent of her seclusion, and the reasons for it:

> ...for several years, my Lexicon—was my only companion.... You ask of my Companions—Hills—Sir—and the Sundown—and a Dog—large as myself, that my Father bought me—They are better than Beings—because they know—but do not tell....[13]
>
> Could you believe me—without? [Higginson had asked for a picture] I had no portrait, now, but am small, like the Wren, and my Hair is bold, like the Chestnut Bur—and my eyes, like the Sherry in the Glass, that the Guest leaves—Would this do just as well? It often alarms Father—He says death might occur, and he has Molds of all the rest—but he has no Mold of me....[14]
>
> Of "shunning Men and Women"—they talk of Hallowed things, aloud—and embarrass my Dog—He and I don't object to them, if they'll exist their side. I think Carlo would please you—He is dumb, and brave....[15]
>
> You noticed my dwelling alone.... I do not cross my Father's ground to any House or town....[16]

Dickinson would never have allowed herself to become the focus of a community deathwatch. Years later, Kafka felt the same way:

> A happy man does not see the dark side of reality. His sense of life suppresses the gnawing woodworm of the consciousness of death. One forgets that instead of walking, one is falling. It's as if one were drugged. So it's a direct offense to be asked after one's health. It's as if one apple asked another apple: "How are the worms that the insect bites gave you?" Or if one blade of grass asked another: "How are you withering? How goes your esteemed decomposition?" ... Inquiries about one's health increases one's consciousness of dying, to which as a sick man I am particularly exposed.... I cannot forget it. I have nothing which would drive it out of my mind.[17]

"How are you withering?" The Dickinsons were the First Family in a village where each resident was a target for gossip and innuendo, and where a person's misfortune quickly became the topic of the day. There are no reports that Emily advertised her grief, or surrendered to crying fits, or gave the impression that she was an invalid. Nevertheless, she may have worried that the shadow of disease was visible on her face and form, that she was marked by consumption. When Amherst celebrated the 1853 opening of rail service, Emily hid in the woods, caught a glimpse the train and then, as she reported in a letter to Austin, "ran home again for fear somebody would see me, and ask me *how I did*."[18] When she kept the outside world from getting a long hard look at her, was it because she wanted no one to know she was *hurting?*

753

> Grief is a Mouse—
> And chooses Wainscot in the Breast
> For His shy House—
> And baffles quest—
>
> Grief is a Thief—quick startled—
> Pricks His Ear—report to hear
> Of that Vast Dark—
> That swept His Being—back—
>
> Grief is a Juggler—boldest at the Play—
> Lest if He flinch—the eye that way
> Pounce on His Bruises—One—say—or Three—
> Grief is a Gourmand—spare His luxury—
>
> Best Grief is Tongueless—before He'll tell—
> Burn Him in the Public square—
> His Ashes—will
> Possibly—if they refuse—How then know—
> Since a Rack could'nt coax a syllable—now [1863]

Shielding herself from those who would attempt a closer look, Emily may have been hiding a *double* wound: disease and impenitence. The wounded deer is an apt metaphor. Perhaps she used that figure of speech because of its earlier use by Charlotte Brontë. "The Wounded Stag," was written by Brontë years before *Jane Eyre*. The poem opens:

> Passing amid the deepest shade
> Of the wood's sombre heart,
> Last night I saw a wounded deer
> Laid lonely and apart.
>
> Such light as pierced the crowded boughs
> (Light scattered, scant and dim),
> Passed through the fern that formed his couch
> And centred full on him.
>
> Pain trembled in his weary limbs,
> Pain filled his patient eye,
> Pain-crushed amid the shadowy fern
> His branchy crown did lie.

> Where were his comrades? where his mate?
> All from his death-bed gone!
> And he, thus struck and desolate,
> Suffered and bled alone.[19]

Charlotte Brontë repeated the image in her second novel, *Shirley*, written in 1848 as her sister Emily Brontë was near death. Shirley Keeldar visits with Caroline Helstone, and senses that Caroline is concealing something. Shirley gets right to the point: "A pretty expression you have in your countenance.... Wonderfully self-supported you look, *you solitude-seeking, wounded deer. Are you afraid Shirley will worry you, if she discovers that you are hurt, and that you bleed?*"[20]

Dickinson revered Charlotte Brontë, calling her *Queen* at a time when many of her Amherst neighbors were labeling the English novelist *coarse* and *heathenish*. When she returned *Jane Eyre* to its owner late in 1849, she attached a bouquet of fragrant box leaves and this note: "If all these leaves were altars, and on every one a prayer that Currer Bell might be saved—and you were God—would you answer it?"[21] Several years later, beginning to write poems, and knowing by then that "Currer Bell" was Charlotte Brontë, Dickinson answered her own question: "Oh what an afternoon for Heaven, / When 'Brontë' entered there!"[22]

Charlotte once gave this somewhat rosy assessment of Emily Brontë's seclusion:

> My sister's disposition was not naturally gregarious: circumstances favoured and fostered her tendency to seclusion; except to go to church, or take a walk on the hills, she rarely crossed the threshold of home.... Her imagination, which was a spirit more sombre than sunny—more powerful than sportive—found in such traits material whence it wrought creations like Heathcliff, like Earnshaw, like Catherine....
>
> Had she but lived, her mind would of itself have grown like a strong tree—loftier, straighter, wider-spreading—and its matured fruits would have attained a mellower ripeness and sunnier bloom....[23]

Charlotte's prediction that her sister would have grown into a "strong tree" is open to challenge. None of Emily Brontë's poems are marked by a sense of hope or even by the sort of wry humor employed by Dickinson. The "circumstances" contributing to Emily Brontë's seclusion were fixed in place, and there is nothing to suggest that her consumption was subject to remission. Added grief would have been her only reward for living on, for she would have been there for the deaths of her beloved sisters Anne and Charlotte, and of Charlotte's unborn child. And after Patrick Brontë's death in 1861, she would have been the sole survivor in a family of eight. Life for her had been a forest fire. How would she have grown "loftier, straighter, wider-spreading"?

Emily Brontë and Emily Dickinson became reclusive in similar circumstances: disease, the loss of close friends and relatives to consumption, an aversion to conventional religion, the comforts of a sturdy two-story home, a home library, a favorite writing table. But these are factors that are measurable—reclusion is also a state of mind. Brontë was truly dysfunctional and hermitic, Dickinson much less so. On a measure of reclusive behavior, Emily Brontë would be at or near the top of the scale, at a considerable distance from Emily Dickinson.

Brontë's intense solitude was due, in large measure, to her West Yorkshire location. Haworth was bordered on the east by class-ridden mill towns, on the west by gray and desolate moorland. Other factors affecting Brontë but not Dickinson were deaths in the immediate family, the unremitting progress of her illness, and the chronic consumption of her brother Bramwell and sisters Anne and Charlotte. Dickinson knew all the details from Elizabeth Gaskell's *The Life of Charlotte Brontë* (1857). Commiserating with Elizabeth Holland after the death of Dr. Holland in 1881, Dickinson referenced "gigantic Emily Brontë, of whom her Charlotte said 'Full of ruth for others, on herself she had no mercy.' The hearts that never lean, must fall. To moan is justified."[24]

Everyone who knows the story of the Brontës understands the source of Emily Brontë's moan. She was 3 when her mother died. At age 6 she and Charlotte, two years older, joined their sisters, Elizabeth, 10, and Maria, 12, at the Clergy Daughters' School at Cowan Bridge. The four girls were taught "godly" habits of prayer, cleanliness and self-denial, and punished when they showed too much spirit or any sign of vanity. Living conditions were Spartan, and meals so badly prepared as to be all but inedible. Maria and Elizabeth began to cough and lose weight and, removed from school by their father, died soon after. Emily Brontë was then not quite 7 years old. Except for a bit of schooling in 1835, half a year of teaching in 1837 and a 10-month sojourn in Brussels with her sister Charlotte in 1842, where she studied music and foreign languages, she stayed at home in Haworth with her father and three remaining siblings. Branwell, her brother, died first, in September 1848. When Emily Brontë died shortly after, at age 30, her wasted body was placed in a coffin only 16 inches wide. Almost immediately, Anne Brontë began to fail, and she too expired in 1849. When Charlotte realized that she was about to lose Anne, her only remaining sibling, her resolve and spirit broke. She turned to the God she had rebuked in *Jane Eyre* and other writings: "I must confess that, in the time which has elapsed since Emily's death, there have been moments of solitary, deep, inert affliction.... I have learnt that we are not to find solace in our own strength; we must seek it in God's omnipotence. Fortitude is good; but fortitude itself must be shaken under us to teach us how weak we are!"[25]

This is where Charlotte and Emily Brontë parted ways. Ingrid Geerken observed in 2004 that Emily Brontë "rejected the God and the church of her father (Patrick Brontë was a Evangelical clergyman) in favor of what she calls 'the God within my breast.' Emily refused to teach at Sunday school and did not attend church regularly. According to Stevie Davies, her attitude toward Christian piety 'varied from the cool to the contemptuous.' As Christianity could not assuage her mourning, the novel became the medium of Brontë's reparative work."[26] Like Dickinson, Brontë had little use for a conventional heaven. Brontë uses Catherine Earnshaw as her spokesperson: "I dreamt once that I was [in heaven] ... heaven did not seem to be my home; and I broke my heart with weeping to come back to earth; and the angels were so angry that they flung me out, into the middle of the heath on the top of Wuthering Heights where I woke sobbing for joy."[27]

Dickinson, reading of the lives and writings of the "electric" Brontës, as she called them, infused herself into their story. She, too, had encountered dread disease, had imagined herself dying, had doubted God and heaven, had written poetry in an upstairs bedroom.

247

The Lamp burns sure—within—
Tho' Serfs—supply the Oil—
It matters not the busy Wick—
At her phosphoric toil!

The Slave—forgets—to fill—
The Lamp—burns golden—on—
Unconscious that the oil is out—
As that the Slave—is gone. [1861]

But Dickinson wasn't truly alone. Her environment was invigorating, and her social interaction more robust than that of the Brontës. Amherst was located in the scenic and unspoiled Connecticut River Valley. Trees, flowering shrubs, fruit orchards, flower and vegetable gardens were everywhere. An unusual number of Amherst inhabitants were college graduates; almost every family owned their own home; the village supported a bookstore and one of the best country newspapers in New England, *The Hampshire and Franklin Express*. Emily regularly read *Harper's* and *Atlantic Monthly* and the *Springfield Republican*. The Dickinson family was responsible for making Amherst a college town. The Dickinson children knew the story of how their grandfather, Samuel Fowler Dickinson, had ruined himself financially to spearhead the effort to create Amherst College as a West Massachusetts counterweight to the growing religious liberalism in Boston and Worcester. The Dickinsons were the village's unofficial First Family. Both Edward and Austin Dickinson served long terms as Treasurer of Amherst College, and Austin conceived and supervised projects to beautify the village.

Emily Dickinson, to her dying day, always had Austin and Lavinia at her side for support and protection. In stark contrast, all six Brontë children died of consumption. Imagine if Austin had been snatched away in the mid-1850s, and Lavinia a few years later—Dickinson's poems, if written at all, might have turned out to be fully as dark as the poems of Emily Brontë. Dickinson's immediate family surrounded her throughout her most creative years. Edward Dickinson was the first to die, in 1874. Emily's mother followed eight years later, *after resting at home for the second half of her 78 years*. After his marriage to Sue Gilbert, Austin lived next door to the Dickinson homestead at Evergreens, a fashionable Italianate house built for the couple by Edward Dickinson, a place that Sue used as a literary salon (Emerson, among others, visited there).

Even in seclusion, Emily was a social being, her relationships widening and deepening through the mails, Over her lifetime, she sent out as many as ten thousand letters, and in turn received a like amount. Her withdrawal was, at least in part, *a kind of self-quarantine*—she might not have known that others might *catch* her disease, but she may have been convinced that they were eager to *catch on* to it.

Dickinson had easy access to the latest novels. She was particularly excited by Lady Georgiana Fullerton's novel, *Ellen Middleton*. Austin Dickinson, still in Boston in 1852, sent the book as a gift to her. She thanked him: "I have read 'Ellen Middleton' and now Mat [Sue Gilbert's sister, Martha] has it. I need'nt tell you I like it, *nor need I tell you more, for you know already*."[28] The title character, Ellen, is plunged into melodrama: an orphan, she is taken in by an uncle and his wife; bitterness develops between Ellen and her stepsister, Julia, who is upset because her mother adores Ellen; Julia furiously taunts Ellen, who lashes back in a moment of anger, striking Julia and accidentally knocking her down a steep flight of steps leading to a raging mountain stream, into which Julia falls and drowns. Ellen is unaware that the incident has been witnessed. She now stands to inherit the family estate. She falls in love with Edward Middleton, a cousin, but soon after they marry, the story of the "crime" is revealed. Edward turns Ellen out of the house:

Edward had forbidden my name to be uttered before him.... I would take another, and bury myself in a seclusion where I might linger through the increasing symptoms of that illness which, during the last few days, I had detected, and recognized by the hectic spots on my cheeks, by a racking cough, and nightly sweats. There I would live alone, and suffer alone, and die alone.[29]

Mrs. Denley, the landlady at Ellen's new lodgings, is concerned about Ellen's appearance, and judges that she is "dying by inches—of something—the Lord only knows what—for Dr. Reid doesn't." Mrs. Denley brings flowers for Ellen's room:

She caught my hand ... and her hand, sir!—why it was more like one of those bits of hot coal there, than the little white soft thing it looked like, and when I looked at her face, there was a bright fever spot on each cheek, and her lips were as white as could be. "You are very ill, ma'am," says I to her; "your hand is burning hot." She put it to her forehead and "it does not feel hot to me," says she ... but now ... she has taken to her bed, and is in a very bad way indeed...."[30]

Ellen's hectic and her fever are signs of advanced consumption. Lady Fullerton leaves no doubt that the end result will be fatal. The moral of the story is clear: thwarted romantic desire leads to pulmonary consumption and then to the grave. Emily wrote to Sue Gilbert (who was then teaching in Baltimore, and not yet engaged to Austin): "You and I will have an hour with 'Edward' and 'Ellen Middleton,' sometime when you get home—*we must find out if some things contained therein are true, and if they are, what you and me are coming to!*"[31] Was Emily Dickinson harboring a terrible crime? Had she caused someone death? Had she been banished from wedlock? Of course not. What Emily and Sue were "coming to" might well have been etched in the disease that blackened their family histories: Sue's mother had died of consumption; both of Emily's grandmothers had succumbed to the disease, and Emily's mother was housebound with a mysterious, unidentified malady. The two 21-year-old women were dealing with complex romantic issues—Ben was off in Worcester, married, and Austin seemed at times more interested in Sue's older sister, Martha. For Emily and Sue, the future may have seemed a slippery slope at best. But at least they had each other to confide in.

1853 was an oppressive year for Emily. Ben died, Austin became engaged to Sue, and it seemed everyone was either dying or crowding into Christ's camp. Emily's guard was up. Her reluctance to show herself in Amherst may have been intensified by articles she was now reading in *Harper's New Monthly Magazine*. The publication started up in June, 1850, and Vinnie's subscription began soon after, never to lapse. The two sisters anticipated each issue, devouring the contents.

For Emily, reading *Harper's* was a double-edged sword. Some articles lifted the spirit, others made the skin crawl. Even then, magazines capitalized on the news value of dread disease. Consumption was referenced time and again, often in terms of God's will, and often in lurid clinical detail, as in an eruption of blood from the mouth. A reasonable assumption is that articles dealing with the disease caught Dickinson's eye, especially pieces featuring deathbed scenes.

> 1726
>
> The right to perish might be thought
> An undisputed right
> Attempt it, and the Universe
> Upon the opposite
> Will concentrate it's officers—
> You cannot even die
> But nature and mankind must pause
> To pay you scrutiny—[undated]

In its description of oncoming winters, *Harper's* was less than sensitive: "In the country, the season, however splendid, is sad; for the pilgrim of the year understands that these brilliant days are the last green points of the pleasant summer along which he has been idly coasting, and that he must now stretch straight away into the barren winter. He gazes wistfully at the landscape; but its crimson green is only the hectic of disease."[32]

In March, 1852, *Harper's* ran "Blighted Flowers," the story of one man's infatuation with two girls he saw frequently on the street, a beautiful girl of seventeen, an embroideress, and her even more lovely younger sister. But soon "the unmistakable indications of consumption made their appearance: the harassing cough, the hectic cheek, the deep-settled pain in the side, the failing breath.... All the world knows the ending of such a hopeless strife as this."[33] The man becomes their benefactor and watches on, helplessly, as the two girls waste away and die.

The October 1852 *Harper's* featured "The Life and Death of Paganini." It turns out that Nicolo Paganini suffered the same kind of indignities that had been visited on Frédéric Chopin and George Sand in Majorca:

> On his arrival at Naples, Paganini found ... his health daily becoming worse, [and] it was reported that he was consumptive. At Naples, the opinion prevails that consumption is contagious. His landlord, alarmed at having in his house one who was supposed to be dying of this malady, had the inhumanity to turn him into the street, with all he possessed.
>
> Paganini was dying.... The medical men advised him to proceed to Marseilles, the climate of which they considered favorable to his health. He

followed this advice.... Vain hope! [He] resolved on passing the winter at Nice. Nice was destined to be his last abode. The progress of his malady was rapid, his voice became almost extinct, and dreadful fits of coughing, which daily became more frequent, and, finally, reduced him to a shadow. The sinking of his features, a certain token of approaching death, was visible in his face....[34]

In 1853, *Harper's* included a small, scary and decidedly unscientific piece, "A Slight Cold":

Consider "a slight cold" to be in the nature of a chill, caught by a sudden contact with your grave; or as occasioned by the damp finger of death laid upon you, as it were, to mark you for HIS.... [Beware of those who] choose to NEGLECT A SLIGHT COLD. Let not these complain of being bitten by a reptile, which they have cherished to maturity in their very bosoms, when they might have crushed it in the egg!

Now, if we call "a slight cold" the egg, and pleurisy—inflammation of the lungs—asthma—CONSUMPTION, the enormous reptile.... There are many ways in which this egg may be deposited and hatched. Going suddenly, slightly clad, from a heated into a cold atmosphere, especially if you can contrive to be in a state of perspiration, sitting or standing in a draught, however slight—it is the breath of death, reader, and laden with the vapors of the grave![35]

Pulmonary consumption and the literature of the macabre went hand in hand. Like Edgar Allan Poe, who watched on as tuberculosis laid waste to his delicate young wife, Emily Dickinson was drawn to write, repeatedly, of the fine line separating life and death:

308

I breathed enough to take the Trick—
And now, removed from Air—
I simulate the Breath, so well—
That One, to be quite sure—

The Lungs are stirless—must descend
Among the cunning cells—
And touch the Pantomime—Himself,
How numb, the Bellows feels! [1862]

"Extracts From the Portfolio of an Excitement Seeker" ran in Harper's in 1853. A boy tells Grandfather of a near-death episode: "the most curious part ... was the acuteness of my sense of hearing when every other sense was dead and still. The ear seemed ten times more sensitive than ever, when the whole of the rest of the body was dead." Grandfather: "that can be easily accounted for.... Hearing is a sense which depends less upon volition than any other. You must open your eyes to see; you must open your mouth to taste; you must expand your nostrils to smell; but sound walks in, without asking your leave."[36]

In 1859, Dickinson read in *Harper's* of a buzzing fly:

> In the autumn there are some preternaturally still, shadowed days ... when single leaves, at intervals drop quietly to the ground, like tears that fall without sobbing; and the landscape seems to be utterly self-involved, meditating its own decay. There is a more conscious sadness in such days than in all others of the year. The trees make no effort to hold their leaves; the warm, rich softness of the air seems a mockery over the brown meadows, like a sweet south wind, full of life, and hope, and joy, blowing over the face of one who lies dying of consumption.... The eye steals away to the fields and sees the great haystack roofed for snow—sees the last stooks of cornstalks removed ... and although the sun shines and the air is warm, and a late fly buzzes upon the window, there is a foreshadowing silence—the sweetness of placid and resigned decay.
>
> In the feeling of these days is one of perfect resignation. They are as effortless as the outline of a flower... They are like the last serene hours of a good man, who passes from life to life as a king from chamber to chamber of his palace; who lies, sweet and silent, remembering the early days, the old friends, the tender ties, the sympathies, joys, and sorrows, that have made the world dear and sacred....[37]

The 1853 and 1859 pieces in *Harper's* may have contributed to Dickinson's striking poem, "I heard a Fly buzz—when I died—," a poem that turns the traditional Calvinist deathwatch upside down. The speaker in the poem spends her dying moments attentive, not to Jesus, but to a fly. The poet John Ciardi thought of the fly as "the last kiss of the world, the last buzz of life."[38]

591

I heard a Fly buzz—when I died—
The Stillness in the Room
Was like the Stillness in the Air—
Between the Heaves of Storm—

The Eyes around—had wrung them dry—
And Breaths were gathering firm
For that last Onset—when the King
Be witnessed—in the Room—

I willed my Keepsakes—Signed away
What portion of me be
Assignable—and then it was
There interposed a Fly—

With Blue—uncertain—stumbling Buzz—
Between the light—and me—
And then the Windows failed—and then
I could not see to see—[1863]

One suspects that Emily Brontë would have relished "I heard a Fly buzz—." A study of Brontë by Ingrid Geerken speaks of *corpsing* incidents in *Wuthering Heights*, including one in which we see Catherine Earnshaw

> "dashing her head against the arm of the sofa, and grinding her teeth," before "stretch[ing] herself out stiff, and turn[ing] up her eyes, while her cheeks, blanched and livid, assumed the aspect of death." ... Heathcliff cradles her body—her arms suddenly relax, and her head hangs down.... Corpsing makes the experience of death accessible by representing what it feels like to be dead. In this way, corpsing is motivated both by a desire to simulate a state close to that of a dead loved one, and to experience our own death—paradoxically—in a way that we can communicate and remember.[39]

Corpsing, observes Geerken, pops up time and again in nineteenth century creative works. Poe comes immediately to mind, and the pale slender women in Pre-Raphaelite paintings. Geerken focuses on Emily Dickinson and Christina Rossetti:

> Emily Dickinson can begin a poem (remarkably) by saying "I heard a Fly buzz—when I died—." Christina Rossetti, in another register, expresses a state of disembodiment in which not only the material body, but the entire physical world, is erased.... Poems such as Dickinson's "I felt a Funeral, in my Brain," and Rossetti's After Death describe the sensation of death in material and empirical terms. The agent—in an expression of impossible agency—still sees, hears and smells even as she inhabits what Rossetti calls the "death apartment." Like these poets, Brontë desentimentalizes the typical features of Victorian deathbed accounts (such as the visible rising of the soul or mist, the last look, of the metaphor of Death as teacher and deliverer), transforming them from the inside out through empirical observation.[40]

Christina Rossetti was born five days before Emily Dickinson, and outlived her by eight years. She was seriously ill through much of her life with Graves disease and with the cancer that eventually killed her. She came near to marrying twice, before retiring into quiet seclusion.

In November, 1857, *Harper's* gave their readers "Joseph Thorne—His Calling." It's likely that Emily thought of Ben Newton as she read the story: a boy and a girl meet and have long talks on summer evenings; the boy speaks to the girl's father of his intentions; the father rejects the notion; the boy goes off to further a career, the girl pines for him; "hectic on his wasting cheek," he sickens and dies of consumption; she vows to keep his spirit alive until they unite in Heaven. Some excerpts:

> ... Joseph Thorne and pretty Mabel Emerson.... Thorne, unknown to himself, was a poet ... he was the only one who had ever looked into her heart.... Her father, the richest and busiest farmer in all Westvale, had never found time to

learn any thing of her inner nature. Perhaps he was not even capable of understanding her.

[It] was many months, even after they each believed themselves dearer to the other than any thing else on earth, before any binding vows of love were spoken.... But the charmed hour came at last....

"I love your daughter, and she loves me, will you consent that she shall be my wife?" ... "Your wife! my daughter Mabel! What are your prospects? What is your business? What would you keep her on? ... I am sorry, I am truly sorry ... but, if such is the life you have marked out, I can not give her to you."

... the light of her life seemed to have gone out and her soul shuddered—alone in the darkness.... There was no visible change, save that her lips smiled a little more seldom, and her cheek was white as marble.... One afternoon in May she sat alone under the trees.... Her father's step along the highway disturbed her reverie. There were tears in his eyes.... "Poor Mabel!" he said.... I have seen Joseph Thorne. He came home this afternoon, as I think, to die. He wants you. Go to him, Mabel."

... The cottage door was open.... Mabel had crossed the room; her arms were folded about his neck, her lips clung to his in a long kiss of love and despair. For six weeks she was his constant nurse.... Mabel felt then how truly she was part of himself—that their two souls, separated though they might be for years, must be reunited before either could be a symmetrical and perfect whole. His summons came on a June twilight.... "Mabel, my life's angel, I will wait for you where it needeth not to marry or be given in marriage...."

Mabel Emerson's work is not yet done. She is wedded to a hope and a memory.... Wherever trouble is, wherever hearts are struggling with sorrow, her presence is at the door; and she whom Joseph Thorne loved to call the angel of his life will go to her last rest crowned with the blessings of those ready to perish. "Her works they shall follow her."[41]

Was Emily Dickinson, like Mabel in this story, wed to a hope and to a memory? The letters from Ben—emotional nourishment—were always close at hand. In stark contrast, Emily Brontë had no letters from a loved one to read and re-read. In fact, Emily Brontë had few letters of *any* kind to read. She seldom corresponded—only three letters are on record. Charlotte *pushed* her sister Emily to publish her poems and her one novel. Walking the moors was Emily Brontë's chief balm—the hills, the sunshine, the breeze posed no threat. In "Shall Earth No More Inspire Thee," she lodged her trust, her soul, and *the voice of the poem* in Mother Earth:

> I know my mountain breezes
> Enchant and soothe thee still—
> I know my sunshine pleases
> Despite thy wayward will.

When day with evening blending
Sinks from the summer sky,
I've seen thy spirit bending
In fond idolatry.

I've watched thee every hour—
I know my mighty sway—
I know my magic power
To drive thy griefs away.

Few hearts to mortals given
On earth so wildly pine,
Yet none would ask a Heaven
More like the Earth than mine.

Then let my winds caress thee—
Thy comrade let me be—
Since naught beside can bless thee,
Return and dwell with me.[42]

Dickinson had something Brontë lacked—an impish streak. Even when comparing earthly to everlasting life, Dickinson could be a bit droll:

544

"Heaven" has different Signs—to me—
Sometimes, I think that Noon
Is but a symbol of the Place—
And when again, at Dawn,

A mighty look runs round the World
And settles in the Hills—
An Awe if it should be like that
Opon the Ignorance steals—

The Orchard, when the Sun is on—
The Triumph of the Birds
When they together Victory make—
Some Carnivals of Clouds—

The Rapture of a finished Day
Returning to the West—
All these—remind us of the place
That Men call "Paradise"—

Itself be fairer—we suppose—
But how Ourself, shall be
Adorned, for a Superior Grace—
Not yet, our eyes can see—[1863]

The two poems argue that *heaven can wait*. The two Emilys write of glorious sunsets, warm sunshine, mountain breezes, geese flying in formation, cloud-pictures, and both wonder how, in the afterlife, God can improve on all this. Dickinson's style is coy. Brontë is didactic, convinced there is no God, but only Mother Nature: "naught beside can bless thee / Return and dwell with me."

Because both Emilys wrote out of private pain, and not for publication, their impressions, emotions, attitudes and convictions are authentic. While it's true that Dickinson mailed her poems to Holland, Bowles and Higginson, all men of letters, it was not publication she craved so much as validation as a poet or, at the least, positive feedback. Published poets became celebrities, subject to public scrutiny. Dickinson had her reasons for wanting to remain a *nobody*.

1095

When I have seen the Sun emerge
From His amazing House—
And leave a Day at every Door
A Deed, in every place—

Without the incident of Fame
Or accident of Noise—
The Earth has seemed to me a Drum,
Pursued of little Boys [1865]

Dickinson first began writing poems in 1858, not long after she read "Joseph Thorne." The numbness she had felt at the loss of her daisies was then transmuting into a profound sadness. There is a difference between *depression* and *sadness*. Gloria Steinem, the co-founder of *Ms.* Magazine, married for the first time in the year 2000 to a man she adored, a humanitarian and animal activist, David Bale. He died, three years later, of brain lymphoma. Steinem was asked afterwards if she had fallen into depression. Losing her husband, she replied, helped her to understand that, in depression, nothing matters, but that in sadness, everything matters. This is what, on the brink of becoming a poet in 1858, Emily Dickinson came to realize: *everything mattered*. Her heart went out to Emily Brontë, who fought a losing battle to physical and emotional pain. Dickinson understood: "To moan is justified."

Wuthering Heights is the literary equivalent of Edvard Munch's iconic painting, "The Scream." In boyhood, Munch lost his mother and sister Sophie to tuberculosis, and he himself was often sick. His first major work, "The Sick Child," begun when he was 18, was based on Sophie's death. He titled other works "Death in the Sickroom," "Anxiety," "Vampire," "The Blossom of Pain." His early paintings are bleak: limp figures with featureless or hidden faces, over which loom the threatening shapes of heavy trees and brooding houses. His women are, alternately, innocent sufferers or lurid, life-devouring vampires.

Franz Kafka once told a friend that the poet's "song is only a scream," and that the poet "is not a giant, but only a brightly plumaged bird in the cage of existence."[43]

360

The Soul has Bandaged moments—
When too appalled to stir—
She feels some ghastly Fright come up
And stop to look at her—

Salute her, with long fingers—
Caress her freezing hair—
Sip, Goblin, from the very lips
The Lover—hovered—o'er—
Unworthy, that a thought so mean
Accost a Theme—so—fair—

The soul has moments of escape—
When bursting all the doors—
She dances like a Bomb, abroad,
And swings opon the Hours,

As do the Bee—delirious borne—
Long Dungeoned from his Rose—
Touch Liberty—then know no more—
But Noon, and Paradise—

The Soul's retaken moments—
When, Felon led along,
With shackles on the plumed feet,
And staples, in the song,

The Horror welcomes her, again,
These, are not brayed of Tongue—[1862]

> How well I remember that last, awful night! ... Zillah Bliss ... sat beside her.... "Richard," she cried ... save her!" ... With a convulsive effort, my mother sat erect.... Blood burst anew from her mouth and nostrils.... I wiped away the life-blood oozing from between my mother's lips. I kissed them again and again.
> —Josephine Franklin, *Rachel*, 1860

8. Terror

In September 1861, Emily Dickinson experienced a *volcanic* event. "I had a terror—since September—I could tell to none," she informed Thomas Wentworth Higginson, "and so I sing, as the Boy does by the Burying Ground—because I am afraid."[1]

Of what was Dickinson afraid? And why could she tell no one? After failing to locate a telltale event, a smoking gun, leading scholars decided that the "terror" was self-generated, the product of an overwrought imagination. Thomas H. Johnson in 1955 argued that the crisis was "precipitated by [Rev. Charles] Wadsworth's acceptance of a call to the Calvary Church in San Francisco.... To Emily Dickinson, Wadsworth's removal was terrifying because she feared she might never be able to control her emotions or her reason without his guidance."[2]

At the time Johnson was writing this (in the pre-feminist 1950s), three letters drafted by Dickinson came to light—in *An Emily Dickinson Encyclopedia*, Marianne Noble calls them "three long, anguished love letters."[3] The first was written in 1858, the other two in 1861. The letters are addressed to some unnamed "Master." Richard Sewall was certain the Master Letters were "vital indeed," and the key to Dickinson's terror in 1861: "There is no doubt of the importance of these three letters," he wrote in 1974, even while admitting that, to him, the letters were "baffling."[4]

Sewall fell into *a priori* thinking. Unable to find an overt cause for Dickinson's "terror," he pointed to the Master letters and, like Johnson, supported a "troubled romance" theory. Paula Bennett was one of the many critics to go along with this seemingly snug logic: "all the evidence of her letters and poems suggests that the September terror had to do with a breakdown that occurred in her relationship with a man that she had been writing to since 1858. It is this man whom critics and biographers, following the poet's lead, have chosen to call the Master since his true identity can probably never be confirmed."[5]

At the time Sewall was writing *The Life of Emily Dickinson*, those debating the identity of the so-called "Master" had narrowed the field of candidates to two: Reverend Charles Wadsworth and Samuel Bowles. Sewall saw this result as premature, and hesitated to make a choice. He finally tilted towards Bowles, but just barely: "we look in vain in all three letters for the living presence of either one of them."[6] Cynthia Wolff was adamant; she maintained that "no detail is precise enough to identify any man in particular. Wadsworth and Bowles have both been conjectured, but these are unlikely choices."[7] Wolff puzzled over the romance scenario: "For a long time critics supposed that this 'terror' was some disappointment in love. Common sense in some measure argued against such a inference: she scarcely knew Higginson at the time of this letter, and it would be astonishing to find her alluding to such an intimate matter in so early a note. Moreover, 'terror' is a curious word to use about a broken love affair: 'loss' or 'disappointment' would surely be more apt."[8] Wolff's theory was that a crisis of *health* was the cause of the "terror since September." But it was not tuberculosis that Wolff had in mind. She believed that Dickinson was afraid of losing her eyesight.[9]

Habegger rejects the thinking of Johnson, Sewall *and* Wolff. "The enigmatic statement ["I had a terror…"] has been explained chiefly in two ways," he writes, "that she had early symptoms of her eye trouble of 1864 and 1865 and feared she was going blind, and that she felt deserted when she learned that Wadsworth would accept the pastorate at San Francisco's Calvary Presbyterian Church. Under scrutiny, neither explanation holds up. There is no real evidence of eye trouble in 1861, and no reason to think this would be a problem she could 'tell to none.' As to the minister … it was not till December 9 that the congregation voted to call Wadsworth."[10]

Unable, like the others, to pinpoint any one event as the cause for the 1861 crisis, Habegger substitutes generalities, describing Dickinson's terror as "profound and systemic and ongoing," the "thing Dickinson had been booked to fall into," an abject fear related to a "disconnection between her heart's absolutism and the realities of life."[11] Even, perhaps, a form of *paranoia*: "Dickinson felt deserted by everyone who was dearest and could understand her, and on whom she most depended."[12]

Without intending to, Johnson, Sewall, Wolff and Habegger all undercut a great poet. It is sexist to say that the bottom fell out of Dickinson's life when Wadsworth relocated to California, or when Bowles went to Europe in search of health. To say she lived in terror as a result of an eye problem is to paint her a hypochondriac, or hysterical. To imply, as Habegger does, that she was mired in a "sense of isolation, abandonment, rejection,"[13] is to deny that she lived in seclusion by choice. Dickinson selects words meticulously. She writes of a terror *since* September, an ongoing *condition* of terror, not an encapsulated event such as the relocation of a loved one. She cannot speak to anyone of the trigger event, certainly not to Higginson, and not even to those close to her: not Vinnie, not her sister-in-law Sue, not Elizabeth Holland, *no one*. Perhaps that's because it's easier to speak of a broken heart than of broken lungs, especially if you're a member of the first family of Amherst, and the only impenitent member of that family in a town where penitence was prized. Emily's loyalty to those in her family, and especially to Father, ran deep; it may have been one reason she wrote *in slant*. That way, she could *tell all the truth*, as she saw it, about disease and dying, and yet safeguard her family from charges of religious backsliding, from scandal.

Readers of Dickinson might want to take a long look at the tail end of her "terror" statement—"and so I sing, as the Boy does by the Burying Ground—because I am afraid." A *cemetery* is not an abstraction, nor does it call to mind bad eyesight or a failed romance. It seems that Dickinson's TB continued well beyond the 1846–1852 period spotlighted by Dr. Hirschhorn. In the second of three Master Letters (dated "early 1861" by Franklin), she lets on that "Wonder wastes my pound, you said I had no size to spare," and informs Master of a "cough as big as a thimble" and "a Tomahawk in my side."[14] Considerable weight loss and pain under the sternum are signs that her condition had worsened. Was her sputum flecked with blood? Was Emily terrified by something life-threatening: *an eruption of blood from the lungs?*

> 422
>
> Give little Anguish—
> Lives will fret—
> Give Avalanches—
> And they'll slant—
> Straighten—look cautious for their Breath—
> But make no syllable—like Death—
> Who only shows his Marble Disc—
> Sublimer sort—than Speech—[1862]

A hemorrhage needs no poetry, Dickinson implies; the gravestone, with clarity, tells it all.

In Dickinson's day, bleeding from the lungs was an occasion for panic.

An American doctor, J. H. Pulte, addressed the problem in 1857: "Spitting or coughing up of blood is generally considered by persons such a dangerous, and, for the life of the patient, fatal symptom, that they lose, when it occurs, all presence of mind, frequently incapacitating them for the right action in the case."[15] The death scene in *Rachel* rings true. Ellen brings up blood from the lungs. The blood is *everywhere*—on the hands of her husband, on the pillows and sheets, on the white dress of Zillah, her son's fiancé. Zillah knows what it means: "Richard, save her—save her!" But it is already too late. Blood pours from Ellen's nose and mouth. Understandably, no one knows what to do next. Richard, out of his mind, kisses his mother's blood-soaked lips repeatedly. She dies in his arms.

The image of a son kissing his mother's bloodied lips must have given pause to New Englanders who knew stories of persons who had died of consumption, only to return from the dead to feed on the blood of family members, causing them to waste away. Vampire crazes—there was one in the Connecticut River Valley in the mid–1800s—have long been associated with pulmonary tuberculosis. The term *nosferatu*, popularized by Bram Stoker's *Dracula*, is an archaic term derived from the Greek *nosophorus*, meaning "plague carrier." To "kill" such vampires, New Englanders exhumed and mutilated a number of cadavers. Occasionally, a corpse was found to have blood on its lips, surely an alarming sight, but one that often occurs naturally as the corpse decomposes.

Henry David Thoreau, struggling in 1859 with TB, recorded in his journal: "I have just read of a family in Vermont who, several of the members having died of consumption, just burned the lungs, heart and liver of the last deceased, in order to prevent any more from having it."[16] Thoreau made a desperate attempt to beat the disease. Unable in 1861 to afford a stay in the West Indies or the south of Europe, he went off in May to Minnesota instead. Yes, Minnesota! The *New Englander and Yale Review* had trumpeted the latest fad, the "healthfulness of Minnesota, ... already an asylum for invalids from all parts of the land.... The victims of pulmonary disease ... are sent, not, as formerly, to the warm latitudes, but to cold ones. The dry, bracing air of Minnesota has proved peculiarly remedial, as the high, cool districts of Switzerland have done."[17] In Minnesota, Thoreau investigated the flora and fauna of the West, and visited with Sioux Indians. His excursion—3,000 miles over two months—was cut short when his cough worsened, and he returned to Concord. Ten months later, at the age of 44, Thoreau died of TB. Dickinson admired the man deeply, and four years after his death wrote to Sue Gilbert Dickinson, vacationing at Cape Cod: "Was the sea cordial? Kiss him for Thoreau."[18]

Thoreau, the hardheaded naturalist, had been grasping at straws. Lacking reliable facts about the disease that was killing him, he had run off to Minnesota. And who could blame him? Everything about consumption—its cause, its prognosis, its cure—was up for grabs. One physician who tried to cut through the fog of ignorance was John Ware, President of the Massachusetts Medical Society from 1848 to 1852. In his *On Hemoptysis as a Symptom* (1860), he reported his detailed 40-year study of 300 consumptives. Dr. Ware listed the age at which each patient experienced his or her first attack of bleeding[19]:

Age at 1st Hemoptysis	Male	Female	TOTAL
Under 15	1	3	4
15–20	12	27	39
21–25	31	32	63
26–30	36	40	76
31–35	31	12	43
36–40	18	16	34
41–50	15	15	30
51–60	5	13	18
61–70	1	4	5
Over 70	3	2	5
TOTAL	153	164	317

In September, 1861, Emily Dickinson was 30 years old, an age at which consumptives were at high risk for a first hemorrhage. This is not, of course, evidence that she had one. Or she may have first bled from the lungs a few years earlier. But it is far from unthinkable that someone at age 30, with a family history of pulmonary problems, sharp pain in the side and a persistent cough should begin to raise some blood. Around the time of her "terror" letter to Higginson, Dickinson wrote the following:

465

The name—of it—is "Autumn"—
The hue—of it—is Blood—
An Artery—opon the Hill—
A Vein—along the Road—

Great Globules—in the Alleys—
And Oh, the Shower of Stain—
When Winds—upset the Basin—
And spill the Scarlet Rain—

> It sprinkles Bonnets—far below—
> It gathers ruddy Pools—
> Then—eddies like a Rose—away—
> Opon Vermillion Wheels—[1862]

Cynthia Chaliff, in an essay she contributed to *Poetry, the Healer* (1970), saw Dickinson's fears as "phantoms" arising from an "obscure psychological crisis of her middle years."[20] Chaliff characterized "The name—of it—is 'Autumn'" as a "vivid evocation not of a desperate situation, but of desperate emotions that result when man finds himself, for whatever reason, devoid of hope."[21] Chaliff suggested that Dickinson was detached from reality: "What is described is a literal bloodbath, like the scene of some wholesale retribution, and the poet is the unwitting perpetrator, for she creates and reports it ... [out of] her thirst for blood and revenge."[22]

Reacting to the surfeit of blood, Chaliff describes Dickinson as someone out of control, someone with the attributes of a vampire. This is a sad and unseeing approach. Emily Dickinson was not rabid, nor rancorous, nor the only tubercular poet to associate autumn with blood. Lesya Ukrainka, the foremost woman writer in Ukrainian literature, a leading figure in its modernist movement, had her first acute lung problems in 1901, when she was 30 years old. Seeking cures in Davos, Switzerland and in Egypt, Ukrainka survived TB for another 12 years. When she wrote about her struggles, she was dealing with an intractable disease, not with "phantoms." Ukrainka's autumn poem (in translation) is considerably more self-revealing than the one written by Dickinson:

<u>Autumn</u>

Autumn with fingers all bloodstained hastes on,
Longing to meet with her dear distant sun.
Blood on her garments enhances her charm,
Spattering them like brocade.

Thus for the sun is fair Autumn adorned,
Robed like a princess for festival rites.
All that the world hath of beauty she takes,
Garbing herself in its sheen.

Ah, but the days swiftly shorten and change,
Sometimes the sun gleams, then shadows his face.
Fast-fading Autumn now grieves and laments,
Hopes of the spring-time are gone.

Autumn goes on, but invisible thorns
Tear at her body and wear it away;
Yet, though despairing, she smiles as she cries:
"Sun, look upon me, I smile!"

> Yonder the sun sinks behind the dark hills,
> Blasts of raw wind springing up from the frost,
> Massive gray clouds slowly pile in the sky,
> Winter replies: "Lo, I come!"
>
> Autumn then tears at her garment, bloodstained,
> Down at their feet they lie strewn in a heap;
> Naked, defenceless, she stands as she groans:
> "Come then, for now is the time!"[23]

An apt title for either of these two Autumn poems might be "Hemorrhage." That Dickinson lived on for 25 years after her "terror in September" does not rule out the possibility that she spit up blood in 1861. Despite the "death warrant" analogy, not everyone died, like Ellen in *Rachel*, hard upon a first hemoptysis. And some lived on for years and even decades. Dr. Ware sorted his research population into three groups, roughly equal in numbers. Class One: those in which hemoptysis occurred as the first symptom, or very early in the disease, followed by a quick and steady plunge to death. Matilda Hoffman, Washington Irving's fiancée, and Emma Washburn, who perished so quickly at Mount Holyoke, fit this category. Class Two: those who lived on after the first hemoptysis, displaying distinct marks of consumption, but whose decline was slow, and not always progressive. They had periods of remarkable relief and even remission, before dying of TB, death occurring at various periods following the first hemoptysis, from two to forty years. Ukrainka falls into this grouping, along with Ellen Tucker Emerson. Class Three: those who lived on after the first hemoptysis, perhaps with one or more episodes, but who regained their health, with no return of the disease. Some were still alive, in ordinary health; others died of something other than consumption at periods from 2 to 37 years following the initial hemorrhage.[24] Francis March, the suitor dumped by Emily Fowler, meets this description, and perhaps Robert Louis Stevenson. And if Emily Dickinson brought up blood from the lungs in 1861, then she too belongs in this category.

One case study in post-hemoptysis survival stands out. Paul Hamilton Hayne was born in the same year as Emily Dickinson, 1830, and followed her in death by only seven weeks in 1886. He was raised in the South Carolina home of a wealthy and cultured uncle, Robert Y. Hayne, a U. S. Senator famous for debating Daniel Webster on the issue of states' rights. Complaining of "the lung trouble" in the 1850s, Paul Hamilton Hayne abandoned a career in law to take up the writing of poems.[25] He became known as "The Poet Laureate of the South," and maintained close ties to the two other famous post–Civil War poets of the South, Henry Timrod and Sidney Lanier. Timrod died of pulmonary TB at age 38, and Lanier of the same disease at age 39.

In the year that Timrod died, 1867, Hayne, then 37, was suffering violent bleedings from the lungs. To "a dear old friend," he wrote what he thought might be his last letter. He was sure he was about to die:

> Just now, I am so sick, weary & despondent, that it is with an effort I am able even to scribble these few lines.... If I live long enough (which is doubtful, for I have had several severe hemorrhages lately), my design is to publish.... I will leave the MSS with you.... The room turns round, & round, as I glance up from the paper, & sometimes, I can, with great difficulty, catch my breath. Ah! the great secret we all pant to discover, seems very near to me now.[26]

Seven years later, Hayne contacted America's most beloved poet, Henry Wadsworth Longfellow: "Since I saw you last ... I have suffered from illness so *severe*, that *twice* I confidently expected a removal from this strange world ... that terrible autumn 'Panic' struck me down."[27] And four years after that, once more to Longfellow: "I would have thanked you long ago ... but have been *ill* from several attacks of hemorrhage."[28] In 1879, Hayne's wife, Mary, wrote to Longfellow that Hayne had suffered a "constant loss of blood (for nearly a year)."[29] Hayne confided in March of 1881 to one of his admirers that "I *still* suffer from occasional attacks of Hemorrhage,"[30] and two months later he opened up to a fellow author whose health was "frail & uncertain": "Here, *truly* I can sympathize with you, because during 25 years (a sad quarter of a century), I myself have not known a solitary day of strength, or freedom from pain & lassitude."[31]

Paul Hamilton Hayne suffered dozens of hemorrhages, yet lived to the age of 56, eventually dying of TB. Dr. Ware, In his 1860 report, correctly noted that hemoptysis, "often so fearfully apprehended by the patient, and so appalling to his friends when it occurs,"[32] was rarely fatal. Even in Class One, almost all patients died as a result of their consumption, and not because they had bled from the lungs. Only a few died by suffocating in their own blood. Ware was careful to tack on this warning: "no patient who has once had hemoptysis, however slight, can ever afterward be regarded as entirely secure from the development of tubercular disease."[33] And there's the rub. We all know that terror need strike but once, in sufficient force, to hold those victimized and those around them in terror for years afterward.

457
Nature—sometimes sears a Sapling—
Sometimes—scalps a Tree—
Her Green People recollect it
When they do not die—

> Fainter Leaves—to Further Seasons—
> Dumbly testify—
> We—who have the Souls—
> Die oftener—Not so vitally—[1862]

Dickinson's "terror" followed a series of TB-related deaths. Martha Snell struggled at her family's South Pleasant Street home in Amherst for two years before she succumbed. Her sister Mary, four years older, had been one of Emily Dickinson's "special Amherst friends."[34] Mary had visited with Emily at Mount Holyoke in December 1847, bringing along a letter from Austin, and she was also close to Vinnie, with whom she corresponded. Martha and Mary were the daughters of Ebenezer Strong Snell, a brilliant professor of mathematics and natural philosophy at Amherst College from 1834 to 1876. One of Snell's colleagues remarked on his "quiet humor and a happy turn of expression," which contrasted "so singularly with his serious air and his mathematical exactness ... and helps to make him one of the most genial of companions and colleagues as well as one of the most admired and beloved of teachers ... the puns, bons mots, pleasantries and pungencies which have dropped from his lips ... would make a racy volume."[35] Professor and Mrs. Snell attended all the commencement gatherings at the Dickinson Homestead, and Emily is known to have sat with them at a time when she was still attending church. It's safe to assume that Emily monitored the ups and downs of Martha Snell's battle with consumption.

There is a first-hand account of Martha's last years, written shortly after her February 1860 death by her betrothed, Henry S. Kelsey (Amherst College, Class of 1855). Kelsey began his memoir in the fall of 1857, when Martha was turning 22:

> Martha contracted a severe cold. Being somewhat liable to coughs, no marked attention was given to it either by herself or her parents.... The cold became gradually more deeply seated, and the cough more frequent. Still to the cautions and anxieties of friends she ever offered a cheerful and hopeful answer. Indeed no one entertained any fear & no one knew how closely deadly disease was coiling around the springs of life.... Dear Mattie was balancing between life and death....
>
> Slowly strength returned and we received her as one from the dead ... she was strong enough to sit for an hour or two....
>
> There too, and thus early, I learned the depth and sincerity of her Christian character, and how ready she was to submit to the will of God. "I felt almost sorry," said she, "when I found myself growing strong again. I had given up the world, and it would have been sweet to go to rest. Now I know that I must go through it all again." ... Care and tenderness added to elasticity of constitution did their work, and we rejoiced to see her once again in her

place by the fireside.... On bright days in Feb. and March [1858] ... she was sometimes seen moving slowly and cautiously towards a neighbor's. She loved the mild air and the sunshine ... she had recovered so much as to feel comparatively well....

[One] day the shadow went backward on the sundial of hope. It never returned to its place again.... She plainly raised blood from the lungs. This new drain ... not only removed its scarlet flood but also ... robbed her of courage to fight for life ... it would seem as if she must die....

For a time she seemed to stand still or even retrograde. But, before long, out of door exercise and the balmy air of early summer began to do their work, & ... it was manifest that she was gaining slowly in weight & strength ... to our great joy, on a sudden, this grievous disease left her almost entirely.... It was a happy sight to see her now. She could run and shout and sing like a girl of sixteen.... Health and strength had in great measure returned, her cough had chiefly disappeared and in many aspects she was the Martha of former days. As the autumn [of 1858] waned into winter ... she remained, as it seemed, about stationary. We all had hope....

It was the 20th of Jan. It was a bright day and Mattie was in fine spirits. As we walked through the hall she said to me with great cheerfulness and animation, "Oh I do feel so well today! If I could only be so well all the time!" We were sitting together on the sofa. I noticed she stopped twice in the midst of a sentence to cough ... she stepped to the front door to clear her mouth. I sat thinking of her all the time with pride and affection. In a moment she returned trembling with agitation & sinking at my side whispered with quivering lip, "I raised a mouthful of pure blood." ... It was a dreadful blow.... From this day the struggle of the preceding year was renewed and carried forth daily, but against more fearful odds.[36]

Martha Snell held on for another thirteen months. At the end, Kelsey described his fiancée, "wrenched and sore by the racking of a terrible cough, and exhausted by the loss of blood.... It seemed as if there was literally a fire in her bones and she was consuming alive before us."[37] If Martha Snell had been a part of Dr. Ware's study, she would have been designated a Class Two consumptive, one who lived on after the first hemoptysis, regularly displaying the symptoms of pulmonary tuberculosis, in a slow decline, but with periods of relief and even remission, death by TB occurring any time after two years.

John Ware, a physician, trained himself to be detached and clinical. The chronically ill and those who love them, on the other hand, can become intensely emotional. This was the case with Emily Dickinson. Weeks after Martha Snell's funeral (did Emily attend?), Emily's favorite aunt, Lavinia, became the latest Norcross female to die of pulmonary consumption. Vinnie, who had gone to Boston to help Aunt Lavinia and her two children,

Louise and Frances, wrote back to Amherst with the bad news. Devastated, Emily entered into a tumultuous period of anxiety and grief. Emily wrote to Vinnie: "I sob and cry till I can hardly see my way 'round the house again; and then sit still and wonder if she sees us now, if she sees me.... And I thought she would live I wanted her to live so, I thought she could not die!"[38]

Emily was drawn to those who, like her, were bereaved because of consumption. In 1859 she met Catharine Turner, who was visiting with Susan Dickinson. Emily and Kate hit it off, although it wasn't until 1860 that Emily learned of Kate's widowhood, and that her husband of two years, Campbell Turner, had died of pulmonary tuberculosis at the age of 26. Learning of the details, and perhaps flashing back to Ben Newton and all the others, Emily wrote to Kate: "There is a subject dear—in which we never touch.... I, too went out to meet the "Dust" early in the morning. I, too in Daisy mounds possess hidden treasure—therefore I guard you more."[39] It's likely that Dickinson was thinking of Ben Newton, buried in Northborough, and not of Charles Wadsworth or Samuel Bowles, both very much alive.

In September, the month of "terror" in 1861, TB claimed two persons Emily knew and admired; Caroline Dutch Hunt died on the 8th, Lucy Elizabeth Dwight on the 11th. Prior to her marriage, Caroline Dutch had taught Emily's mother, and after becoming a widow with five children, she returned to Amherst Academy to become one of Emily's teachers. She was, according to Habegger, "clearly, the dominant woman instructor in 1840–1843,"[40] receiving praise in 1841 (Emily was then 10 years old) for improved student performance in the areas of composition, botany and intellectual philosophy.

Emily referred to Lucy Dwight as "my little Sister." Lucy's husband, Rev. Edward Strong Dwight, preached at the First Church in Amherst, from 1854 to 1860. Emily was attracted to his sermons from the beginning, and took to visiting the Dwight home weekly, informing Sue Gilbert in 1854: "Mr. and Mrs. Dwight are a sunlight to me.... They are sweet and loving."[41] Lucy was seven years older than Emily, and Emily's "little" sister only in the sense that she was wasting away from TB (because of her ill health, Rev. Dwight had hesitated taking the pulpit in Amherst). Writing to Sue from Washington in 1855, Emily passed along "love" to "dear Mr. and Mrs. Dwight."[42] Even after Emily stopped attending church services, she remained a loyal friend to the couple, and gifts and notes passed between the "sisters." Lucy died in Gorham, Maine. In sympathy, Emily sent some dried flowers (or possibly, a few poems), along with a note of two lines: "Will little Ned lay these on Mama's pillow? *Softly*—not to wake her!"[43] Lucy had left behind two children, Annie, age 10, and Edward (Ned), age 5.

Emily could not let go of Lucy. Three months later, she again wrote to Edward Strong Dwight:

> Upon those winter nights I have much recollections of evenings passed with you—and her—at the "parsonage"—and the fire crackles—still—and her cheek softly reddens—as we talk—and laugh....
> I took her notes today.... I put them in my breast—to see if I could warm them—and then the tears fell so—I feared that they would blot them out—as they were but in pencil—and so I laid them back.[44]

It seems obvious from other parts of this letter that Emily had held frequent and frank discussions with the Dwights on the nature and utility of God and Heaven: "I suppose your friend [God]—the Stranger—can comfort more than all of us—but that is Dusk—to me.... I presume it is better—where she is—and holier—and safer—but then I like my little friend where I can see it's face, and *that's* so far—"[45]

Emily continued to listen to her wound, her grief. In January of 1862, she wrote again to Dwight, thanking him for a photograph of Lucy:

> My little sister's face—so dear—so unexpected—filled my eyes with the old rain.... I do not ask if you are "better"—because split lives—never "get well"—but the love of friends—sometimes helps the Staggering—when the Heart has on it's great freight.[46]

David Higgins grasped the importance to Emily of Lucy Dwight's death, calling it "perhaps ... a greater shock to Emily than extant letters indicate," and wondering if it might not be one source of the "terror since September."[47] There's no denying the impact on Emily of the deaths of Aunt Lavinia, Martha Snell, Caroline Dutch Hunt, and Lucy Dwight, all by pulmonary consumption.

354

If Anybody's friend be dead
It's sharpest of the theme
The thinking how they walked alive—
At such and such a time—

Their costume, of a Sunday,
Some manner of the Hair—
A prank nobody knew but them
Lost, in the Sepulchre—

How warm, they were, on such a day,
You almost feel the date—
So short way off it seems—
And now—they're Centuries from that—

> How pleased they were, at what you said!
> You try to touch the smile
> And dip your fingers in the frost—
> When was it—Can you tell—
>
> You asked the Company to tea—
> Acquaintance—just a few—
> And chatted close with this Grand Thing
> That dont remember you—
>
> Past Bows, and Invitations—
> Past Interview, and Vow—
> Past what Ourself can estimate—
> That—makes the Quick of Wo! [1862]

September 1861 crashed in on Dickinson. "If any event of the outside world ... shook the American poet to the roots of her vocal cords," Ellen Moers argued, "it was the death in [June of] 1861 of Elizabeth Barrett Browning."[48] Yet Moers can't explain why this was so: "between Elizabeth Barrett Browning and Emily Dickinson there was *no affinity whatsoever* but their sex ... all that one loves in Elizabeth Barrett Browning, all that Alice Meynell itemizes as her 'fruitful genius, her passion for good, her abundance, her nobility, her tenderness, and her strength'—must be put in the negative to produce a likeness of Emily Dickinson. Dickinson was no realist, no feminist, no reformer, no agitator, no daughter of the epic age."[49]

Gary Lee Stonum agrees: "In style and theme ... Browning is more nearly Dickinson's opposite than model."[50] But Stonum doesn't leave it at that; he points out that Dickinson felt close to Browning, not for literary reasons, but *because of Browning's death*: "Until Browning's death Dickinson never once refers to her in any of the surviving poems, letters, or rumors and reports of conversation. In the year to year and a half afterward, however, Dickinson mentions her in five letters ... and writes at least three memorial poems."[51] The three are "Her last poems" (Fr600), "I went to thank her" (Fr637), and "I think I was enchanted" (Fr627). Stonum believes that one other poem, "Ourselves were wed one summer—dear" (Fr596), "likewise reads ... as an elegy for Barrett Browning."[52] Dickinson wrote 849 poems in the years 1862 to 1865, almost half her total output. Was she soldiering on in place of a fallen comrade? Stonum thinks so: "Following the Englishwoman's death, Dickinson at times imagined herself as invisibly bidding to fill the place Browning had occupied in English poetry."[53]

Moers and Stonum lacked knowledge of Dickinson's TB. Dickinson and Browning led parallel lives, growing up in well-placed families, suffering early lung disease, entering into seclusion as young adults. But Browning moved on, daring everything that, to Emily, seemed moot: vaulting to literary fame, marrying against a father's wishes, moving to Italy, giving birth to a baby. The Dickinson family library contained Browning's 1852 poems and 1859 verse-novel, *Aurora Leigh*, both with markings by Dickinson.[54] Browning was, in Dickinson's words, *a Queen*, and her death brought on several Dickinson poems. Jane Donahue Eberwein calls the one below a "joyous response to Elizabeth Barrett Browning's poems."[55]

627

I think I was enchanted
When first a sombre Girl—
I read that Foreign Lady—
The Dark—felt beautiful—

And whether it was noon at night—
Or only Heaven—at noon—
For very Lunacy of Light
I had not power to tell—

The Bees—became as Butterflies—
The Butterflies—as Swans—
Approached—and spurned the narrow Grass—
And just the meanest Tunes

That Nature murmured to herself
To keep herself in Cheer—
I took for Giants—practising
Titanic Opera—

The Days—to Mighty Metres stept—
The Homeliest—adorned
As if unto a Jubilee
'Twere suddenly confirmed—

I could not have defined the change—
Conversion of the Mind
Like Sanctifying in the Soul—
Is witnessed—not explained—

'Twas a Divine Insanity—
The Danger to be sane
Should I again experience—
'Tis Antidote to turn—

To Tomes of Solid Witchcraft—
Magicians be asleep—
But Magic—hath an element
Like Deity—to keep—[1863]

What Dickinson knew of Elizabeth Barrett Browning before Browning's death in 1861 came primarily from a profile in *Harper's* written in 1852 by a grand old lady of letters, Mary Russell Mitford, a piece Emily would have been certain to read, and to save. Mitford made it seem as if Barrett Browning's health problems had been non-threatening and no longer of any consequence:

> My first acquaintance with Elizabeth Barrett commenced about fifteen years ago ... a slight, delicate figure, with a shower of dark curls falling on either side of a most expressive face, large tender eyes richly fringed by dark eyelashes, a smile like a sun-beam.... I saw much of her during my stay in town ... in spite of the difference of age, intimacy ripened into friendship....
>
> The next year [1837, when Browning was 31] was a painful one to herself and to all who loved her. She broke a blood vessel upon the lungs, which did not heal. If there had been consumption in the family, that disease would have intervened. There were no seeds of the fatal English malady in her constitution, and she escaped ... she began the life which she continued for so many years, confined to one large and commodious but darkened chamber, admitting only her own affectionate family and a few devoted friends....
>
> Gradually her health improved. About four years ago [1848] she married Mr. Browning, and immediately accompanied him to Pisa. They then settled at Florence; and this summer I have had the exquisite pleasure of seeing her once more in London, with a lovely boy at her knee, almost as well as ever, and telling tales of Italian rambles, of losing herself in chestnut forests, and scrambling on mule-back up the sources of extinct volcanoes. May Heaven continue to her such health and such happiness![56]

Taking in these details in 1852, Emily may have felt that love had conquered all! But Barrett Browning's health had been overstated. In 1838, Barrett Browning had mailed a direct command to Mrs. Mitford: "*Do not say much about my health when you write,*"[57] insisting in a follow-up that "there is not at present, any ulceration of the lungs,"[58] and that "the spitting of blood is very little."[59] By 1839, she was more open with Mrs. Mitford: "I have been very ill ... have not left my bedroom for six weeks."[60] "I took two draughts of opium last night—but even the second failed to bring sleep.... Opium—opium—night after night—!"[61] "The spitting of blood has never intermitted from last March twelvemonth, and my voice has never been able to lift itself above a whisper."[62]

Emily, of course, had no way of knowing that Browning was 15 when she first developed lung disease, or that Browning's habit of taking opiates had begun at that time, or that the woman she called "my Anglo-Florentine" had endured two miscarriages before delivering, at age 43, the baby she nicknamed "Pen." Imagine how disturbed she must have been to read, for the first time, details of the collapse and death of one of her Queens. The dreadful news came in the mail, a long tribute in her monthly issue of *Atlantic Monthly*. And the month? *September 1861.*

> Mrs. Browning's life was a prolonged combat with disease.... Confined to her room ... Elizabeth Barrett developed into the great artist and scholar. From her couch went forth those poems which have crowned her as "the world's greatest poetess" ... she lay almost speechless at times, and seeing none but those friends dearest and nearest....
>
> Patient in long suffering, she never spoke of herself, except when the subject was forced upon her by others.... Books and humanity ... were foremost in her thoughts.... I speak not of religion, for with her everything was religion. Her Christianity was not confined to church and rubric....
>
> Mrs. Browning's illness was only of a week's duration. Having caught a severe cold of a more threatening nature than usual, medical skill was summoned; but ... there was no whisper of great danger until the third or fourth night.... At half-past four, on the morning of the 29th of June, Elizabeth Barrett Browning died of congestion of the lungs.... Mrs. Browning's death is not without a sad consolation. From the shattered condition of her lungs, the physician feels assured that existence could not at the farthest have been prolonged for more than six months. Instead of a sudden call to God, life would have slowly ebbed away; and, too feeble for the slightest exertion, she must have been denied the solace of books, of friends, of writing, perhaps of thought even. God saved her from a living grave, and her husband from protracted misery.[63]

A year later, Dickinson responded to the loss in verse:

>   517
> A still—Volcano—Life—
> That flickered in the night—
> When it was dark enough to do
> Without erasing sight—
>
> A quiet—Earthquake style—
> Too subtle to suspect
> By natures this side Naples—
> The North cannot detect
>
> The solemn—Torrid—Symbol—
> The lips that never lie—
> Whose hissing Corals part—and shut—
> And Cities—ooze away—[1863]

It was as if, with Barrett Browning's death, a massive support system had suddenly given way. Dickinson must have thought long and hard on the tragic event, for she remembered the summer when she first read Browning's *Aurora Leigh*:

596

Ourselves were wed one summer—dear—
Your Vision—was in June—
And when Your little Lifetime failed,
I wearied—too—of mine—

And overtaken in the Dark—
Where You had put me down—
By Some one carrying a Light—
I—too—received the Sign.

'Tis true—Our Futures different lay—
Your Cottage—faced the sun—
While Oceans—and the North must be—
On every side of mine

'Tis true, Your Garden led the Bloom,
For mine—in Frosts—was sown—
And yet, one Summer, we were Queens—
But You—were crowned in June—[1863]

Dickinson imagined herself vaulting the oceans to be in Florence, Italy, looking down on Browning's grave:

637

I went to thank Her—
But She Slept—
Her Bed—a funneled Stone—
With Nosegays at the Head and Foot—
That Travellers—had thrown—

Who went to thank Her—
But She Slept—
'Twas Short—to cross the Sea—
To look opon Her like—alive—
But turning back—'twas slow—[1863]

Death was crowding in. Emily wrote to Loo and Fanny: "That Mrs. Browning fainted, we need not read *Aurora Leigh* to know, when she lived with her English aunt; and George Sand 'must make no noise in her grandmother's bedroom.' Poor children! Women now, queens, now! And one in the Eden of God."[64] Emily, still thinking of Barrett Browning's death, and of Robert Browning's grief, wrote to Mary Bowles, who had just given birth to a baby boy: "will you call him Robert—for me. He is the bravest man—alive—but *his* Boy—has no mama—*that* makes us all weep—don't it?"[65] Emily's received portraits of Barrett Browning from friends; one was framed, and became a fixture on her' bedroom wall. When Samuel Bowles was in

Italy in 1862, Emily sent along this note: "Should anybody where you go, talk of Mrs. Browning, you must hear for us—and if you touch her Grave, put one hand on the Head, for me—her unmentioned Mourner."[66]

Emily Dickinson had reason to be terrified in 1861. She had lived for too long with a monster. In the "terror" letter, she writes: "I read Miss Prescott's 'Circumstance,' but it followed me, in the Dark—so I avoided her." Why was the *Atlantic Monthly* piece so unsettling? "Circumstance" opens in the woods of northern Maine, where a young wife has gone off some distance to look in on a terminally ill (*consumptive?*) neighbor:

> ... so busy had she been with care and sympathy that she did not at first observe the approaching night.... Home lay some three miles distant, across a copse, a meadow, and a piece of woods.... She was ... rather depressed by the pain she had witnessed and the fatigue she had endured.... Walking rapidly now, and with her eyes wide-open, she distinctly saw in the air before her what was not there a moment ago, a winding-sheet—cold, white, and ghastly, waved by the likeness of four wan hands—that rose with a long inflation, and fell in rigid folds, while a voice, shaping itself from the hollowness above, spectral and melancholy, sighed—"The Lord have mercy on the people! The Lord have mercy on the people!" Three times the sheet with its corpse-covering outline waved beneath the pale hands....
>
> Suddenly, a swift shadow, like the fabulous flying-dragon, writhed through the air before her, and she felt herself instantly seized and borne aloft. It was that wild beast—the most savage and serpentine and subtle and fearless of our latitudes—known by hunters as the Indian Devil, and he held her in his clutches on the broad floor of a swinging fir-bough. His long sharp claws were caught in her clothing ... and she saw instinctively the fierce plunge of those weapons, the long strips of living flesh torn from her bones, the agony, the quivering disgust....
>
> She did not think at this instant to call upon God. She called upon her husband. It seemed to her that she had but one friend in the world; that was he; and again the cry, loud, clear, prolonged, echoed through the woods. It was not the shriek that disturbed the creature.... It must have been the echo, most musical, most resonant, repeated and yet repeated, dying with long sighs of sweet sound, vibrated from rock to river and back again ... she saw that while the beast listened he would not gnaw—and this she felt directly, when the rough, sharp, and multiplied stings of his tongue retouched her arm....
>
> She had heard that music charmed wild beasts ... and when she opened her lips the third time, it was not for shrieking, but for singing....
>
> The monster raised his head and flared the fiery eyeballs upon her, then fretted the imprisoned claws a moment and was quiet.... Her voice, at first faint and fearful, gradually lost its quaver, grew under her control and subject to her modulation; it rose on long swells, it fell in subtle cadences, now and then its tones pealed out like bells from distant belfries on fresh sonorous mornings....

> What rending pains were close at hand! Death! and what a death! worse than any other that is to be named! ... No gnawing disease can bring such hideous end as this; for that is a fiend bred of your own flesh....⁶⁷

"Circumstance" pitches forward, with the Indian Devil tearing away pieces of his captive's flesh, and she creating new songs to keep from panicking, and to soothe the beast. Finally, the woman's husband, who has gone out looking for her, with their sleeping baby in his arms, hears her song, and rushes to the rescue, killing the beast with a well-aimed rifle shot. Reunited, husband and wife cross the hills to their home—and to Prescott's surprise ending:

> There is no home there. The log-house, the barns, the neighboring farms, the fences, are all blotted out and mingled in one smoking ruin. Desolation and death were indeed there, and beneficence and life in the forest. Tomahawk and scalping-knife, descending during that night, had left behind them only this work of their accomplished hatred and one subtle foot-print in the snow.⁶⁸

Jerome Loving seems to know, intuitively, why Dickinson fled from Harriet Prescott's story:

> [The captive] strains her voice to save her life. Whenever it failed her, "the long red tongue [of the monster] was thrust forth again. Before it touched, a song sprang from her lips."
> To sing was [was Dickinson's way] to fill the darkness with words. "You wonder why I write—so," she told her friend Mary Bowles that spring. "Because I cannot help" Almost a year later ... she told her cousins [Aunt Lavinia's daughters, Loo and Fanny] "Let Emily sing for you because she cannot pray." The woman in the story cannot pray either, cannot project herself into a safer future: "She did not think this instant to call upon God. She called upon her husband." But the calls are useless until they metamorphose into song: "Just this point between life and death intensified every faculty...."
> For Dickinson at the height of her poetic powers, these moments were almost routine: "I had a terror—since September—I could tell to none—and so I sing, as the Boy does by the Burying Ground—because I am afraid."⁶⁹

The analogy stares us in the face. The early poems of Emily Dickinson are comparable to the songs of the victim in "Circumstance." After a day of serving the needs of Mother, Emily is in her bedroom, writing poems. Emily Norcross Dickinson, the mother, lies close by, in the clutch of an unnamed illness. Emily Elizabeth Dickinson, the daughter, sings to remain sane, and to hold off a fiend bred of her own flesh:

425

'Twas like a Maelstrom, with a notch,
That nearer, every Day,
Kept narrowing it's boiling Wheel
Until the Agony

Toyed coolly with the final inch
Of your delirious Hem—
And you dropt, lost,
When something broke—
And let you from a Dream—

As if a Goblin with a Guage—
Kept measuring the Hours—
Until you felt your Second
Weigh, helpless, in his Paws—

And not a Sinew—stirred—could help,
And Sense was setting numb—
When God—remembered—and the Fiend
Let go, then, Overcome—

As if your Sentence stood—pronounced—
And you were frozen led
From Dungeon's luxury of Doubt
To Gibbets, and the Dead—

And when the Film had stitched your eyes
A Creature gasped "Reprieve"!
Which Anguish was the utterest—then—
To perish, or to live? [1862]

"Mrs. Philbrick, I fear that your mother cannot live through another winter in this climate...." "You think she might live in comparative comfort? It would not be merely prolonging her life as a suffering invalid?" ... "Oh, yes, undoubtedly," said the doctor. "She need never die of consumption at all, if she could breathe only inland air.

—"no name" [Helen Maria Fiske Hunt Jackson], *Mercy Philbrick's Choice*, 1876

9. Afterlife

In 1876, a "no name" novelist sent her heroine, Mercy Philbrick, *inland* from Cape Cod to the hills of Western Massachusetts, in search of better air. Ten years earlier, that novelist-to-be, Helen Maria Fiske Hunt, hoping to carve out a new life, had come *to* the seashore, to Newport, Rhode Island, largely for the same reason. "She was familiar with the town," writes her most recent biographer, Kate Phillips, "having lived there for a time ... she enjoyed the 'constant *tonic*' of the local climate, reputed to be healthy for consumptives."[1] Phillips points out that Helen, over the course of her life, "endured a vast, baffling variety of ailments. In some of her letters it is difficult to discern exactly what is wrong with her.... Above all, she suffered from severe respiratory problems ... she seems to have lived in fear of dying from the same disease that had shattered the lives of her parents."[2]

It was in February, 1866 that Helen Hunt took a room in Hannah Dame's boardinghouse in Newport, across the hall from Thomas Wentworth Higginson, the most accomplished author in a resort and spa town filled with authors. Higginson liked to impress and amuse his circle of admirers by showing off some strange poems he had been receiving, and he did so with Helen Hunt, his latest female protégé. She must have been astonished to discover that they were written by her childhood playmate, Emily Dickinson. In 1866 Higginson held two dozen Dickinson poems, including the love poems "There came a day at summer's full" and "Your riches taught me poverty," and he allowed Helen to copy them into a keepsake volume of her own.

With that transfer, the poems were placed, for the first time, in the right hands. Higginson had been flattered when Dickinson called him

"Preceptor," and asked him to judge if her verse was "alive," if it "breathed."[3] Even if his first impression was of an "original poetic genius,"[4] he was "bewildered"[5] by the poems, and put off by their punctuation and capitalization. Over the years, Dickinson gifted him with more than 100 poems. He found them unsuited for publication because of their "defiance of form,"[6] at first thinking of Dickinson as utterly careless. He remarked that she "almost always grasped whatever she sought, but with some fracture of grammar and dictionary on the way. Often, too, she was obscure and sometimes inscrutable."[7] He suggested exact rhyme, standard punctuation, correct grammar and, of course, *titles*.

Dickinson's replies were mock deferential, and she did nothing to alter her complex style. If anything, she became even more intent on *not* making the poems accessible to a larger public. That had never been her purpose. She was coming to realize that being alive, being a part of the world, and not shut up in a box, was reward enough.

776

Drama's Vitallest Expression is the Common Day
That arise and set about Us—
Other Tragedy

Perish in the Recitation—
This—the best enact
When the audience is scattered
And the Boxes shut—

"Hamlet" to Himself were Hamlet—
Had not Shakespeare wrote—
Though the "Romeo" left no Record
Of his Juliet,

It were infinite enacted
In the Human Heart—
Only Theatre recorded
Owner cannot shut—[1863]

Helen Hunt, unlike Higginson, had no reservations about the worth of Emily's verse. She fell in love with the poems from the start. Kate Phillips notes Helen's "relish" of "the moral and aesthetic daring of Dickinson's innovative work," and argues that Helen "sympathized with Dickinson's poetic rebellion against a rigidly orthodox Calvinist upbringing, tied to Amherst College."[8] Phillips may want to be a bit more precise. Emily and Helen were members of the same species. What they found truly objectionable was the Calvinist approach to disease, death and salvation. Two decades had passed since the two, as thirteen-year-olds, had watched on at the funeral of Helen's mother, Deborah Vinal Fiske. In 1866 both women were emerging from a long cycle of loss, pain, and deep sadness. Nathan Fiske died in 1847, like his wife a victim of TB, leaving Helen an orphan at age 16. Five years later, she married a U.S. Army engineer, Edward Bissell Hunt, brother of a former New York governor. Their first child, Murray, died in infancy in 1854. Then Major Hunt suffocated in 1863 while testing his newly designed underwater naval vessel. Two years later, the remaining child, her beloved "Rennie," succumbed to diphtheria. Alone and grief-stricken, Helen came to Newport for the remainder of the winter. Latching on to Higginson, she hoped for a career in writing.

At the time of her father's death, Helen was given a box containing the family correspondence. One letter, mailed to Deborah Fiske in 1838 by a consumptive friend living in Woburn, Massachusetts, is emblematic of a Calvinist mindset irksome to both Helen and Emily, that is, that God is *all* and humankind is *naught*, and that life on earth is of little use or meaning:

> You may have heard of ... my new attack of pulmonary difficulties.... [I] began at an early hour in the morning to expectorate blood quite freely for six days. Then it ceased & I have since been rapidly gaining to the surprise of my friends & physicians. I am now quite comfortable though feeble—have been able to attend Church four half days & to resume my labours in the Sabbath School.
>
> I have surely great reason to be humble & grateful that God has dealt so kindly in his chastisement & in judgment remembered mercy. My health has been so precarious of late that it seems as if one foot stood upon life, the other upon death. What God deigns to do—whether to continue life & protract disease—or to destroy—or to heal—remains among the uncertainties ... but of one thing there is a certainty that I am in the hands of Him who does all things well, & knows infinitely better than his short-sighted creatures what is best for them....[9]

Helen took a different stance. On the eve of her 21st birthday, she told her guardian, Julius Palmer, of her dislike of the "entire, absolute, unconditional" measures required of a convert to Christ: "I love *dress*; I love *company*; I love *all* sorts of reading; I love *simple* intellectual exertion, without any view to an end.... I love, in short, the world: I *know* I am not willing to give it up."[10]

A career in writing would bring her fully into that world. With Higginson's guidance, she would place hundreds of poems and stories and articles and book reviews in America's leading newspapers and magazines, and then become a successful novelist. When Ralph Waldo Emerson was asked in the 1870s if Helen Hunt Jackson might not be the best woman poet in

America, he agreed, but was said to have added "Perhaps we might as well omit the *woman*."[11]

When Helen Hunt first read Dickinson's poems, she was unaware that Emily was, like herself, at a turning point in life. "I can wade Grief— / Whole Pools of it— / I'm used to that—" (Fr312), Dickinson had recorded in an early poem. But in the mid-1860s, the terror and grief was coming to an end for Emily, and the years ahead would be marked by a degree of self-possession that only love or suffering can bring. Alfred Habegger recognizes the dramatic turnaround in Dickinson's mental and emotional state:

> Beginning in 1858, the poet's heroic production had been driven in part by the working-out of inner matters. Eighteen sixty-five, the last year she kept up her blistering pace, resulted in more than two hundred poems.... During the next five years ... she composed only seventy poems.... There were fewer letters as well....
>
> Remarkably, of the seven poems written in the first person singular from 1866 to 1869, only one has the speaker engaged in reviewing the past.... The writer who had lavished herself on acts of memory, exploring her history, her singularity, her starved triumphs, her hard-won mastery, had for the first time stopped trying to tell her story....[12]

"Dickinson had achieved," Habegger concludes, "a relaxed sense of security, a mature and detached perspective on herself."[13] But neither Habegger nor anyone has explained *why* Dickinson's great poetic drive suddenly came to an end after 1865. Perhaps the simplest answer is that she had reached the fifth and final stage of the grieving process, the stage of *acceptance*. One needn't be a grief therapist to locate the emotions of *denial*, *anger*, *bargaining*, and *depression* in dozens of Dickinson's early poems. By the time she had reconnected with Helen Fiske Hunt, Dickinson's health had stabilized, and no one she loved was nearing death by TB. No longer a wounded deer, or a *smitten* rock that gushes, she averaged only 15 new poems a year from 1866 to 1870. Love poems became rare, and after 1864, she stopped threading her verse into fascicles.

> 1094
> We outgrow love, like other things
> And put it in the Drawer—
> Till it an Antique fashion shows—
> Like Costumes Grandsires wore. [1865]

Emily had (literally) given up the ghost. Mourning Ben Newton and other daisies, speaking out for them, she had emerged a poet. She had bargained to keep Ben nearby, where he might hear her songs. Now, granite silence suggested there would be no feedback, no reunion.

894

The Overtakelessness of Those
Who have accomplished Death—
Majestic is to me beyond
The Majesties of Earth—
The Soul her "Not at Home"
Inscribes opon the Flesh,
And takes a fine aerial gait
Beyond the Writ of Touch. [1865]

A spirit-bride fantasy, one of Goth's bromides, had kept her afloat; now sentiment was giving way to observable truth, to the dictates of nature. There was no longer a need for a dowry. Her poems are the evidence that she was moving on:

857

She rose to His Requirement—dropt
The Playthings of Her Life
To take the honorable Work
Of Woman, and of Wife—

If ought She missed in Her new Day,
Of Amplitude, or Awe—
Or first Prospective—or the Gold
In using, wear away,

It lay unmentioned—as the Sea
Develope Pearl, and Weed,
But only to Himself—be known
The Fathoms they abide—[1864]

Emily Dickinson began to look to the *outside* world, to those around her, and to nature, for her topics. In a letter to Elizabeth Holland in early May, 1866, she luxuriated in the enchantments of spring, and playfully chided Elizabeth for her comments about the slow change of the season: "Friday I tasted life. It was a vast morsel. A circus passed the house—still I feel the red in my mind though the drums are out.... The lawn is full of south and the odors tangle, and I hear today for the first the river in the tree. You mentioned spring's delaying—I blamed her for the opposite. I would eat evanescence slowly."[14]

1127

After the Sun comes out
How it alters the World—
Wagons like messengers hurry about
Yesterday is old—

> All men meet as if
> Each foreclosed a news—
> Fresh as a Cargo from Balize
> Nature's qualities—[1866]

While Habegger's word, *repose*, is well suited to Dickinson's outward observable behaviors, the word *acceptance* speaks more to her inner traits of fortitude and will power, and to her new-found ability to meet each new day with fresh eyes. It was with *this* Emily Dickinson that Helen Hunt became reacquainted in the late 1860s. Helen was favorably impressed by Emily's depth and demeanor, and expressed an envy of Emily's abilities as a poet.

Was *Mercy Philbrick's Choice* Helen's tribute to Emily Dickinson? Habegger notes that the novel is set in a New England village modeled on Amherst, and that the protagonist is "a woman poet whose 'choice' was not to marry. Locally, it was rumored that Dickinson had helped to write the novel."[15] *Mercy Philbrick's Choice*, George Whicher was careful to point out, "is not a fictional biography of Emily Dickinson, but rather a novel into which have been inserted some traits of appearance and character borrowed from her and some allusions to her actual history.... Lavinia stated that Mrs. Jackson asked Emily's help on a novel that she had already projected and begun to write, and that when Emily could not or would not contribute her share, her friend mischievously put her into the story."[16]

Whicher catches glimpses of Ben Newton in *Mercy Philbrick's Choice*: "There can be no doubt ... that some circumstances in Emily Dickinson's life are quite literally transcribed. Her friendship with Ben Newton, for example, is paralleled in the brief account of Mercy Philbrick's relations with the young minister Harvey Allen."[17] Helen Hunt created this account of Harvey and Mercy:

> Mr. Allen, who had been Mercy's teacher for three years, had early seen in her a strong, poetic impulse, and had fostered and stimulated it by very means in his power.... It would have been very easy for him to love Mercy ... he felt himself strangely stirred whenever he looked into her sensitive, orchid-like face....
> "I might make her think she loved me, perhaps," he said to himself. "She is so lonely and sad, and has seen so few men; but it would be base.... I will never try to make her love me."
> And he never did. He taught her and trained her, and developed her, patiently, exactingly, and yet tenderly, as if she had been his sister ... but he never betrayed to her, even by a look or tone, that he could have loved her as his wife. No doubt his influence was greater over her for this subtle, unacknowledged bond.... Probably a change must have come, had they lived thus closely together a year or two longer ... six months after her departure, he had loyally and lovingly promised to be the husband of another.[18]

After she moves to Western Massachusetts, Mercy's romantic interest centers on Stephen White. Again, there are intimations of Ben Newton. Stephen White is a lawyer in his twenties. He falls in love with Mercy, and the bond between the two grows stronger each time they meet. But then he tells her he cannot yet marry because of his commitments to his invalid mother, with whom he lives.

> On the threshold of the door, he [Stephen White] turned and fixed his eyes upon her with one long look of sorrow, compassion, and infinite love. Her heart thrilled under it. She made an eager step forward. If he had returned, she would have thrown herself into his arms, and cried out, "O Stephen, I do love you, I do trust you." But Stephen made an inexorable gesture of his hand, which said more than any words, "No! no! do not deceive yourself," and was gone.
>
> And thus they parted for ever, this man and this woman who had been for two years all in all to each other, who had written on each other's hearts and lives characters which eternity itself could never efface.[19]

64

Heart! We will forget him!
You and I—tonight!
You may forget the warmth he gave—
I will forget the light!

When you have done, pray tell me
That I may straight begin!
Haste! lest while you're lagging
I remember him! [1859]

Whicher suggests that Helen Hunt Jackson patterned Mercy Philbrick on Emily Dickinson, and especially in three ways: "Mercy ... [is] marked by an uncompromising love of truth. She hides herself from unwelcome callers lest she be forced to speak or act a social lie in greeting them. Her ailing mother, a 'comparatively helpless, aged child,' awakens 'all the deep maternal instincts of her strong nature.'"[20]

Mercy is marked by an uncompromising love of truth. Mercy's rock-solid integrity is at the core of her habit of seclusion. She confesses to Harvey Allen that "many a time when I have seen tiresome or disagreeable people coming to our house, I have run away and hid myself, so as not to be found; not in the least because I could not bear the being bored by them, but because I could not bear the thought of the lies I should speak, or at least act, if I saw them."[21] Reverend Allen tries to get Mercy to see that one needs to tell a white lie on occasion, to make others more comfortable, but Mercy thinks to herself that this is a "very dangerous doctrine."[22]

A lie's a lie, let whoever will call it fine names, and pass it off as a Christian duty. The Bible does not say, "Thou shalt not lie, except when it is necessary to lie, to avoid hurting thy neighbor's feelings." It says, "Thou shalt not lie." Oh, what a horrible word "lie" is! It stings like a short, sharp stroke with a lash.[23]

Although Dickinson hated lies, she nonetheless realized it might be impolitic, and certainly unkind, to confess her beliefs in their most naked form. Her solution was new kind of poetry:

> 1263
>
> Tell all the truth but tell it slant—
> Success in Circuit lies
> Too bright for our infirm Delight
> The Truth's superb surprise
> As Lightning to the Children eased
> With explanation kind
> The Truth must dazzle gradually
> Or every man be blind—[1872]

Mercy hides herself from unwelcome callers lest she be forced to speak or act a social lie in greeting them. In her discussions and correspondence with Emily, and in reading her poems, Helen Hunt might readily have concluded that her old friend was intensely protective of her own space, but not anti-social. And so it was with Mercy Philbrick:

> ... to so exceptional a nature as Mercy's, a certain amount of isolation was inevitable, all through her life, however fortunate she might be in entering into new and wider relations. The loneliness of intense individuality is the loneliest loneliness in the world,—a loneliness which crowds only aggravate, and which even the closest and happiest companionship can only in part cure.[24]

Richard Chase sensed the reasons why Dickinson kept to herself:

> There were many elements of passivity and retreat in her reclusive life, responses to panic, insecurity, bereavement, sickness.... Her seclusion was a way of maintaining in her inner life that precarious hold on sanity and vitality of which her poems often speak.... Her antagonist was nothing less than society itself, and the public opinion through which the values of society were forced upon the individual.[25]

Emily Dickinson knew that others labeled her a recluse, but she did little to either justify that fact, or to explain it away.

409

The Soul selects her own Society—
Then—shuts the Door—
To her divine Majority—
Present no more—

Unmoved—she notes the Chariots—pausing—
At her low Gate—
Unmoved—an Emperor be kneeling
Opon her Mat—

I've known her—from an ample nation—
Choose One—
Then—close the Valves of her attention—
Like Stone—[1862]

Mercy's ailing mother, a "comparatively helpless, aged child," awakens "all the deep maternal instincts of her strong nature." Helen Hunt knew, first-hand, of the relationship between a daughter and an invalid mother. In childhood, she had been the keeper of leeches used to treat her mother, Deborah Fiske. There can be little doubt that Helen would know, or at least suspect, a consumptive when she saw one. In the years leading up to *Mercy Philbrick's Choice*, she visited and talked with Emily at the Homestead, and the two exchanged a number of letters. Helen was well positioned to assess the medical condition of Emily Norcross Dickinson and to take in details of the relationship between Emily, the mother, and Emily, the daughter. It may be more than a coincidence that, in the novel, Mercy and her mother have the same first name. Mercy Philbrick treats her mother, Mercy Carr, with "never-failing respect," and Mrs. Carr profits from the "love and kindness and shelter and direction" provided by Mercy.[26]

There were a number of times in the 1850s and early 1860s when Emily, in her letters, belittled or denigrated her mother—"I never had a Mother," she complained to Higginson. Emily's negativism toward Mother may have been fueled by denial and anger over the deaths of those she loved, and especially Ben Newton. But by the time she became reacquainted with Helen Hunt, she was at the end of a cycle of deep grief. As she gained in health, her feelings for her mother softened and deepened. At the time of her deepest depression (the 5 years following Newton's death), nothing mattered. Now, *everything mattered*. Richard Sewall notes that "Emily enjoyed at least something of what she called, when her mother was helpless, a "holier demand...." One need not be a sentimentalist to see in Emily's ultimate feeling for both her mother and father a tenderness and humane understanding that redeem, if they do not contradict, her earlier posturings."[27]

982

If I can stop one Heart from breaking
I shall not live in vain
If I can ease one Life the Aching
Or cool one Pain

Or help one fainting Robin
Unto his Nest again
I shall not live in vain. [1865]

By the time she wrote this poem, Emily Dickinson had become an enlarged being, with a wider reach of sympathy, a finer tenderness, a strength of endurance. It was only then that she came to the realization that Mother was *also* a wounded deer, that the two of them were members of the same species.

Helen Hunt Jackson moves Mercy Philbrick along the same path. At the start, Mercy's poems, resembling Emily's early poems, are dark and intense, "so largely subjective in tone that it was hard for her readers to believe that they were not all drawn from her own individual experience."[28] But as she moves on, she writes "more and more ... to do a little towards making people glad, towards making them kind to one another, towards opening their eyes to the omnipresent beauty."[29] As Emily Dickinson gained some distance from the years of trauma, she did all of that, and also occasionally kicked up her heels:

1356

A little Madness in the Spring
Is wholesome even for the King,
But God be with the Clown—
Who ponders this tremendous scene—
This whole Experiment of Green—
As if it were his own! [1875]

And even when she touched upon the predicaments and pitfalls of life, and the unforeseeable sequel to life on earth, she could be a little silly:

1335

Floss wont save you from an Abyss
But a Rope will—
Notwithstanding a Rope for a Souvenir
Is not beautiful—

But I tell you every step is a Trough—
And every stop a well—
Now will you have the Rope or the Floss?
Prices reasonable—[1874]

And there were occasions when she would let go and become deliciously silly!

1355

> His Mansion in the Pool
> The Frog forsakes—
> He rises on a Log
> And statements makes—
> His Auditors two Worlds
> Deducting me—
> The Orator of April
> Is hoarse Today—
> His Mittens at his Feet
> No Hand hath he—
> His eloquence a Bubble
> As Fame should be—
> Applaud him to discover
> To your chagrin
> Demosthenes has vanished
> In Waters Green—[1875]

Emily looks at the frog with the eyes of a child—with eyes wide open. And why not? She had run a grisly gauntlet, and had survived. She shared her enthusiasm for living with Loo and Fanny Norcross:

- 1864—Every day life feels mightier, and what we have the power to be, more stupendous.[30]

- 1872—We turn not older with the years, but newer every day.[31]

- 1873—Life is a spell so exquisite that everything conspires to break it.... The mysteries of human nature surpass the "mysteries of redemption," for the infinite we only suppose, while we see the finite.[32]

- 1873—Each of us gives or takes of heaven in corporeal person, for each of us has the skill of life.[33]

What Emily was communicating to her orphaned "little sisters" was the essence of her humanity; what she was asking of them in return was the recognition—and deepening—of their humanity in response to hers. It is what she asks of us, the readers of her poems:

1338

> Time does go on—
> I tell it gay to those who suffer now—
> They shall survive—
> There is a Sun—
> They dont believe it now—[1874]

9. Afterlife

In *Helen Hunt Jackson: A Literary Life*, Kate Phillips maintains that Dickinson was not on Helen Hunt's mind when she developed *Mercy Philbrick's Choice* and that, in fact, the lead character, Mercy, is imbued with *Helen's* characteristics and values. This is an argument for another day. Jackson opens her final chapter with an account of Mercy's later life. The passage may or may not have been meant as a song of praise to Dickinson, but it will do quite nicely as a description of Dickinson's *afterlife* until something better comes along:

> Mercy Philbrick lived thirty years after the events described in these pages. It was a life rich to overflowing, yet uneventful, as the world reckons: a life lonely, yet full of companionship; sad, yet full of cheer; hard, and yet perpetually uplifted by an inward joy.... This was largely the result of her unquenchable gift of song, of the true poet's temperament, to which life is for ever new, beautiful, and glad.
>
> It was also the result of her ever-increasing spirituality of nature. This took no shape of creed, worship, or what the world's common consent calls religion.... But her realization of the solemn significance of the great fact of being alive deepened every hour; her tenderness, her sense of brotherhood to every human being, and her sense of the actual presence and near love of God. Her old intolerance was softened, or rather it had changed from antagonisms on the surface to living principles at the core. Truth, truth, truth, was still the war-cry of her soul....[34]

>   882
>
>   The Truth—is stirless—
>   Other force—may be presumed to move—
>   This—then—is best for confidence—
>   When oldest Cedars swerve—
>
>   And Oaks untwist their fists—
>   And Mountains—feeble—lean—
>   How excellent a Body, that
>   Stands without a Bone—
>
>   How vigorous a Force
>   That holds without a Prop—
>   Truth stays Herself—and every man
>   That trusts Her—boldly up—[1864]

The last word on Emily Dickinson belongs to the children she befriended. MacGregor Jenkins was a neighbor and playmate of Martha Dickinson, Emily's niece "Mattie," who lived next door at Evergreens. During their play outside the Dickinson Homestead, the neighborhood children were delighted whenever Emily lowered a basket of gingerbread loaves, each topped with a flower. In 1930 Jenkins recollected his childhood comings and goings at the Dickinson Homestead in the late 1870s:

> In that house Emily Dickinson was leading her exquisite, vibrant life, not as a morbid recluse, but as an enthusiastic observer of all the great things that make a soul a soul.... And the children felt this. They knew Miss Emily well. She was not shy with them. She was a splendid comrade and a staunch champion. Her ready smile, her dancing eyes, her quick reply made us tingle with pleasure when we were near her....
>
> She made us feel near a thousand things we did not understand ... vague intimations of forces that we felt about us, but no one could explain to us; a feeling that there were a million things in life that were sweet and beautiful that our hungry lips could not taste or our eager hands touch.
>
> I recall her as usually dressed in white, which added to the effect of fragility and unreality that always baffled me. Baffled me because Miss Emily was not really fragile; she was far too dynamic a person to create any such impression, and she certainly was real. Her participations in our games, her stout defense of us in times of stress, her defiance of Maggie [the strong-minded Dickinson family maid] in raiding the pantry that we should be well supplied with cookies or doughnuts, all these were the attributes of a very real and very human friend and comrade.
>
> But it was baffling, for in the midst of her boldest raid on our behalf, a footstep would be heard outside the kitchen door and our laughing goddess of plenty would become the flutter of the edge of a white skirt behind a closing door.
>
> It was baffling. Her attitude toward this perplexing habit of precipitous flight was puzzling. It was not panic, we knew that. It was not timidity nor was it unfriendliness. We knew her to be the bravest person in the world; the fact that she was not afraid of Maggie proved that. She certainly was not unfriendly—her constant thought of us and her other friends belied any such imputation—and yet she always impressed us as a bird poised for flight. The slightest incursion from the outside would cause her to disappear suddenly and completely. There would be no cry of alarm, no ruffling of feathers, no undignified haste, but smoothly, silently, and often with a swift parting smile, she would vanish.[35]

And so has a Daisy vanished.

Appendix A:
Excerpts from American Novels, 1850–1876

1. OMITTED CENTER

"Bless me, mother! It can't be possible that you have been sitting up for me all this time!" said Margaret.

"You have stayed late, but that can't be helped now. How do you feel?"

"Oh, very well," was replied with an effort to speak cheerfully and appear unconcerned: "only I am a little hoarser than I was."

"You breathe with difficulty," said Mrs. Ellis. "Have you no pain in your breast?"

"A slight pain in my side, and some pain here," placing her finger on the throat-pit....

It was nearly day-dawn before Margaret found sufficient relief.... Mrs. Ellis ... dispatched a servant for their physician.... The patient complained of great oppression and pain in the breast, that was increased by a full inspiration.... "Do you think her lungs affected, doctor?" the parents anxiously inquired....

"There is some inflammation there," replied the doctor, evasively.... By the end of a week ... her expectoration, though not abundant, was sometimes tinged with blood; she was so weak as to be unable to sit up in bed.... Hope died in the hearts of the parents and friends.... Tears filled the eyes of the sufferer ... something rose in her throat, which she threw up with a slight effort. It was bright red blood! ... She became deadly pale.

"My good resolutions are all in vain," she murmured.... "It is too late!"

A hurried message was sent for the physician.... He came immediately, and succeeded in checking the rapid flow of blood from the lungs ... what had seemed a fatal change in the disease, proved to be a beneficial one. All inflammation subsided, and nature had only to heal the lacerations ... and aid the whole system in a return to health. This return was very slow, and ... an imperfect one. The glow of health, which had given to the face of Margaret so much brightness and beauty, never came back, except as a hectic flush....

"Were you really in earnest, mother," said Margaret one day, after she was so far recovered as to be able to sit up and walk across her room, "when you spoke about parents transmitting to their children a predisposition to the particular diseases from which they suffered?"

... "Deeply in earnest," replied Mrs. Ellis. "It follows from this immutable law in nature, that like produces like.... My mother died of consumption; I have a marked predisposition to that fatal disease; and I need not tell you that your lungs are peculiarly sensitive."

—T. S. Arthur, *Seed-time and Harvest*. Philadelphia: Lippincott, Grambo, 1851, pp. 65–72.

2. Dread Disease

Eva ... began to fail rapidly. [Augustine] St. Clare was at last willing to call in medical advice—a thing from which he had always shrunk, because it was the admission of an unwelcome truth. But, for a day or two, Eva was so unwell as to be confined to the house; and the doctor was called.

Marie St. Clare had taken no notice of the child's gradually decaying health and strength, because she was completely absorbed in studying out two or three new forms of disease to which she believed she herself was a victim...

Ophelia [Augustine's New England cousin, imported to run the Louisiana plantation household] ... tried to awaken her ... about Eva; but to no avail.

"I don't see as anything ails the child," she [Marie, to Ophelia] would say; "she runs about, and plays."

"But she has a cough."

"Cough! you don't need to tell me about a cough. I've always been subject to a cough.... When I was of Eva's age, they thought I was in a consumption.... Mammy used to sit up with me. O! Eva's cough is not anything."

"But she gets weak, and is short-breathed."

"Law! I've had that, years and years; it's only a nervous affection."

"But she sweats so, nights!"

"Well, I have, these ten years...."

"It's true," said [Augustine] St. Clare, "that Eva is very delicate ... and that she has grown so rapidly as to exhaust her strength.... But just now she is only prostrated by the heat of the weather and by the excitement of her cousin's visit.... The physician says there is room for hope."

In a week or two, there was a great improvement of symptoms—one of those deceitful lulls, by which her inexorable disease so often beguiles the anxious heart, even on the verge of the grave. Eva's step was again in the garden, in the balconies, she played and laughed again, and her father, in a transport, declared that they should soon have her as hearty as anybody ... the physician alone felt no encouragement from this illusive truce....

What is it that sometimes speaks in the soul so calmly, so clearly, that its earthly time is short? Is it the secret instinct of decaying nature, or the soul's impulsive throb, as immortality draws on? Be it what it may, it rested in the heart of Eva, a calm, sweet, prophetic certainty that Heaven was near; calm as the light of sunset, sweet as the bright stillness of autumn.

—Harriet Beecher Stowe, *Uncle Tom's Cabin,
or, Life Among the Lowly*, Vol. 2. Boston:
J. P. Jewell, 1852, pp. 81–83

3. IMPENITENCE

Lily was not long in discovering that her mother was wasting away.... The cough, the uneasiness, the unnatural brilliancy of the eye, and the hectic glow upon the cheek, all indicated ... that awful disease, which comes creeping, like a serpent, upon the victim which it has charmed ... Day by day Mrs. Lanier wasted away. Not a murmur escaped her lip.... She glided, like a spirit, from room to room, in the discharge of her household duties.... Like a guardian angel, Lily ever hovered about her mother. No word had ever escaped either the daughter or mother on the subject which was disturbing the peace of the former and was haunting the cheek of the latter.

One beautiful evening in September, Lily and her mother were sitting on the steps of the front portico.... "My child, I know that I am dying.... Lily, let's calm ourselves, and with Christian fortitude talk of the future ... this affliction is from the hands of 'Him who doeth all things well,' and that we owe all our blessings to his bounty.... I have taught you how to pray, how vain is all the pomp of this poor paltry world, how fleeting and uncertain is life, how hopes decay and beauties wither, how disappointments come and dim the eye and blanch the cheeks; and have pointed out to you the bleeding form of our Saviour upon the cross of Calvary, pouring out his warm life's blood that we might not die but have eternal life.... Trust, my child, in Him, and when your mother sleeps in death, He will be your friend and father...."

From that night Mrs. Lanier rapidly declined. She complained frequently of severe headaches, and of increasing pain of the side ... the chilling winds of bleak November began to blow [and] she seldom left her room.... It is indeed a solemn thing to stand beside the death-bed of those whom we have loved.

But oh! what a triumph it is to die the Christian's death, as did the good Aurelia Lanier! It is a victory, greater, by far, than has ever been achieved upon bloody battle-fields.... The poet's laurel may wither and die—the bold achievements of the warrior may soon be lost amid revolutions and counter-revolutions—the most daring flight of human intellect may be touched by the cheerless waves of oblivion, but the Christian dying in the firm faith of a Saviour's love, and with the glory of a new and brighter world streaming upon the fading vision, is a victory the like of which cannot be found in all the pomp and glitter of earthly magnificence.

Such a death unhinges the subtlest philosophy of the atheist and sends him cowering into a deeper gloom than he has ever known, for it unveils the truth, "So boldly, plainly, perfectly distinct, That none the meaning can mistake or doubt."

—Philip Goodwin, *Lily White*. Philadelphia: Lippincott, 1858, pp. 51–61.

4. Ben Newton

I say, doctor ... that this very inward waste ... has done more to teach me of the imperishableness of that true self—the true I—than all the sermons and readings could have done.... My father died whilst I was in my fifteenth year.... The physician said he had hemorrhage from the lungs.... From that moment I imbibed the most powerful dread lest my fate should be sealed like my father's....

During one of my excursions I met with one so pure, so gentle, and beautiful, that life assumed a new interest.... My every sense was filled—I was a man again. One day, Juliette and myself were enjoying a sail in a small pleasure-boat, when of a sudden the wind changed, and ere we could return a cold drizzling rain set in.... That night I awoke with a sharp pain in my chest, and was burning with fever.... Inflammation of the lungs had attacked me....

Then came upon me the bitterest self-reproaches. I would not, I could not marry the being I so tenderly loved ... I could not make her the mother of children doomed to die by an inheritance! I spoke of friendship to her; yes, friendship, when I was a self-immolated sacrifice to my love. We parted. Her young heart seemed crushed. I could not explain my fearful apprehensions. She thought me insincere—my God, when I suffered equally. See, here is a copy of a note I addressed to her containing a ring: 'DEAR JULIETTE, In the olden time ... a ring was held sacred ... a symbol of unity, foreshadowing golden days ... let it be the silent token of my constant thought and unswerving love.'

Then commenced the dewy sweats.... My clothes were now too large over my chest. Day by day I gradually wasted, and my breath grew short on slight exertion. One evening something salt welled up into my throat, and, with a slight cough, bright blood fell upon the cloth before me. I rose, locked my door, and bled alone! Not even my mother discovered it....

"She comes—she comes!" ... the servant was rapidly escorting a young lady. Her silken hair fell over his pillow, as she bent her ear to catch his voice.... "Can you now forgive me, dear Juliette?" he faintly asked. "Do you not read the fatal secret that dashed the cup of joy from our lips? Was this wretched body a fit mate for thine?"

"Oh, speak not thus to me, George. It was not the body I loved—thy spirit mated mine. See, upon this hand I have ever worn the ring; am I not thy spirit-bride?"

Again it is May—the churchyard is green again. Two tombs lie together. One seems but freshly made.... On this new tomb is inscribed, "Juliette."

—Edward H. Dixon, *Scenes in the Practice of a New York Surgeon.* New York: DeWitt & Davenport, 1855, pp. 270-286.

5. First Love

She [the fantasy wife] is there—her tears softening yours, her smile lighting yours ... sweetest and fairest.... How you study the color on that cheek, if it grow not fainter; How you tremble at the lustre in those eyes, if it be not the lustre of Death; How you totter under the weight of that muslin sleeve—a phantom weight! ... she has whispered to you her fears, and in the same breath—soft as a sigh, sharp as an arrow—bid you bear it bravely....

But your little Bessy, your favorite child is pining ... that blanched cheek ... those little thin lips.... Thinner and thinner they grow; plaintive and more plaintive her sweet voice.... She is gone. She cannot hear you: she cannot thank you for the violets you put within her stiff white hand. And then—the grassy mound—the cold shadow of head-stone!

... *Her* lip is rich and full; her cheek delicate as a flower. Her frailty doubles your love. And the little one she clasps—frail too—too frail; the boy you had set your hopes and heart on. You have watched him growing ever prettier, ever winning more and more upon your soul ...And, now, with his pale sister in the grave, all *that* love has come away from the mound, where worms feast, and centers on the boy.... How often you steal to his bed late at night, and lay your hand lightly upon the brow ... and watch ... the little lips half parted, and listen—your ear close to them—if the breathing be regular and sweet! But the day comes—the night rather—when you can catch no breathing.

... that childless wife clinging to you.... That wife, over whom your love broods, is fading.... What anxiety! ... How you struggle to fancy—there is no danger; how she struggles to persuade you—there is no danger! ... Your eye follows the physician as he leaves your house: is he wise, you ask yourself; is he prudent? is he the best? ... And now the hand that touches yours, is it no thinner—no whiter than yesterday? Sunny days come when she revives; color comes back; she breathes freer; she picks flowers; she meets you with a smile: hope lives again. But the next day of storm she is fallen. She cannot talk even; she presses your hand...

... They have sent for you. She is lying down; her eyes half closed; her breathing long and interrupted. She hears you; her eye opens; you put your hand in hers; yours trembles—hers does not. Her lips move; it is your name. "Be strong," she says. "God will help you!" She presses harder your hand;—"Adieu!" A long breath—another—you are alone again.

A coffin ... they have clothed the body in decent grave clothes, and the undertaker is screwing down the lid, slipping round on tip-toe. Does he fear to waken her? ... The coffin is gone out. The stupid mourners have wept—what idle tears! She, with your crushed heart, is gone out!

—Ik Marvel [Donald Grant Mitchell], *Reveries of a Bachelor*. New York: Baker & Scribner, 1850, pp. 33–48.

6. Spirit-Bride

Many said that my sister was too beautiful for this world. They frequently made this remark after the red began to deepen and burn on her cheek, and she at first coughed a little, and then more and more.... Our parents were alarmed, and sent for the family physician. He took a little blood, and gave some medicine, which my father said was mostly opium.... I wondered very much that the doctor should cut a hole in my sister's white arm, and take away that cup of blood.... After a few days, Emma declared that she was a great deal better ... and again she insisted on being allowed to go to the winter parties...

One very cold evening she returned late.... She began to cough early, and the blood rushed from her lungs into the trachea in such quantities as nearly to strangle her.... The minister came, and asked if she repented of her sins.... My father declared that the minister was a fool ... the young and earnestly-believing minister [attempted] to refute my father's heresies....

"O Mr. Lyndon," said he, "Jesus is our Saviour. He came to seek and to save the lost." "When the work is done I'll send in my allegiance, Mr Barker. For the present, I have no proof that the lost are found, or saved, or any thing of the kind." "But you must have faith; you must believe that he is your Saviour...."

Barker ... argued on with my father, as if success were sure ultimately to crown his efforts. He might as well have argued with a windmill ... he used to kneel down and pray fervently by Emma's bedside, that we all might be saved, that God would have mercy on his servant who did not yet believe in his beloved Son, and not allow him to descend faithless into ... and then he begged that father and child might not be separated ... the one to go away into outer darkness ... while the other was received into Life Eternal.... I looked at my father as the minister offered up his petition. The muscles of his under lip quivered, and I almost thought I saw a tear fill his eye, but he did not allow it to burst forth....

My sister faded almost imperceptibly ... the young and ardent minister ... was so honest, so much in earnest, so kind, and so happy in his faith ... that Emma came to have a tender regard for this Christian young man.... She was now weak from constant bleeding at the lungs.... She loved music, and Barker sang the sweetest melodies set to Methodist hymns, and promised her plenty of music in heaven.... There she would rest from all her pains; her fever would be quenched ... and, sweetest of all, she would live among music.... She was happy....

Emma's conversion brought with it some ... meddling [Christian] brethren and sisters. The most formidable was a maiden lady of very uncertain age.... She had a large stock of what my father called "spiritual pride".... She hated the enemies of Jesus Christ with a holy hatred. She said that God was angry with the wicked ... and she hurled her anathemas ... against my father....

> —Mary Sargeant Gove Nichols, *Mary Lyndon, or Revelations of a Life*. New York: Stringer and Townsend, 1855, pp. 33–38.

7. Queen Recluse

I have noticed that persons with consumptive diseases are ashamed of them.... A consumption is called a "cough," a "cold," a "throat disease," a "bronchial difficulty," a "catarrhal disorder," a "pulmonary tendency," a "pain in the chest," a "weakness of the lungs," a "tendency to secretion," "profuse expectoration," an "attack of asthma," a "weakness and loss of strength."

The victim of consumption carries around with him into society for a long time, often, his pale, wan, or unnaturally flushed face, and holds out his card of health to everybody. He suspiciously conjectures that everyone who meets him, notices his peculiar disorder in his features, and makes remarks at his leisure, the general aim of which is to show that "he is dying of the consumption!"

Now, a man with a disordered, unhealthy system, whose heart, blood, liver, stomach, are diseased, whose nerves are disordered, in whom a ... fever, or paralysis ... will crush him in a week, goes cheerily forth, imbibes his ale, smokes his cigar, guides with a strong hand his fiery bays ... and every one says of him, "what a fine specimen of health and long life!"

Alas! the poor, pale, unstrung, coughing pulmonaryist may outlive him years; but shame on his disease, he can not hide it!

> —Samuel H. Elliot, *Dreams and Realities in the Life of a Pastor and Teacher*. New York: J. C. Derby, 1856, pp. 436–437.

8. Terror

I was a man ... when my mother died.... How well I remember that last, awful night! The apartment was large and brilliantly lighted. The rich curtains were looped back; bouquets of delicate spring flowers ... everywhere. It had not the air of a sick-chamber, because my mother had been stricken down but that very evening. She had ruptured, suddenly, a blood-vessel. I had retired for the night; awakened, hurriedly, from slumber, I went down to her room.

As I entered, her face was hidden from me by the pillows in which it was buried. Zillah Bliss ... my affianced wife, sat beside her on the bed, her head bowed on her bosom, her hands tightly locked one in the other. On seeing me, a quick gleam of something, which, if it were not hope, had all its beauty, passed rapidly over her features. "Richard," she cried, wildly advancing to meet me, "Richard, save her—save her!" Before I could reply, a voice from the other side of the bed uttered in a low, sonorous, but self-possessed tone, "It is too late!" It was my [step-]father. On his hands were great red spots of blood; the pillows, the sheets were marked with it; and on the white dress of Zillah Bliss glittered, also, fresh crimson stains. "She is dying," continued my father. "Aid is of no consequence now. Again, I say, it is too late." ...

I approached.... My mother raised her head, and, oh, the unutterable anguish writhing in her eyes, bright, almost unto fierceness, with the despair of death! The heavy masses of hair, flowing around her face, gave her ghastly complexion a still more unearthly hue. Life, I saw, was ebbing fast—mortality verging into immortality. Little as I knew of death, I recognized it then. My father sat on the bed's edge, clasping one of those colorless hands in his own. He ... bent over the dying woman with a repentant tenderness that seemed to crave forgiveness for past sin. "Ellen," he whispered fervently, "do you—can you hear me? If you can, for the love of mercy, give me some signal."

She did not speak. The eyes, which were gradually assuming a dull, hazed appearance, closed wearily and opened again very slowly.... With a convulsive effort, my mother sat erect.... Blood burst anew from her mouth and nostrils.... Whatever might have been the rights of her husband in that last solemn hour, I felt that I had mine, also. I put aside his hand ... and with my own gently wiped away the life-blood oozing from between my mother's lips. I kissed them again and again. There was no struggle, but there was that gathering shadow on the white forehead which is so terribly understandable. Not a sound broke the deep silence of the chamber, but the indistinct and oppressed breathing of her whose lamp of life was even then vibrated by chill winds.... I thought this breathing grew fainter, and I bent down to listen ... the faint respiration suddenly ceased, and a slow pallor crept over the still features ... the shadow deepened, fell, and she expired.

—Josephine Franklin, *Rachel*. Boston: Thayer and Eldridge, 1860, pp. 270–275.

9. Afterlife

The young widow, Mercy Philbrick, and her old and almost childish mother, Mercy Carr, were coming by slow and tiring stage journeys up the dreary length of Cape Cod. For thirty years the elder woman had never gone out of sight of the village graveyard in which her husband and four children were buried. To transplant her was like transplanting an old weather-beaten tree, already dead at the top. Yet the physicians had said that the only chance of prolonging her life was to take her away from the fierce winds of the sea. She herself, while she loved them, shrank from them. They seemed to pierce her lungs like arrows of ice-cold steel, at once wounding and benumbing. Yet the habit and love of the seashore life were so strong upon her that she would never have been able to tear herself away from her old home, had it not been for her daughter's determined will.

Mercy Philbrick was a woman of slight frame, gentle, laughing, brown eyes, a pale skin, pale ash-brown hair, a small nose; a sweet and changeful mouth, the upper lip too short, the lower lip much too full; little hands, little feet, little wrists…. She confronted grief as she would confront an antagonist force of any sort: it was something to be battled with, to be conquered. Fate should not worst her: come what might, she would be the stronger of the two. When the doctor said to her,

"Mrs. Philbrick, I fear that your mother cannot live through another winter in this climate…."

"You think, then, that she might be well in a different climate?"

"Perhaps not well, but she might live for years in a dryer, milder air. There is as yet no actual disease in her lungs," the doctor replied.

Mercy interrupted him.

"You think she might live in comparative comfort? It would not be merely prolonging her life as a suffering invalid?" …

"Oh, yes, undoubtedly," said the doctor. "She need never die of consumption at all, if she could breathe only inland air. She will never be strong again, but she may live years without any especial liability to suffering."

"Then I will take her away immediately," replied Mercy, in as confident and simple a manner as if she had been proposing only to move her from one room into another.

—"no name" [Helen Maria Fiske Hunt Jackson], *Mercy Philbrick's Choice*. Boston: Roberts Brothers, 1876, pp. 22–24.

Appendix B: Dickinson Poems Used in This Work

The Dickinson poems in this work are from R. W. Franklin's *The Poems of Emily Dickinson: Reading Edition*, The Belknap Press of Harvard University Press, 1998. The chart below shows the numbering of each poem as it also appears in Thomas H. Johnson's *The Complete Poems of Emily Dickinson*, Little, Brown and Company, 1960.

Poem # in Franklin	Dated by Franklin	Dickinson Poems Used in This Work	Poem # in Johnson
		Introduction	
567	1863	It knew no Medicine	559
		The Omitted Center	
100	1859	What inn is this	115
528	1863	'Tis not that dying hurts us so	335
19	1858	So has a daisy vanished	28
20	1858	If those I loved were lost	29
22	1858	A brief but patient illness	18
26	1858	Distrustful of the gentian	20
1632	1884	Quite empty quite at rest	1606
470	1862	That first day when you praised me sweet	659
325	1862	There came a day at summer's full	322
640	1863	Death sets a thing significant	360
		Dread Disease	
210	1861	If I should'nt be alive	182
485	1862	The whole of it came not at once	762
138	1860	To fight aloud is very brave	126

Appendix B

Poem # in Franklin	Dated by Franklin	Dickinson Poems Used in This Work	Poem # in Johnson
40	1858	I hav'nt told my garden yet	50
202	1861	"Faith" is a fine invention	185
288	1862	My first well day since many ill	574

Impenitence

533	1863	I reckon when I count at all	569
91	1859	Some too fragile for winter winds	141
245	1861	God permits industrious angels	231
1752	undated	God is indeed a jealous God	1719
1260	1872	Is heaven a physician	1270
581	1863	Of course I prayed	376

Ben Newton

719	1863	If he were living—dare I ask	734
712	1863	I could suffice for him I knew	643
688	1863	To know just how he suffered would be dear	622
951	1865	Unable are the loved to die	809

First Love

442	1862	I see thee better in the dark	611
461	1862	We cover thee sweet face	482
363	1862	I know a place where summer strives	337
867	1864	I felt a cleaving in my mind	937
79	1859	New feet within my garden go	99
1516	1879	One thing of thee I covet	1464
1781	undated	The distance that the dead have gone	1742
6	1858	Adrift! A little boat adrift	30

Spirit-Bride

471	1862	To make one's toilette after death	485
775	1863	Suspense is hostiler than death	705
75	1859	Sexton! My master's sleeping here	96
200	1861	The rose did caper on her cheek	208
261	1861	I held a jewel in my fingers	245
454	1862	I rose because he sank	616

Queen Recluse

181	1860	A wounded deer leaps highest	165
753	1863	Grief is a mouse	793
247	1861	The lamp burns sure within	233
1726	undated	The right to perish might be thought	1692

Dickinson Poems Used in This Work

Poem # in Franklin	Dated by Franklin	Dickinson Poems Used in This Work	Poem # in Johnson
308	1862	I breathed enough to take the trick	272
591	1863	I heard a fly buzz when I died	465
544	1863	"Heaven" has different signs to me	575
1095	1865	When I have seen the sun emerge	888
360	1862	The soul has bandaged moments	512

Terror

422	1862	Give little anguish	310
465	1862	The name of it is "autumn"	656
457	1862	Nature sometimes sears a sapling	314
354	1862	If anybody's friend be dead	509
627	1863	I think I was enchanted	593
517	1863	A still volcano life	601
596	1863	Ourselves were wed one summer—dear	631
637	1863	I went to thank her	363
425	1862	'Twas like a maelstrom with a notch	414

Afterlife

776	1863	Drama's vitalest expression is the common day	741
1094	1865	We outgrow love like other things	887
894	1865	The overtakelessness of those	1691
857	1864	She rose to his requirement—dropt	732
1127	1866	After the sun comes out	1148
64	1859	Heart! We will forget him	47
1263	1872	Tell all the truth but tell it slant	1129
409	1862	The soul selects her own society	303
982	1865	If I can stop one heart from breaking	919
1356	1875	A little madness in the spring	1333
1335	1874	Floss won't save you from an abyss	1322
1355	1875	His mansion in the pool	1379
1338	1874	Time does go on	1121
882	1864	The truth is stirless	780

Chapter Notes

The source for all Dickinson poems in this work is *The Poems of Emily Dickinson: Reading Edition*, ed. R. W. Franklin. Cambridge, Mass.: The Belknap Press of Harvard University Press, 1999.

Abbreviations for Frequently Used Sources

HABEGGER — Habegger, Alfred. *My Wars Are Laid Away in Books: The Life of Emily Dickinson.* New York: Random House, 2001.

HIRSCHHORN — Hirschhorn, Norbert. "Was It Tuberculosis? Another Glimpse at Emily Dickinson's Health." *New England Quarterly* 72 (March 1999).

LETTERS — Johnson, Thomas H., ed. *The Letters of Emily Dickinson.* One-volume edition. Cambridge, Mass.: The Belknap Press of Harvard University Press, 1986.

LEYDA — Leyda, Jay. *The Years and Hours of Emily Dickinson.* 2 vols. New Haven: Yale University Press, 1960.

SEWALL — Sewall, Richard B. *The Life of Emily Dickinson.* New York: Farrar, Straus and Giroux, 1974.

TUTT — *Helen Hunt Jackson Papers.* Special Collections, Tutt Library, Colorado College, Colorado Springs, Colorado.

WHICHER — Whicher, George. *This Was a Poet: A Critical Biography of Emily Dickinson.* Ann Arbor: University of Michigan Press, 1957.

WOLFF — Wolff, Cynthia G. *Emily Dickinson.* New York: Knopf, 1986.

Introduction

1. LEYDA, p. xxi, vol. 1.
2. T. S. Eliot, *On Poetry and Poets* (New York: Farrar, Straus & Giroux, 1957), p. 124.
3. Emily Dickinson, *The Poems of Emily Dickinson: Reading Edition*, ed. R. W. Franklin (Cambridge, Mass.: The Belknap Press of Harvard University Press, 1999), p. 255.
4. Marjorie Gibson and Lynn Betlock, "Tuberculosis and Our Ancestors," *New England Ancestors* 6:3 (Summer 2005), p. 19.
5. SEWALL, p. 138.
6. SEWALL, p. 138.
7. SEWALL, p. 138.
8. SEWALL, p. 138 (emphasis added).
9. *History of the Town of Amherst* (Amherst, Mass.: Press of Carpenter & Morehouse, 1896), p. 441.
10. "Tuberculosis Declines to Historic Low in the U.S.," *The New York Times*, March 24, 2006, Section A, p. 11.

11. David M. Morens, "At the Deathbed of Consumptive Art," *Emerging Infectious Disease* 8:11 (November 2002). p. 1357.
12. Morens, p. 1353.

1. THE OMITTED CENTER

1. HIRSCHHORN, p. 102.
2. HIRSCHHORN, pp. 117–118.
3. HABEGGER, p. 262.
4. WOLFF, p. 64.
5. WOLFF, p. 109.
6. WOLFF, p. 109.
7. WOLFF, p. 133.
8. WOLFF, p. 133.
9. WOLFF, p. 134.
10. WOLFF, p. 135.
11. WOLFF, pp. 205–206.
12. WOLFF, pp. 269.
13. Sheila Rothman, *Living in the Shadow of Death: Tuberculosis and the Social Experience of Illness in American History* (New York: Basic, 1994), p. 23.
14. Camille Paglia, *Sexual Personae: Art and Decadence from Nefertiti to Emily Dickinson* (New York: Vintage, 1991), pp. 633–636.
15. Paglia, p. 673.
16. Paglia, p. 636.
17. LETTERS, L 265, p. 408.
18. LETTERS, L 271, p. 415.
19. Charles Dickens, *Nicholas Nickleby* (New York: Oxford University Press, 1990), pp. 637–638.
20. J. D. B. DeBow, *Mortality Statistics of the Seventh Census of the United States, 1850* (Washington, D.C.: A. O. P. Nicholson, Printer, 1855), pp. 124–125.
21. DeBow, pp. 124–125.
22. DeBow, pp. 124–125.
23. HABEGGER, p. 170.
24. HABEGGER, p. 170.
25. Heman Humphrey, "The Woman that Feareth the Lord: A Discourse Delivered at the Funeral of Mrs. D. W. V. Fiske," February 21, 1844, pp. 33–36.
26. TUTT, Ms0020, Box 1, Folder 1, Letter, mid–September, 1833.
27. TUTT, Ms0020, Box 1, Folder 1, Letter, September 29, 1833.
28. Rothman, p. 126.
29. Rothman, pp. 126–127.
30. Rothman, p. 126.
31. LETTERS, L 11, p. 32.
32. HABEGGER, p. 174.
33. LETTERS, L 503, p. 583.
34. HABEGGER, p. 175.
35. LETTERS, L 10, p. 28.
36. LETTERS, L 17, p. 52.
37. Dickinson, p. 324.
38. HABEGGER, p. 217.
39. LETTERS, L 27, p. 75.
40. Charlotte Brontë, *Jane Eyre* (London: J. M. Dent, 1922), p. 73.
41. Judith Farr, *The Passion of Emily Dickinson* (Cambridge, Mass.: Harvard University Press, 1992), p. 251.
42. Vivian R. Pollak, *Dickinson: The Anxiety of Gender* (Ithaca: Cornell University Press, 1984), p. 38.
43. LETTERS, L 457, p. 551.
44. David Higgins, *Portrait of Emily Dickinson: The Poet and Her Prose* (New Brunswick, N.J.: Rutgers University Press, 1967), p. 69.
45. Harriette M. Plunkett, *Josiah Gilbert Holland* (New York: Scribner's, 1894), p. 7.
46. Plunkett, p. 70.
47. LETTERS, L 174, p. 308.
48. James D. Hart, *The Popular Book: A History of America's Literary Taste* (Berkeley: University of California Press, 1963), p. 134.
49. J. G. Holland, *Bitter-Sweet: A Poem* (New York: Scribner's, 1863), pp. 19–21.
50. Holland, p. 34.
51. Holland, pp. 34–36.
52. Holland, pp. 36–39.
53. Francis DeWitt, *Fourteenth Report to the Legislature of Massachusetts, Relating the Registry and Returns of Births, Marriages, and Deaths For the Year Ending December 31,1855* (Boston: William White, Printer to the State, 1857), p. 24.

2. DREAD DISEASE

1. Harriet Beecher Stowe, *Uncle Tom's Cabin: Or, Life Among the Lowly*, vol. 2 (New York: Thomas Y. Crowell, 1897), p. 247.
2. HABEGGER, third page of photographs following p. 366.
3. WHICHER, p. 28.
4. LEYDA, p. 44, vol. 1.
5. Millicent Todd Bingham, *Emily Dick-*

inson's Home: Letters of Edward Dickinson and His Family. With Documentation and Comment by Millicent Todd Bingham (New York: Harper, 1955), p. 413.

6. Bingham, p. 413.
7. Rothman, Living in the Shadow of Death, p. 7.
8. LETTERS, L 182, p. 324.
9. "Balsam of Liverwort," Springfield Republican, February 20, 1844, p. 4.
10. Mary Frazaer, Early Engagement: and Florence (a sequel) (Cincinnati: Moore, Anderson, Wilstach & Keys, 1854), p. 193.
11. René and Jean Dubos, The White Plague: Tuberculosis, Man, and Society (New Brunswick, N.J.: Rutgers University Press, 1987), pp. 32–33.
12. Mrs. H. C. Gardner, Rosedale: A Story of Self-Denial (Cincinnati: Poe & Hitchcock, 1863), p. 210.
13. Richard A. Schaefer, Legacy: Daring to Care, Chapter 10: "How Much More Could They Bear?" http://www.llu.edu/info/legacy/Legacy11.html
14. TUTT, Ms0020, Box 1, Folder 1, Letter, October 19, 1829.
15. TUTT, Ms0020, Box 1, Folder 2, Letter, October 2, 1833.
16. TUTT, Ms0020, Box 1, Folder 2, Letter, October 7, 1833.
17. TUTT, Ms0020, Box 1, Folder 4, Letter, July, 1836.
18. Chet Raymo, "Thus We Behold a Deadly Beauty," The Boston Globe, September 28, 1998, p. C2.
19. "Tuberculosis," Love To Know 1911 Online Encyclopedia, http://53.1911encyclopedia.org/T/TU/TUBERCULOSIS.htm
20. "Gene That Controls Susceptibility to Tuberculosis Discovered," McGill University, Montreal. http://www.sciencedaily.com/releases/2003/05/030514081028.htm
21. WOLFF, pp. 60–61.
22. LETTERS, L 401, p. 515.
23. HABEGGER, pp. 93–94.
24. HIRSCHHORN, p. 115.
25. HABEGGER, p. 211.
26. HABEGGER, p. 148.
27. LETTERS, L 9, p. 26.
28. LETTERS, L 13, p. 36.
29. HIRSCHHORN, p. 114.
30. LETTERS, L13, p. 37
31. LETTERS, L 15, p. 45.
32. LETTERS, L 16, p. 48.
33. HIRSCHHORN, p. 105.
34. LETTERS, L 23, p. 66.
35. HIRSCHHORN, p. 109.
36. George Capron, New England Popular Medicine (Providence: J. F. Moore, 1846), p. 161.
37. Thomas Dormandy, The White Death: A History of Tuberculosis (London: Hambledon, 1999), p. 49.
38. William C. Richards, Great in Goodness: A Memoir of George N. Briggs (New York: Sheldon, 1866), pp. 334–335.
39. LETTERS, L 18, p. 56.
40. WOLFF, p. 501.
41. LETTERS, L 23, pp. 65–66.
42. Jack L. Capps, Emily Dickinson's Reading, 1836–1886 (Cambridge, Mass.: Harvard University Press, 1966), p. 16.
43. HIRSCHHORN, p. 116.
44. LETTERS, L 45, p. 118.
45. HIRSCHHORN, p. 107
46. James Jackson, Letters to a Young Physician Just Entering upon Practice (Boston: Phillips, Sampson, 1855), pp. 173–190.
47. Jackson, Letters to a Young Physician, p. 36.
48. LETTERS, L 55, p. 143.
49. LETTERS, L 57, p. 147.
50. LETTERS, L 64, p. 159.
51. LETTERS, L 72, p. 174.
52. LETTERS, L 76, p. 179.
53. LETTERS, L 84, p. 192.
54. LETTERS, L 87, p. 200.
55. LETTERS, L 122, p. 248.
56. LETTERS, L 129, p. 259.
57. LETTERS, L 132, p. 263.
58. LETTERS, L 141, p. 271.
59. LETTERS, L 145, p. 276.
60. LETTERS, L 148, p. 278.
61. LETTERS, p. 279.
62. LETTERS, L 152, p. 281.
63. LETTERS, L 156, p. 287.
64. HIRSCHHORN, p. 111.
65. HABEGGER, p. 262.
66. LETTERS, p. 279.
67. James Jackson Papers (H MS c 8.1), Harvard Medical Library in the Francis A. Countway Library of Medicine, Boston.
68. James Jackson, Another Letter to a Young Physician (Boston: Ticknor and Fields, 1861), p. 32.
69. Jackson, Another Letter, p. 34.

70. Jackson, *Another Letter*, p. 33.
71. TUTT, Ms 0020, Box 1, Folder 4, Letter, July, 1836.
72. TUTT, Ms 0020, Box 1, Folder 4, Letter, July 22, 1836.
73. TUTT, Ms 0020, Box 1, Folder 4, Letter, July 22, 1836.
74. TUTT, Ms 0241, Box 3, Folder 24, Letter, September 19, 1837.
75. TUTT, Ms 0241, Box 3, Folder 24, Letter, February 14, 1839.
76. TUTT, Ms 0241, Box 3, Folder 24, Letter, 1839.
77. TUTT, Ms 0020, Box 1, Folder 8, Letter, September 19, 1841.
78. TUTT, Ms 0020, Box 1, Folder 5, Letter, October 15, 1841.
79. TUTT, Ms. 0020, Box 1, Folder 5, Letter, October 24, 1841.
80. George Canning Hill, *Our Parish, or, Annals of Pastor and People*. Boston: L. P. Crown, 1854, pp. 233–234.
81. DeWitt, *Fourteenth Report of the Legislature of Massachusetts*, pp. 244–246.
82. TUTT, Ms0020, Box 1, Folder 8, Letter, October 14, 1841 or 1842.
83. TUTT, Ms0020, Box 1, Folder 6, Letter, July 13, 1843.
84. William Cranch Bond Fifield Collection (B MS c 3.3.), Boston Medical Library in the Francis A. Countway Library of Medicine, Boston.

3. IMPENITENCE

1. LETTERS, L 261, p. 404.
2. LETTERS, L 342b, p. 475.
3. WOLFF, p. 59.
4. Charles Grandison Finney, "The Nature of Impenitence and the Measure of its Guilt," *The Oberlin Evangelist*, January 21, 1846.
5. LETTERS, L 11, pp. 30–31.
6. LETTERS, L 10, pp. 27–28.
7. LETTERS, L 13, p. 38.
8. Donald Scott, "Evangelicalism, Revivalism, and the Second Great Awakening," National Humanities Center, http://www.nhc.rtp.nc.us:8080/tserve/nineteen/nkeyinfo/nevanrev.htm
9. LETTERS, L 18, p. 56.
10. WOLFF, p. 100.
11. LEYDA, p. 136, vol. 1.
12. "Life and Labors of Mary Lyon," *New Englander and Yale Review* 10:38 (May 1852), pp. 271–276.
13. LETTERS, L 23, p. 67.
14. Rebecca Fiske, *Mount Holyoke Journal Letters, 1843–1891*, May 22, 1848, p. 53. http://clio.fivecolleges.edu/mhc/journal_letters/, Mount Holyoke College Archives and Special Collections.
15. Fiske, May 22, 1848, p. 53.
16. Fiske, May 22, 1848, p. 54.
17. Fiske, May 22, 1848, p. 54
18. Asahel Cornwell Washburn, *The Young Christian's Victory; or, Memoir of Emma G. Washburn* (Hartford: Edwin Hunt, 1849), p. 74.
19. Washburn, p. 57.
20. Washburn, p. 62
21. Washburn, pp. 63–64.
22. Fiske, May 24, 1848, p. 55.
23. Fiske, May 25, 1848, p. 56.
24. Isaac Watts, *Psalms, Hymns, and Spiritual Songs* (Boston: Crocker & Brewster, 1856), pp. 392–393.
25. Washburn, p. 70.
26. HABEGGER, p. 218.
27. LETTERS, L 261, p. 404.
28. HABEGGER, p. 313.
29. Edward Everett Hale, *How to Do It* (Boston: James R. Osgood, 1871), p. 11.
30. Hale, *How to Do It*, pp. 12–13.
31. Edward Everett Hale, Jr., ed., *The Life and Letters of Edward Everett Hale*, 2 vols. (Boston: Little Brown, 1917), p. 183, vol. 1.
32. Edward Everett Hale, "Let Life Teach the Value of Life," Sermon at the Church of the Unity, Worcester, Massachusetts, June 28, 1847.
33. Elizabeth A. Petrino, *Emily Dickinson and Her Contemporaries: Women's Verse in America, 1820–1885* (Hanover, N.H.: University Press of New England, 1998), pp. 53–54.
34. LETTERS, p. 926.
35. Magdalena Zapedowska, "Wrestling with Silence: Emily Dickinson's Calvinist God," *ATQ* (*The American Transcendental Quarterly*) 20.1 (March 2006), p. 382–394.
36. WOLFF, p. 102.
37. LEYDA, Vol. 1, pp. 170–171.
38. LETTERS, L 35, p. 94.
39. HABEGGER, p. 336.

40. Habegger, p. 336.
41. Richard Chase, *Emily Dickinson* (New York: Dell, 1951), p. 192.
42. Chase, p. 154.
43. Chase, pp. 173–174.
44. Chase, p. 177.
45. Chase, p. 165.
46. Gustav Janouch, *Conversations with Kafka* (New York: New Directions, 1971), p. 100.
47. Edith Södergran, *Love & Solitude: Selected Poems, 1916-1921*, transl. and with an introduction by Stina Katchadourian (San Francisco: Fjord, 1981), p. 9.
48. Södergran, p. 59.
49. Södergran, p. 9.
50. Letters, L 932, p. 837.
51. Letters, L 234, p. 376.
52. Beth Maclay Doriani, "God," in *An Emily Dickinson Encyclopedia*, ed. Jane Donahue Eberwein (Westport, Conn.: Greenwood, 1998), pp. 126–127.

4. Ben Newton

1. Chase, *Emily Dickinson*, pp. 158–159.
2. Jerome Loving, *Emily Dickinson: The Poet on the Second Story* (New York: Cambridge University Press, 1986), p. 10.
3. Farr, *The Passion of Emily Dickinson*, pp. 248–249.
4. Farr, p. 5.
5. Wolff, p. 412.
6. Wolff, p. 588.
7. Wolff, p. 135.
8. Sewall, p. 445.
9. Letters, L 170, p. 302.
10. Leyda, p. 319.
11. Leyda, p. 309.
12. "Editor's Drawer," *Harper's New Monthly Magazine* 9:51 (August, 1854), p. 424.
13. "Editor's Drawer," p. 424.
14. Whicher, p. 102.
15. Charles Wadsworth, "Rev. & Dear Brother," Letter, February 26, 1852, Schaffer Library Collections, Union College, Schenectady, New York.
16. "Died March 28, at the parsonage, Watervliet" [reprint of article in *Christian Intelligencer*], *The Litchfield Enquirer*, April 28, 1853.
17. Letters, L 776, pp. 744–745.
18. Wolff, p. 398.
19. Habegger, p. 376.
20. Stephen G. Weisner, *Embattled Editor: The Life of Samuel Bowles* (New York: University Press of America, 1986), p. 142.
21. George S. Merriam, *The Life and Times of Samuel Bowles*, 2 vols. (New York: Century, 1885), p. 22, vol. 1.
22. Merriam, p. 308.
23. Merriam, p. 308
24. Leyda, p. 35, vol. 2.
25. Weisner, p. 48.
26. Leyda, p. 281, vol. 2.
27. Letters, L. 300, pp. 437–438.
28. Whicher, p. 82.
29. Letters, L 30, p. 84.
30. Letters, L 34, pp. 91–92.
31. Jay Mack Holbrook, "Fitchburg Births, Marriages and Deaths," *Massachusetts Vital Statistics, 1751-1895* [microfiche] (Oxford, Mass.: Holbrook Research Institute, 1987), card 39, p. 72.
32. Letters, L 44, p. 116.
33. Whicher, p. 140.
34. Letters, L 110, p. 236.
35. Whicher, p. 92.
36. Letters, L 122, p. 248.
37. Paula Bennett, *My Life a Loaded Gun: Female Creativity and Feminist Poetics* (Boston: Beacon, 1986), pp. 38–39.
38. "Death of Benjamin F. Newton," *Daily Morning Transcript* (Worcester, Massachusetts), March 25, 1853.
39. "Funeral Solemnities of the Late B. F. Newton," *Daily Morning Transcript* (Worcester, Massachusetts), March 28, 1853.
40. Holbrook, "Fitchburg Births, Marriages and Deaths," card 39, p. 72.
41. Franklin P. Rice, *Worcester Births, Marriages and Deaths* (Worcester, Massachusetts: The Worcester Society of Antiquity, 1894), p. 194; Ermina Newton Leonard, *Newton Genealogy* (De Pere, Wisc.: Bernard Ammidown Leonard, 1915), p. 133.
42. Worcester (Mass.) Assessor's Office, "State and County Taxes, 1819," *Records, 1819-1857*.
43. Worcester (Mass.) Assessor's Office, "Personal Income and Value of Estates, 1820," *Records, 1819-1857*.
44. *United States Census, 1860, Rhode Island, Providence County, Smithfield*, p. 149.

45. Franklin P. Rice, *Vital Records of Shrewsbury, Massachusetts, to the End of the Year 1849* (Worcester: Franklin P. Rice, 1904), p. 194.
46. George F. Whicher, "Emily Dickinson's Earliest Friend," *American Literature*, 6:1 (March 1934), p. 8.
47. United States Census, 1860, Rhode Island, Providence County, Smithfield, p. 149.
48. Rhode Island Death Records, 1885–1888 [Microfilm], Roll #50, 1886, p. 658.
49. Frances L. Eaton, *Vital Records of Berlin, Massachusetts, to the End of the Year 1899* (Marlboro, Mass.: Eaton, 1935), p. 78.
50. *United States Census Office, Census Records for Worcester County, 1850–1870*, p. 160, vol. 3.
51. Gilman Bigelow Howe, *Vital Records of Northborough, Massachusetts, to the End of the Year 1850* (Worcester: F. P. Rice, 1901), p. 101.
52. Eaton, *Vital Records of Berlin*, p. 332.
53. Holbrook, "Fitchburg Births, Marriages and Deaths," card 39, p. 72.
54. WHICHER, p. 86.
55. HABEGGER, pp. 699–700.
56. Henry S. Nourse, ed., *Birth, Marriage and Death Register, Church Records & Epitaphs of Lancaster, Massachusetts, 1643 to 1850* (Lancaster: Printed by W. J. Coulter, 1890), p. 267.
57. United States Census, 1850, Massachusetts, Suffolk County, Boston, Ward 11.
58. "A Good Appointment," *Massachusetts Spy* (Worcester, Massachusetts), May 26, 1852.
59. "Thoughts at the Funeral Service of the Late B. F. Newton," *Daily Morning Transcript* (Worcester, Massachusetts), March 29, 1853.
60. "The Late Benjamin F. Newton," *Daily Morning Transcript* (Worcester, Massachusetts), March 26, 1853.
61. "Case #43070: Newton, Benjamin F.," Court of Probate for the County of Worcester, April 5, 1853.
62. "Case #43070: Newton, Benjamin F.," May 3, 1853.
63. "Case #43070: Newton, Benjamin F.," May 17, 1854.
64. "Case #43070: Newton, Benjamin F.," May 17, 1854.
65. *Reports of the Selectmen, Relative to the Expenses of the Town of Concord, for the Year 1850–51* (Concord: Printed at the Freeman Office, 1851), p. 13.
66. "Marriages," *The New England Puritan* (Boston), August 31, 1854.
67. *Annual Report of the School Committee of the Town of Concord for the Year Ending April 1855* (Concord: Silas B. Wilde, Printer, 1855), pp. 4–5.
68. Bradford Kingman, *History of North Bridgewater* (Boston: Published by the Author, 1866), pp. 131–132.
69. "Case #43070: Newton, Benjamin F.," October 3, 1854.
70. *The Boston, Massachusetts City Record & Business Directory for 1860* (Boston: Adams, Sampson, 1859).
71. United States Census, 1870, Massachusetts, Worcester County, Worcester, Ward 6, pp. 53–54.
72. United States Census, 1860, Massachusetts, Worcester County, Lancaster, pp. 106–107.
73. United States Census, 1880, Massachusetts, Worcester County, Lancaster, p. 4.
74. Whicher, "Emily Dickinson's Earliest Friend," p. 7.
75. LETTERS, L 153, pp. 282–283.
76. WHICHER, p. 8.
77. LETTERS, L 298, p. 436.
78. LETTERS, L 265, p. 408.
79. Farr, *The Passion of Emily Dickinson*, p. 251.
80. Calvin Cutter, *Anatomy and Physiology: Designed for School and Families* (Boston: Benjamin B. Mussey, 1846), p. 157.
81. LETTERS, L 127, p. 254.
82. Noah Webster, *An American Dictionary of the English Language*, 2 vols. (Amherst: J. S. and C. Adams, 1844), p. 325, vol. 2.
83. Webster, p. 411, vol. 1.
84. LEYDA, p. 296, vol. 1.
85. HABEGGER, p. 258.

5. FIRST LOVE

1. LETTERS, L 75, p. 178.
2. WHICHER, p. 220.
3. Chase, *Emily Dickinson*, p. 47.
4. HABEGGER, p. 249.
5. SEWALL, p. 679.
6. Ik Marvel [Donald Grant Mitchell],

Reveries of a Bachelor, or A Book of the Heart (New York: Baker and Scribner, 1850), p. 259.

7. LETTERS, L 118, p. 245

8. Wayne R. Kyme, *Donald G. Mitchell* (Boston: Twayne, 1985), p. 1.

9. Waldo H. Dunn, *The Life of Donald G. Mitchell* (New York: Scribner's), 1922, p. 50.

10. Dunn, p. 51.

11. Ik Marvel [Donald Grant Mitchell], *Dream Life: A Fable for the Seasons* (New York: Scribner's, 1851), pp. i–ii.

12. "Recollections of Washington Irving, by One of His Friends," *The Continental Monthly* 1:6 (June 1862), p. 696.

13. "Recollections of Washington Irving," p. 696.

14. Charles Dudley Warner, "Washington Irving," *The Atlantic Monthly* 45:269 (March 1880), p. 401.

15. "Recollections of Washington Irving," pp. 694–695.

16. Washington Irving, *The Sketch-Book* (New York: Putnam, 1861), p. 89.

17. Irving, p. 395.

18. Irving, p. 396.

19. Irving, pp. 400–401.

20. Irving, pp. 182–183.

21. Dubos and Dubos, *The White Plague*, pp. 39–40.

22. Henry F. Pommer, *Emerson's First Marriage* (Carbondale: Southern Illinois University Press, 1967), pp. 28–30.

23. Edith W. Gregg, *One First Love: The Letters of Ellen Louisa Tucker to Ralph Waldo Emerson* (Cambridge, Mass.: The Belknap Press of Harvard University Press, 1962), p. 179.

24. Pommer, p. 13.

25. Pommer, p. 13.

26. Gregg, p. 52.

27. Gregg, p. 82.

28. Janet M. Anderson, "Ellen Emerson and the Tubercular Muse," *Literature and Medicine*, 18:1 (Spring 1999), p. 39.

29. Anderson, p. 50.

30. Anderson, p. 51.

31. Anderson, pp. 52–53.

32. Anderson, p. 53.

33. Anderson, p. 57.

34. Anderson, p. 46.

35. Anderson, p. 47.

36. Anderson, pp. 47–48.

37. Anderson, p. 52.

38. Pommer, p. 43.

39. Pommer, p. 43.

40. William Cullen Bryant, *The Letters of William Cullen Bryant*, ed. William Cullen Bryant II and Thomas G. Voss, 6 vols. (New York: Fordham University Press, 1975), p. 90, vol. 1.

41. Pommer, pp. 45–46.

42. Pommer, p. 48.

43. Pommer, pp. 50–51.

44. Gregg, p. 142.

45. Ralph Waldo Emerson, *The Journals and Miscellaneous Notebooks of Ralph Waldo Emerson*, ed. William H. Gilman and Alfred R. Ferguson, 16 vols. (Cambridge, Mass.: The Belknap Press of Harvard University Press, 1963), p. 244, vol. 3.

46. Emerson, *Journals*, pp. 272–275.

47. Emerson, *Journals*, p. 285.

48. Pommer, p. 55.

49. Ralph Waldo Emerson, *The Letters of Ralph Waldo Emerson*, ed. Ralph L. Rusk, 6 vols. (New York: Columbia University Press, 1939), pp. 12–18, vol. 1.

50. Pommer, p. 81.

51. Ralph Waldo Emerson, *Poems of Ralph Waldo Emerson* (New York: Oxford University Press, 1921), p. 160.

52. Marietta Messmer, *A Vice for Voices: Reading Emily Dickinson's Correspondence* (Amherst: University of Massachusetts Press, 2001), p. 131.

53. Thomas Wentworth Higginson, *Cheerful Yesterdays* (New York: Houghton Mifflin, 1898), pp. 76–77.

54. Maria Lowell, *The Poems of Maria Lowell: With Unpublished Letters and a Biography*, ed. Hope Jillson Vernon, Providence, R.I.: Brown University, 1936), pp. 14–15.

55. Katharine Marie Rodier, "A Career in Letters: Emily Dickinson, T. W. Higginson, and Literary Women." Ph.D. diss., University of Connecticut, 1995, p. 59.

56. Maria Lowell, p. 34.

57. Maria Lowell, pp. 127–128.

58. Maria Lowell, p. 149.

59. Maria Lowell, p. 154.

60. James Russell Lowell, *Letters of James Russell Lowell*, ed. Charles Eliot Norton, 2 vols. (New York: Harper & Brothers, Publishers, 1874), pp. 177–178, vol. 1.

61. Maria Lowell, p. 37.

62. Rodier, p. 68.
63. Rodier, p. 68.
64. Maria Lowell, p. 61.
65. Walker, Cheryl, "Dickinson in Context," in A Historical Guide to Emily Dickinson, ed. Vivian R. Pollack (New York: Oxford University Press, 2004), pp. 189–190.
66. Walker, pp. 190–191.
67. Walker, p. 188
68. Walker, p. 188.
69. Walker, pp. 188–189.
70. Walker, p. 189.
71. Maria Lowell, p. viii.
72. Maria Lowell, p. 37.
73. Maria Lowell, pp. 38–39.
74. James Russell Lowell, "After the Burial," The Atlantic Monthly 21:127 (May 1868), pp. 628–629.
75. LETTERS, L622, p. 649.
76. Rothman, Living in the Shadow of Death, p. 57.

6. SPIRIT-BRIDE

1. Mary Sargeant Nichols, Mary Lyndon, or, Revelations of a Life (New York: Stringer and Townsend, 1855), p. 32.
2. LETTERS, L 6, p. 13.
3. LETTERS, L 8, p. 21.
4. Hogue, Caroline, in 14 by Emily Dickinson, ed. Thomas M. Davis (Fair Lawn, N.J.: Scott, Foresman, 1964), pp. 68–69.
5. Albert J. Gelpi, Emily Dickinson: The Mind of the Poet (New York: W. W. Norton, 1965), p. 112.
6. Gelpi, pp. 112–113.
7. David Baker, "Elegy and Eros," Virginia Quarterly Review 81:2 (Spring 2005), p. 215.
8. George Heath: 'The Midland Poet' http://mysite.wanadoo-members.co.uk/George Heath/index.html
9. Encyclopædia Americana, 14 vols. (Boston: B. B. Massey & Co., 1851), pp. 423–424, vol. 10.
10. Robert Louis Stevenson, The Letters of Robert Louis Stevenson to His Family and Friends, ed. Sidney Colvin, 2 vols. (New York: Scribner's, 1902), p. 25, vol. 2.
11. LETTERS, L 45, p. 118.
12. LETTERS, L 47, p. 123.
13. LETTERS, L 180, p. 321.
14. LETTERS, L 184, pp. 327–328.
15. LETTERS, L 190, pp. 335–336.
16. LETTERS, L 193, p. 338.
17. Barton Levi St. Armand, Emily Dickinson and Her Culture: The Soul's Society (New York: Cambridge University Press, 1984), pp. 42–47.
18. St. Armand, p. 44.
19. St. Armand, pp. 48–51.
20. Edgar Allan Poe, The Works of Edgar Allan Poe (New York: Avenel Books, 1985), p. 714.
21. Daneen Wardrop, Emily Dickinson's Gothic: Goblin with a Gauge (Iowa City: University of Iowa Press, 1996), pp. 54–60. (Emphasis added.)
22. WHICHER, p. 93.
23. WHICHER, p. 94.

7. QUEEN RECLUSE

1. WOLFF, p. 399.
2. LETTERS, L 266, p. 410.
3. HABEGGER, p. 447.
4. Gelpi, Emily Dickinson, p. 163.
5. SEWALL, p. 153.
6. SEWALL, p. 153.
7. Gelpi, pp. 167–168.
8. SEWALL, p. 153.
9. Dubos and Dubos, The White Plague, p. 59.
10. WOLFF, p. 206.
11. Janouch, Conversations with Kafka, p. 33.
12. William Elder, Periscopics, or, Current Subjects Extemporaneously Treated (New York: J. C. Derby, 1854), pp. 88–89.
13. LETTERS, L 261, p. 404.
14. LETTERS, L 268, p. 411.
15. LETTERS, L 271, p. 415.
16. LETTERS, L 330, p. 460.
17. Janouch, Conversations with Kafka, pp. 124–125.
18. LETTERS, L 127, p. 254. (Emphasis added.)
19. Elizabeth Gaskell, The Life of Charlotte Brontë, 2 vols. (New York: Appleton, 1857), pp. 80–81, vol. 1.
20. Charlotte Brontë, Shirley: A Tale, 3 vols. (London: Smith, Elder and Co., 1849), p. 261, vol. 2. (Emphasis added.)
21. LETTERS, L 28, p. 77.

22. HABEGGER, p. 226.
23. Gaskell, vol. 2, pp. 38–39.
24. LETTERS, L 742, p. 721.
25. Gaskell, vol. 2, p. 76.
26. Ingrid Geerken, "'The Dead Are Not Annihilated': Mortal Regret in Wuthering Heights," *Journal of Narrative Theory* 34:3 (Fall 2004), p. 374.
27. Geerken, p. 391.
28. LETTERS, L 90, p. 205. (Emphasis added.)
29. Lady Georgiana Fullerton, *Ellen Middleton: A Tale*, 3 vols. (London: Edward Moxon, 1844), pp. 172–173, vol. 3.
30. Fullerton, vol. 1, pp. 17–18.
31. LETTERS, L 94, p. 212. (Emphasis added.)
32. "Editor's Easy Chair," *Harper's New Monthly Magazine* 7:42 (November 1853), p. 842.
33. "Blighted Flowers," *Harper's New Monthly Magazine* 4:22 (March 1852), p. 550.
34. "Life and Death of Paganini," *Harper's New Monthly Magazine* 5:29 (October 1852), pp. 662–663.
35. "A Slight Cold," *Harper's New Monthly Magazine* 6:32 (January 1853), pp. 258–259.
36. "Extracts from the Portfolio of an Excitement Seeker," *Harper's New Monthly Magazine*, 6:35 (April 1853), p. 646.
37. "Editor's Easy Chair," *Harper's New Monthly Magazine* 20:115 (December 1859), pp. 128–129.
38. John Ciardi, in *14 by Emily Dickinson*, ed. Thomas M. Davis, p. 67.
39. Geerken, p. 381.
40. Geerken, p. 381.
41. "Joseph Thorne—His Calling," *Harper's New Monthly Magazine* 15:90 (November 1857), pp. 803–809.
42. C. W. Hatfield, ed., *The Complete Poems of Emily Jane Brontë* (New York: Columbia University Press, 1941), p. 164.
43. Janouch, p. 16.

8. TERROR

1. LETTERS, L 261, p. 404.
2. Emily Dickinson, *The Poems of Emily Dickinson*, ed. Thomas H. Johnson, 3 vols. (Cambridge: The Belknap Press of Harvard University Press, 1955), p. xxiii, vol. 1.

3. Marianne Noble, "Master," in *An Emily Dickinson Encyclopedia*, ed. Jane Donahue Eberwein (Westport, Conn.: Greenwood, 1998), p. 184.
4. SEWALL, p. 512.
5. Bennett, *My Life a Loaded Gun*, p. 66.
6. SEWALL, p. 528.
7. WOLFF, p. 406.
8. WOLFF, p. 165.
9. WOLFF, p. 165.
10. HABEGGER, pp. 435–436
11. HABEGGER, p. 436.
12. HABEGGER, p. 436.
13. HABEGGER, p. 436.
14. LETTERS, L 248, pp. 391–392.
15. J. H. Pulte, *Homeopathic Domestic Physician: Containing the Treatment of Diseases* (Cincinnati: Moore, Willstach, Keys, 1862), p. 308.
16. Michael E. Bell, *Food for the Dead: On the Trail of New England's Vampires* (New York: Carroll & Graf, 2001), p. 225.
17. Rev. Burdett Hart, "The New Northwest," *New Englander and Yale Review* 17: 68 (November 1859), p. 997.
18. LETTERS, L 320, p. 455.
19. John Ware, *On Hemoptysis as a Symptom* (Boston: David Clapp, 1860), p. 8.
20. Jack J. Leedy, ed., *Poetry, the Healer* (Philadelphia: Lippincott, 1973), p. 36.
21. Leedy, p. 40.
22. Leedy, p. 30.
23. Lesya Ukrainka, *Spirit of Flame: A Collection of the Works of Lesya Ukrainka*, trans. Percival Cundy (Westport, Conn.: Greenwood, 1950), pp. 47–48.
24. Ware, pp. 9–11.
25. Daniel Morley McKeithan, ed., *A Collection of Hayne Letters* (Austin: The University of Austin Press, 1944), p. 120.
26. McKeithan, p. 131.
27. McKeithan, p. 145.
28. McKeithan, p. 159.
29. McKeithan, p. 174.
30. McKeithan, p. 201.
31. McKeithan, p. 76.
32. Ware, p. 16.
33. Ware, p. 24.
34. Bingham, *Emily Dickinson's Home*, p. 68.
35. W. S. Tyler, *Amherst College During the First Half Century* (Springfield, Mass.: Clark W. Bryan, 1873), p. 573.

36. Henry S. Kelsey, *An Account of the Last Two Years of Martha Snell's Life*, April 12, 1860, pp. 5–65. http://clio.fivecolleges.edu/amherst/snell/03diaries/martha-d/account/
37. Kelsey, p. 65.
38. LETTERS, L 217, pp. 361–362.
39. LETTERS, L 222, p. 365.
40. HABEGGER, p. 145.
41. LETTERS, L 176, p. 311.
42. LETTERS, L 178, p. 318.
43. LETTERS, L 237, p. 378.
44. LETTERS, L 243, pp. 383–384.
45. LETTERS, L 243, pp. 383–384.
46. LETTERS, L 246, p. 389.
47. Higgins, *Portrait of Emily Dickinson*, p. 133.
48. Ellen Moers, *Literary Women* (New York: Oxford University Press, 1985), p. 56.
49. Moers, p. 55.
50. Gary Lee Stonum, *The Dickinson Sublime* (Madison, Wisc.: The University of Wisconsin Press, 1990), p. 35.
51. Stonum, p. 40.
52. Stonum, p. 40.
53. Stonum, p. 34.
54. Capps, *Emily Dickinson's Reading*, p. 86.
55. Jane Donahue Eberwein, in Vivian Pollak, *A Historical Guide to Emily Dickinson* (New York: Oxford University Press, 2004), p. 74.
56. Mary Russell Mitford, "Personal Sketches and Reminiscences," *Harper's New Monthly Magazine* 4:22 (March 1852), pp. 506–507.
57. Betty Miller (ed.), *Elizabeth Barrett to Miss Mitford* (London: John Murray, Albemarle St., 1954), p. 28.
58. Miller, p. 34.
59. Miller, p. 38.
60. Miller, p. 42.
61. Miller, p. 60.
62. Miller, p. 60.
63. Kate Field, "Elizabeth Barrett Browning," *The Atlantic Monthly* 8:47 (September 1861), pp. 368–375.
64. LETTERS, L 234, p. 376.
65. LETTERS, L 244, p. 385.
66. LETTERS, L 266, p. 410.
67. Harriet Prescott, "Circumstance," *The Atlantic Monthly* 5:31 (May 1860), pp. 558–561.
68. Prescott, p. 565.
69. Loving, *Emily Dickinson*, pp. 35–36.

9. AFTERLIFE

1. Kate Phillips, *Helen Hunt Jackson: A Literary Life* (Berkeley: University of California Press, 2003), p. 22.
2. Phillips, pp. 19–20.
3. LETTERS, L 260, p. 403.
4. Thomas Wentworth Higginson, "Emily Dickinson's Letters," *The Atlantic Monthly* 68:408 (October 1891), p. 445.
5. Higginson, p. 445.
6. Higginson, p. 446.
7. Higginson, p. 451.
8. Philips, p. 145.
9. TUTT, Ms 0020, Box 1, Folder 27, Letter, January 5, 1838.
10. Phillips, p. 56.
11. Phillips, p. 125.
12. HABEGGER, pp. 498–499.
13. HABEGGER, p. 501.
14. LETTERS, L 318, p. 452.
15. HABEGGER, p. 556.
16. WHICHER, pp. 127–128.
17. WHICHER, p. 128.
18. Helen Hunt Jackson, *Mercy Philbrick's Choice* (Boston: Roberts Brothers, 1876), pp. 88–89.
19. Helen Hunt Jackson, p. 282.
20. WHICHER, p. 128.
21. Helen Hunt Jackson, p. 85.
22. Helen Hunt Jackson, p. 86
23. Helen Hunt Jackson, pp. 86.
24. Helen Hunt Jackson, p. 87–88.
25. Chase, *Emily Dickinson*, p. 268.
26. Helen Hunt Jackson, p. 77.
27. SEWALL, p. 81.
28. Helen Hunt Jackson, p. 269.
29. Helen Hunt Jackson, p. 284.
30. LETTERS, L 298, p. 436.
31. LETTERS, L 379, p. 499.
32. LETTERS, L 389, p. 506.
33. LETTERS, L 388, p. 504.
34. Helen Hunt Jackson, pp. 283–284.
35. MacGregor Jenkins, *Emily Dickinson, Friend and Neighbor* (Boston: Little, Brown, 1930), pp. 21–32.

Bibliography

Anderson, Janet M. "Ellen Emerson and the Tubercular Muse." *Literature and Medicine* 18:1 (Spring 1999).
Annual Report of the School Committee of the town of Concord for the year ending April, 1855. Concord: Silas B. Wilde, Printer, 1855.
Arthur, T. S. *Seed-time and Harvest.* Philadelphia: Lippincott, Grambo, 1851.
Baker, David. "Elegy and Eros." *Virginia Quarterly Review* 81:2 (Spring 2005).
"Balsam of Liverwort." *Springfield Republican*, February 20, 1844.
Bell, Michael E. *Food for the Dead: On the Trail of New England's Vampires.* New York: Carroll & Graf, 2001.
Bennett, Paula. *My Life a Loaded Gun: Female Creativity and Feminist Poetics.* Boston: Beacon, 1986.
Bingham, Millicent Todd. *Emily Dickinson's Home: Letters of Edward Dickinson and His Family.* New York: Harper, 1955.
"Blighted Flowers." *Harper's New Monthly Magazine* 4:22 (March 1852).
The Boston, Massachusetts City Record & Business Directory for 1860. Boston: Adams, Sampson, 1859.
Brontë, Charlotte. *Jane Eyre.* London: J. M. Dent, 1922.
Brontë, Emily Jane. *The Complete Poems of Emily Jane Brontë.* Ed. C. W. Hatfield. New York: Columbia University Press, 1941.
_____. *Shirley: A Tale.* 3 vols. London: Smith, Elder, 1849.
Bryant, William Cullen. *The Letters of William Cullen Bryant.* 6 vols. Ed. William Cullen Bryant II and Thomas G. Voss. New York: Fordham University Press, 1975.
Capps, Jack L. *Emily Dickinson's Reading, 1836–1886.* Cambridge: Harvard University Press, 1966.
Capron, George. *New England Popular Medicine.* Providence, Rhode Island: J. F. Moore, 1846.
"Case #43070: Newton, Benjamin F." *Court of Probate for the County of Worcester*, April 5, 1853.
Chase, Richard. *Emily Dickinson.* New York: Dell, 1965.
Cutter, Calvin. *Anatomy and Physiology: Designed for School and Families.* Boston: Benjamin B. Mussey, 1846.
Davis, Thomas M., ed. *14 by Emily Dickinson.* Fair Lawn, N.J.: Scott, Foresman, 1964.
"Death of Benjamin F. Newton." *Daily Morning Transcript* (Worcester, Massachusetts), March 25, 1853.

DeBow, J. D. B. *Mortality Statistics of the Seventh Census of the United States, 1850.* Washington, D.C.: A. O. P. Nicholson, Printer, 1855.
DeWitt, Francis. *Fourteenth Report to the Legislature of Massachusetts, Relating to The Registry and Returns of Births, Marriages, and Deaths, in the Commonwealth, for the Year Ending December 31, 1855.* Boston: William White, 1857.
Dickens, Charles. *Nicholas Nickleby.* New York: Oxford University Press, 1990.
Dickinson, Emily. *The Poems of Emily Dickinson: Reading Edition.* Ed. R. W. Franklin. Cambridge, Mass.: The Belknap Press of Harvard University Press, 1999.
_____. *The Poems of Dickinson.* 3 vols. Ed. Thomas Johnson. Cambridge: The Belknap Press of Harvard University Press, 1955.
Dixon, Edward H. *Scenes in the Practice of a New York Surgeon.* New York: DeWitt & Davenport, 1855.
Doriani, Beth Maclay. "God." In An Emily Dickinson Encyclopedia. Ed. Jan Donahue Eberwein. Westport, Conn.: Greenwood, 1998.
Dormandy, Thomas. *The White Death: A History of Tuberculosis.* London: Hambledon, 1999.
Dubos, René, and Jean Dubos. *The White Plague: Tuberculosis, Man, and Society.* New Brunswick, New Jersey: Rutgers University Press, 1987.
Dunn, Waldo H. *The Life of Donald G. Mitchell.* New York: Scribner's, 1922.
Eaton, Frances L. *Vital Records of Berlin, Massachusetts to the End of the Year 1899.* Marlboro, Mass.: Eaton, 1935.
Eberwein, Jane Donahue (ed.). *An Emily Dickinson Encyclopedia.* Westwood, Connecticut: Greenwood Press, 1998.
"Editor's Drawer." *Harper's New Monthly Magazine* 9:51 (August, 1854).
"Editor's Easy Chair." *Harper's New Monthly Magazine* 7:42 (November 1853).
_____. *Harper's New Monthly Magazine* 20:112 (December 1859).
Elder, William. *Periscopics, or, Current Topics Extemporaneously Treated.* New York: J. C. Derby, 1854.
Eliot, T. S. *On Poetry and Poets.* New York: Farrar, Straus & Giroux, 1957.
Elliot, Samuel H. *Dreams and Realities in the Life of a Pastor and Teacher.* New York: J. C. Derby, 1856.
Emerson, Ralph Waldo. *The Journals and Miscellaneous Notebooks of Ralph Waldo Emerson.* 16 vols. Ed. William H. Gilman and Alfred R. Ferguson. Cambridge, Mass.: The Belknap Press of Harvard University Press, 1963.
_____. *The Letters of Ralph Waldo Emerson.* Ed. Ralph L. Rusk. Vol. 1. New York: Columbia University Press, 1939.
_____. *Poems of Ralph Waldo Emerson.* New York: Oxford University Press, 1921.
Encyclopædia Americana. 14 vols. Boston: B. B. Mussey, 1851.
"Extracts from the Portfolio of an Excitement Seeker." *Harper's New Monthly Magazine* 6:35 (April 1853).
Farr, Judith. *The Passion of Emily Dickinson.* Cambridge, Mass.: Harvard University Press, 1992.
Field, Kate. "Elizabeth Barrett Browning." *The Atlantic Monthly* 8:47 (September 1861).
Finney, Charles Grandison. "The Nature of Impenitence and the Measure of Its Guilt." *The Oberlin Evangelist,* January 21, 1846.
Fiske, Rebecca. *Mount Holyoke Journal Letters, 1843–1891.* http://clio.fivecolleges.edu/mhc/journalletters/
Franklin, Josephine. *Rachel.* Boston: Thayer and Eldridge, 1860.

Frazaer, Mary. *Early Engagement: and Florence (a sequel)*. Cincinnati: Moore, Anderson, Wilstach & Keys, 1854.
Fullerton, Lady Georgiana. *Ellen Middleton: A Tale*. 3 vols. London: Edward Moxon, 1844.
"Funeral Solemnities of the Late B. F. Newton." *Daily Morning Transcript* (Worcester, Massachusetts), March 28, 1853.
Gardner, Mrs. H. C. *Rosedale: A Story of Self-Denial*. Cincinnati: Poe & Hitchcock, 1863.
Gaskell, Elizabeth. *The Life of Charlotte Brontë*. 2 vols. New York: Appleton and Company, 1857.
Geerken, Ingrid. "'The Dead Are Not Annihilated': Mortal Regret in Wuthering Heights." *Journal of Narrative Theory* 34:3 (Fall 2004).
Gelpi, Albert J. *Emily Dickinson: The Mind of the Poet*. New York: W. W. Norton, 1965.
"Gene That Controls Susceptibility to Tuberculosis Discovered." McGill University, Montreal. http://www.sciencedaily.com/releases/2003/05/030514081028.htm
George Heath: "The Midland Poet." http://mysite.wanadoo-members.co.uk/George-Heath/index.html
Gibson, Marjorie, and Lynn Betlock. "Tuberculosis and Our Ancestors." *New England Ancestors*, 6:3 (Summer 2005).
"A Good Appointment." *Massachusetts Spy* (Worcester, Massachusetts), May 26, 1852.
Goodwin, Philip. *Lily White*. Philadelphia: Lippincott, 1858.
Gregg, Edith W. *One First Love: The Letters of Ellen Louisa Tucker to Ralph Waldo Emerson*. Cambridge, Mass.: The Belknap Press of Harvard University Press, 1962.
Habegger, Alfred. *My Wars Are Laid Away in Books: The Life of Emily Dickinson*. New York: Random House, 2001.
Hale, Edward Everett. *How to Do It*. Boston: James R. Osgood, 1871.
_____. "Let Life Teach the Value of Life." Sermon at the Church of the Unity, Worcester, Massachusetts, June 28, 1847.
Hale, Edward Everett, Jr., ed. *The Life and Letters of Edward Everett Hale*. 2 vols. Boston: Little, Brown, 1917.
Hart, Rev. Burdett. "The New Northwest." *New Englander and Yale Review* 17:68 (November 1859).
Hart, James D. *The Popular Book: A History of America's Literary Taste*. Berkeley: University of California Press, 1963.
Higgins, David. *Portrait of Emily Dickinson: The Poet and Her Prose*. New Brunswick, N.J.: Rutgers University Press, 1967.
Higginson, Thomas Wentworth. *Cheerful Yesterdays*. New York: Houghton Mifflin, 1898.
Hill, George Canning. *Our Parish, or, Annals of Pastor and People*. Boston: L. P. Crown, 1854.
Hirschhorn, Norbert. "Was It Tuberculosis? Another Glimpse at Emily Dickinson's Health." *The New England Quarterly* 72 (March 1999).
History of the Town of Amherst. Amherst, Massachusetts: Press of Carpenter & Morehouse, 1896.
Holbrook, Jay Mack. "Fitchburg Births, Marriages and Deaths." *Massachusetts Vital Statistics, 1751–1895* [microfiche]. Oxford, Mass.: Holbrook Research Institute, 1987.

Holland, Josiah Gilbert. *Bitter-Sweet: A Poem*. New York: Scribner's, 1863.
Howe, Gilman Bigelow. *Vital Records of Northborough, Massachusetts, to the End of the Year 1850*. Worcester, Mass.: F. P. Rice, 1901.
Humphrey, Heman. "The Woman that Feareth the Lord: A Discourse Delivered at the Funeral of Mrs. D. W. V. Fiske." February 21, 1844.
Irving, Washington. *The Sketch-Book*. New York: Putnam, 1861.
Jackson, Helen Hunt. *Mercy Philbrick's Choice*. Boston: Roberts Brothers, 1876.
____. Papers, Tutt Library, Colorado College, Colorado.
Jackson, James. *Another Letter to a Young Physician*. Boston: Ticknor and Fields, 1861.
____. *Letters to a Young Physician Just Entering upon Practice*. Boston: Phillips, Sampson, 1855.
____. Papers, 1800–1867 (H MS C8.1 and B MS C3.3). Harvard Medical Library in the Francis A. Countway Library of Medicine (Boston) Special Collections.
Janouch, Gustav. *Conversations with Kafka*. New York: New Directions, 1971.
Jenkins, MacGregor. *Emily Dickinson, Friend, and Neighbor*. Boston: Little, Brown, 1930.
Johnson, Thomas H. (ed.). *The Letters of Emily Dickinson*. Cambridge: The Belknap Press of Harvard University Press, 1986. [one-volume edition]
"Joseph Thorne—His Calling." *Harper's New Monthly Magazine* 15:90 (November 1857).
Kelsey, Henry S. "An Account of the Last Two Years of Martha Snell's Life." http://clio.fivecolleges.edu/amherst/snell/03diaries/martha-d/account/
Kime, Wayne R. *Donald G. Mitchell*. Boston: Twayne, 1985.
Kingman, Bradford. *History of North Bridgewater*. Boston: Published by the Author, 1866.
"The Late Benjamin F. Newton." *Daily Morning Transcript* (Worcester, Massachusetts), March 26, 1853.
Leedy, Jack L., ed. *Poetry, the Healer*. Philadelphia: Lippincott, 1970.
Leonard, Ermina Newton. *Newton Genealogy*. De Pere, Wisc.: Bernard Ammidown Leonard, 1915.
Leyda, Jay. *The Years and Hours of Emily Dickinson*. 2 vols. New Haven: Yale University Press, 1960.
"Life and Death of Paganini." *Harper's New Monthly Magazine* 5:29 (October 1852).
"Life and Labors of Mary Lyon." *New England and Yale Review* 10:38 (May 1852).
Loving, Jerome. *Emily Dickinson: The Poet on the Second Story*. New York: Cambridge University Press, 1986.
Lowell, James Russell. "After the Burial." *The Atlantic Monthly* 21:127 (May 1868).
____. *Letters of James Russell Lowell*. Ed. Charles Eliot Norton. Vol. 1. New York: Harper & Brothers, 1874.
Lowell, Maria. *The Poems of Maria Lowell: With Unpublished Letters and a Biography*. Ed. Hope Jillson Vernon. Providence, R.I.: Brown University, 1936.
"Marriages." *The New England Puritan* (Boston), August 31, 1854.
Marvel, Ik [Donald Grant Mitchell.] *Dream Life: A Fable for the Seasons*. New York: Scribner's, 1851.
____. *Reveries of a Bachelor: or A Book of the Heart*. New York: Baker and Scribner, 1850.
McKeithan, Daniel Morley, ed. *A Collection of Hayne Letters*. Austin: The University of Texas Press, 1944.
Merriam, George S. *The Life and Times of Samuel Bowles*. 2 vols. New York: Century, 1985.

Messmer, Marietta. *A Vice for Voices: Reading Emily Dickinson's Correspondence.* Amherst: University of Massachusetts Press, 2001.
Miller, Betty, ed. *Elizabeth Barrett to Miss Mitford.* London: John Murray, 1954.
Mitford, Mary Russell. "Personal Sketches and Reminiscences." *Harper's New Monthly Magazine* 4:22 (March 1852).
Moers, Ellen. *Literary Women.* New York: Oxford University Press, 1985.
Morens, David M. "At the Deathbed of Consumptive Art." *Emerging Infectious Diseases* 8:11 (November 2002).
Nichols, Mary Sargeant. *Mary Lyndon, or, Revelations of a Life.* New York: Stringer and Townsend, 1855.
Nourse, Henry S., ed. *Birth, Marriage and Death Register, Church Records & Epitaphs of Lancaster, Massachusetts 1643 to 1850.* Lancaster: W. J. Coulter, 1890.
Paglia, Camille. *Sexual Personae: Art and Decadence from Nefertiti to Emily Dickinson.* New York: Vintage, 1991.
Petrino, Elizabeth A. *Emily Dickinson and Her Contemporaries: Women's Verse in America, 1820–1885.* Hanover, N.H.: University Press of New England, 1998.
Phillips, Kate. *Helen Hunt Jackson: A Literary Life.* Berkeley: University of California Press, 2003.
Plunkett, Harriette M. *Josiah Gilbert Holland.* New York: Scribner's, 1894.
Poe, Edgar Allan. *The Works of Edgar Allan Poe.* New York: Avenel, 1985.
Pollak, Vivian R. *Dickinson: The Anxiety of Gender.* Ithaca: Cornell University Press, 1984.
____. *A Historical Guide to Emily Dickinson.* New York: Oxford University Press, 2004.
Pommer, Henry F. *Emerson's First Marriage.* Carbondale: Southern Illinois University Press, 1967.
Prescott. Harriet. "Circumstance." *The Atlantic Monthly* 5:31 (May 1860).
Pulte, J. H. *Homeopathic Domestic Physician: Containing the Treatment of Diseases.* Cincinnati: Moore, Willstach, Keys, 1862.
Raymo, Chet. "Thus We Behold a Deadly Beauty." *The Boston Globe,* September 28, 1998.
"Recollections of Washington Irving, by One of His Friends." *Continental Monthly* 1:6 (June 1862).
Reports of the Selectmen ... Relative to the Expenses of the Town of Concord, for the Year 1850–51. Concord: Printed at the Freeman Office, 1851.
Rhode Island Death Records, 1885–1888 [Microfilm], Roll #50, 1886.
Rice, Franklin P. *Vital Records of Shrewsbury, Massachusetts, to the End of the Year 1849.* Worcester: Franklin P. Rice, 1904.
____. *Worcester Births, Marriages and Deaths.* Worcester: The Worcester Society of Antiquity, 1894.
Richards, William C. *Great in Goodness: A Memoir of George N. Briggs.* New York: Sheldon, 1866.
Rodier, Katharine Marie. "A Career in Letters: Emily Dickinson, T. W. Higginson, and Literary Women." Ph.D. diss., University of Connecticut, 1995.
Rothman, Sheila. *Living in the Shadow of Death: Tuberculosis and the Social Experience of Illness in American History.* New York: Basic, 1994.
St. Armand, Barton Levi. *Emily Dickinson and Her Culture.* New York: Cambridge University Press, 1984.
Schaefer, Richard A. *Legacy: Daring to Care.* Chapter 10: "How Much More Could They Bear?" http://www.llu.edu/info/legacy/Legacy11.html

Scott, Donald. "Evangelicalism, Revivalism, and the Second Great Awakening." *National Humanities Center.* http://www.nhc.rtp.nc.us:8080/tserve/nineteen/nkeyinfo/nevanrev.htm

Sewall, Richard B. *The Life of Emily Dickinson.* New York: Farrar, Straus and Giroux, 1974.

"A Slight Cold." *Harper's New Monthly Magazine* 6:32 (January 1853).

Södergran, Edith. *Love & Solitude: Selected Poems, 1916–1921.* Trans. with an introduction by Stina Katchadourian. San Francisco: Fjord, 1981.

Stevenson, Robert Louis. *The Letters of Robert Louis Stevenson to His Family and Friends.* 2 vols. Ed. Sidney Colvin. New York: Scribner's, 1902.

Stonum, Gary Lee. *The Dickinson Sublime.* Madison: University of Wisconsin Press, 1990.

Stowe, Harriet Beecher. *Uncle Tom's Cabin, or, Life Among the Lowly.* Vol. 2. Boston: J. P. Jewell, 1852.

"Thoughts at the Funeral Service of the Late B. F. Newton." *Daily Morning Transcript* (Worcester, Massachusetts), March 29, 1821.

"Tuberculosis." *LoveToKnow 1911 Online Encyclopedia.* http://53.1911encyclopedia.org/T/TU/TUBERCULOSIS.htm

"Tuberculosis Declines to Historic Low in the U.S." *The New York Times,* March 24, 2006, Section A, p. 11.

Tyler, W. S. *Amherst College During the First Half Century.* Springfield, Mass.: Clark W. Bryan, 1873

Ukrainka, Lesya. *Spirit of Flame: A Collection of the Works of Lesya Ukrainka.* Trans. Percival Cundy. Westport, Conn.: Greenwood, 1950.

United States Census, 1850. Massachusetts, Suffolk County, Boston Massachusetts, Ward 11.

———, 1860. Massachusetts, Worcester County, Lancaster.

———, 1860. Rhode Island, Providence County, Cranston.

———, 1860. Rhode Island, Providence County, Smithfield.

———, 1870. Massachusetts, Worcester County, Worcester, Ward 6.

———, 1880. Massachusetts, Worcester County, Lancaster.

United States Census Office. Census Records for Worcester County, 1850–1870. Vol. 3.

Wadsworth, Charles. "Rev. Dear Brother." Letter, February 26, 1852. Schaffer Library Collections, Union College, Schenectady, New York.

Walker, Cheryl. "Dickinson in Context." In *A Historical Guide to Emily Dickinson.* Ed. Vivian R. Pollack. New York: Oxford University Press, 2004.

Wardrop, Daneen. *Emily Dickinson's Gothic: Goblin with a Gauge.* Iowa City: University of Iowa Press, 1996.

Ware, John. *On Hemoptysis as a Symptom.* Boston: David Clapp, 1860.

Warner, Charles Dudley. "Washington Irving." *The Atlantic Monthly* 45:269 (March 1880).

Washburn, Asahel Cornwell. *The Young Christian's Victory; or, Memoir of Emma G. Washburn.* Hartford: Edwin Hunt, 1849.

Watts, Isaac. *Psalms, Hymns, and Spiritual Songs.* Boston: Crocker & Brewster, 1856.

Webster, Noah. *An American Dictionary of the English Language.* 2 vols. Amherst: J. S. and C. Adams, 1844.

Weisner, Stephen G. *Embattled Editor: The Life of Samuel Bowles.* New York: University Press of America, 1986.

Whicher, George F. "Emily Dickinson's Earliest Friend." *American Literature* 6:1 (March 1934).
____. *This Was a Poet: A Critical Biography of Emily Dickinson*. Ann Arbor: University of Michigan Press, 1957.
William Cranch Bond Fifield Collection (B MS c 3.3.), Boston Medical Library in the Francis A. Countway Library of Medicine, Boston.
Wolff, Cynthia G. *Emily Dickinson*. New York: Knopf, 1986.
Worcester (Mass.) Assessor's Office, Records, 1819–1857. "Personal Income and Value of Estates, 1820."
____. "State and County Taxes, 1819."
Zapedowska, Magdalena. "Wrestling with Silence: Emily Dickinson's Calvinist God." *ATQ* (*The American Transcendental Quarterly*) 20.1 (March 2006).

Index

*Died from TB

"A brief but patient illness" (ED poem) 9
"A little madness in the spring" (ED poem) 157
"A still volcano life" (ED poem) 143
"A wounded deer leaps highest" (ED poem) 112
"Adrift! A little boat adrift!" (ED poem) 98
"After the Burial" 96–97
"After the sun comes out" (ED poem) 152–153
Amherst 1, 3, 4, 5, 7–8, 9, 11, 14, 15, 16, 18, 33, 35, 36, 37, 41, 42, 48, 50–51, 52, 56, 57, 62, 63, 64, 84, 104, 105, 111, 113–114, 115, 117–118, 119, 130, 138, 153
Amherst College 11, 52, 63, 118, 136, 149; commencements 33, 112, 136
"An Opium Fantasy" 94–95
Anderson, Janet 86–87
"Annabel Lee" 106
"As by the dead we love to sit" (ED poem) 101

Baker, David 102
"Because I could not stop for death" (ED poem) 102
Bennett, Paula 65, 128–129
Bianchi, Martha Dickinson ("Mattie") 57, 159
Bingham, Millicent Todd 24
Bitter-Sweet 19–21
Boston 13, 27, 30, 34–36, 70, 137
Bowles, Mary 61, 144, 146
Bowles, Samuel 18, 38, 57, 61–62, 105, 110–111, 126, 129–130, 138, 144–145

Bremer, Fredrika 93
"A brief but patient illness" (ED poem) 9
Briggs, George Nixon 32–33
Brightwood 18–19
*Brontë, Anne 115, 116
*Brontë, Bramwell 116
*Brontë, Charlotte 11, 14, 17, 26, 49, 61, 80, 114–117, 124
*Brontë, Elizabeth 116
*Brontë, Emily 11, 14, 26, 115–118, 123–126
*Brontë, Maria 116
Brontë, Patrick 115, 117
*Browning, Elizabeth Barrett 26, 77, 80, 140–145
Browning, Robert 76–77, 142, 144
Bryant, William Cullen 87

Calvinism: God's will 13, 21, 42, 43, 47, 81, 101, 105, 120, 150, 164; professing Christ 10, 14, 41–48, 52, 101, 150; religious revivals 10–11, 14, 42, 52, 97–98; rules for baptism 52; salvation 13, 14, 25, 41–43, 51, 81, 101, 105, 149–150, 164, 167; sinfulness 47–49, 50–51, 81
Capps, Jack 34
Chaliff, Cynthia 133
Chase, Richard 53, 56, 80, 155
*Chopin, Frédéric 25–26, 120
Ciardi, John 122
"Circumstance" 145–146
Clark, James D. 60–61
Coleman, Lyman 58–59
*Coleman, Olivia 43–44, 48, 58, 103

193

*Coleman, Eliza 43–44, 57–59, 103
Colorado 62
consumption *see* tuberculosis

Damon, S. Foster 95–96
Davies, Stevie 117
"Death sets a thing significant" (ED poem) 17–18
Dickens, Charles 9
Dickinson, Edward (father) 7, 14, 16, 23–24, 30, 31–33, 34, 41, 52, 61, 63, 64, 69, 101, 113, 118, 130
Dickinson, Emily Elizabeth: Carlo (her dog) 34, 63–64, 80, 113; health 5, 6, 14, 24, 30–33, 34, 39, 44, 103–104, 129–130; joy in life 15–16, 31, 39, 63–64, 125–126, 141, 152–153, 157–160; melancholy (depression) 13, 64–65, 77–78, 98, 126; "Queen Recluse" 34, 110–127, 154–156, 160; reading *Atlantic Monthly* 117, 143, 145–146; reading *Harper's* 117, 119–124, 142; as spirit-bride 56, 76–77, 79, 82–83, 90, 100–109, 124, 151–152; stages of grief 77–78, 98, 151–153, 156–157; "terror since September" 128–147; views on death and dying 5–9, 22, 31, 42, 51, 98, 101–102, 104–105, 120, 122, 149; views on God 8, 13–14, 42–48, 51–55, 56, 79, 125–126, 139; views on immortality (heaven) 14, 15, 48, 51, 56, 79, 101, 104, 105, 117, 125–126, 139, 149; views on Jesus Christ 15, 42–48, 51–54, 122; wearing white 3, 63, 111; with Ben Newton 14–18, 34, 48–50, 56, 62–65, 69, 70, 74, 75–79, 80, 82, 91, 98, 100–109, 112, 123–124, 138, 151–152, 156; with brother, Austin 16, 35–36, 41, 64, 104; with Charles Wadsworth 57–61, 128–130; with father, Edward 7, 16, 24, 32, 41, 130; with mother, Emily 7, 23–24, 41, 57, 110, 146, 156–157; with Samuel Bowles 57, 61–62, 110–111, 129–130; with sister Lavinia ("Vinnie") 16, 18, 24, 41, 52, 111, 130; with sister-in-law, Susan ("Sue") 130, 131
Dickinson, Emily, poetry 1–2, 43, 148–149, 155; compared to Edith Södegran 54; compared to Ellen Emerson 86–87; compared to Emily Brontë 124–126; compared to Maria Lowell 94–96; "daisy" image 6, 8, 9, 61, 91, 138; as a dowry 106–107, 151–152; fascicles 106–108, 151–152; "fly" image 122–123; gothic elements 101–102, 106–107, 127, 152; as grief therapy 8, 151–152; lack of titles 1, 149; "omitted center" 1, 15–21; "robin" image 6–7, 13, 22; unconventional punctuation 87, 149; use of "slant" 2, 6–7, 39, 130, 155; "wounded deer" image 111–112, 114–115, 151
Dickinson, Emily Norcross (mother) 6, 7, 14, 15, 18, 22–24, 29–30, 39, 41–42, 52, 57, 101, 111, 118, 119, 146, 156–157
Dickinson, Lavinia (sister "Vinnie") 14, 16, 18, 24, 29, 34, 41, 52, 78, 101, 104, 110–111, 118, 119, 130, 136, 137–138, 153
*Dickinson, Samuel Fowler (grandfather) 52, 118
Dickinson, Susan Gilbert (sister-in-law) 34, 52–53, 57, 61, 81, 107, 110, 118, 119, 130–131, 138
Dickinson, William Austin (brother "Austin") 14, 16, 31, 34, 35–36, 41, 52–53, 61, 64, 80–81, 101, 104, 110, 114, 118, 119, 136
Dickinson Homestead 1, 56–57, 61, 104, 110, 113, 136, 156, 159–160
"The distance that the dead have gone" (ED poem) 98
"Distrustful of the gentian" (ED poem) 9
Doriani, Beth Maclay 54
Dormandy, Thomas 32
"Drama's vitallest expression is the common day" (ED poem) 149
Dubos, Rene and Jean 112
Dwight, Edward Strong 138–139
*Dwight, Lucy Elizabeth 138–139
"Dying! Dying in the night!" (ED poem) 101–102

Eberwein, Jane Donahue 141
Eliot, T.S. 1
*Emerson, Charles 85, 87–88, 90
*Emerson, Edward 85, 87–88, 90
*Emerson, Ellen Louisa Tucker 85–90, 92, 97, 98, 134
Emerson, Ralph Waldo 17–18, 63, 73, 74, 85–92, 97, 98, 110, 118, 150–151
Emerson, Waldo 90–91
Emerson, William 85, 87, 90
Evergreens 53, 61, 118, 159

"Faith is a fine invention" (ED poem) 38
Farr, Judith 17, 56, 78
Finney, Charles Grandison 42
Fiske, Ann 11, 38
*Fiske, Deborah Vinal 11–12, 24, 27–28, 36–39, 85, 150, 156
Fiske, Helen Maria *see* Jackson, Helen Hunt
Fiske, Humphrey 12
*Fiske, Nathan Welby 37, 38, 150
"Floss wont save you from an abyss" (ED poem) 157
Ford, Gordon 78–79
Fowler, Emily 12–13, 45, 52, 78–79, 96, 134
*Fowler, Harriet 12, 45
Fowler, William 45, 78
Franklin, R.W. 8, 108, 130
Fullerton, Lady Georgianna 118–119

Gaskell, Elizabeth 116
Geerken, Ingrid 117, 123
Gelpi, Albert 101
*Gilbert, Harriet 34, 119
Gilbert, Martha 118
Gilbert, Thomas 34
"Give little anguish" (ED poem) 130
"God is a distant stately lover" (ED poem) 47
"God is indeed a jealous God" (ED poem) 52
"God permits industrious angels" (ED poem) 48
Gould, George 63
Graves, John 57, 104
"Grief is a mouse" (ED poem) 114

Habegger, Alfred 6, 11, 13, 30, 31, 36, 48, 61, 66, 69, 71, 80, 129, 130, 138, 151, 153
Hale, Edward Everett 49–50, 64, 66, 76–77, 78
*Hayne, Paul Hamilton 134–135
"Heart we will forget him" (ED poem) 154
*Heath, George 102
"Heaven has different signs to me" (ED poem) 125
"Her last poems" (ED poem) 140
Higgins, David 18, 139
Higginson, Thomas Wentworth 13, 41, 48, 77–78, 92–93, 113, 126, 128, 129, 130, 132, 148–150, 156

Hirschhorn, Dr. Norbert 5–6, 30–31, 32, 34, 36, 87, 130
"His mansion in the pool" (ED poem) 158
*Hoffman, Matilda 82–84, 97, 98, 134
Hogue, Caroline 101
Holland, Elizabeth 18–19, 24, 116, 130, 152
Holland, Josiah Gilbert 18–21, 116, 126
Holland, Sophia 13, 57
*Holt, Jacob 45, 48
Humphrey, Heman 11–12
Humphrey, Jane 17, 52, 63, 104
*Hunt, Caroline Dutch 138, 139
Hunt, Edward Bissell 150
Hunt, Sereno D. 72–74

"I breathed enough to take the trick" (ED poem) 121
"I can wade grief" (ED poem) 151
"I could suffice for him I knew" (ED poem) 75–76
"I felt a cleaving in my mind" (ED poem) 94–95
"I felt a funeral in my brain" (ED poem) 102, 123
"I hav'nt told my garden yet" (ED poem) 33
"I heard a fly buzz when I died" (ED poem) 102, 122
"I held a jewel in my fingers" (ED poem) 107–108
"I know a place where summer strives" (ED poem) 92
"I like a look of agony" (ED poem) 102
"I reckon when I count it all" (ED poem) 43
"I rose because he sank" (ED poem) 108–109
"I see thee better in the dark" (ED poem) 83
"I think I was enchanted" (ED poem) 140, 141
"I went to thank her" (ED poem) 140, 144
"If anybody's friend be dead" (ED poem) 139–140
"If he were living dare I ask" (ED poem) 64–65
"If I can stop one heart from breaking" (ED poem) 157
"If I should'nt be alive" (ED poem) 22
"If those I loved were lost" (ED poem) 8

Index

Irving, Washington 82–85, 97–98, 134
"Is heaven a physician" (ED poem) 53
"It knew no medicine" (ED poem) 2
"It was not death for I stood up" (ED poem) 102

Jackson, Helen Hunt (née Helen Maria Fiske) 11–13, 38, 96, 148–151, 153–157, 159, 170
Jackson, Dr. James 34–39, 85–90, 93
Jane Eyre 11, 17, 49, 61, 80, 114, 115, 116
Jenkins, MacGregor 159–160
Johnson, Thomas 35–36, 63, 128–129

*Kafka, Franz 53, 112, 113, 127
Katchadourian, Stina 54
*Keats, John 27
Kellogg, John Preston 26
Kelsey, Henry S. 136–137
*Kent, Margaret Tucker 90
Koch, Robert 26, 28

"The lamp burns sure within" (ED poem) 117
*Lanier, Sidney 134–135
Leach, Dr. 28, 36
Leonard, Ermina Newton 66, 68
Leyda, Jay 1
*Lincoln, Levi 69, 71
Lincoln, Susan Amelia Newton 67, 69, 71
"A little madness in the spring" (ED poem) 157
"The Long Ago" 58
Longfellow, Henry Wadsworth 135
Loving, Jerome 56, 146
Lowell, Anna Cabot Jackson 93
Lowell, Blanche 96–97
Lowell, James Russell 92–98
Lowell, Mabel 93
*Lowell, Maria White 92–97, 98
Lowell, Rose 93
Lowell, Walter 93–94
Lyman, Joseph 2–3, 161
Lyon, Mary 14, 44–47

"Maggie" (the Dickinson maid, Margaret Maher) 160
March, Francis 78–79, 103, 134
"Master" figure 57, 61, 128–129, 130
McGill University 29
Mercy Philbrick's Choice 148, 153–157, 159, 170

Merriam, George 61–62
Messmer, Marietta 91
Mitchell, Donald Grant (Ik Marvel) 80–82, 92–93, 98–99, 165–166
Mitford, Mary Russell 142
Moers, Ellen 140
Morens, David 4
Mount Holyoke 14, 30, 31, 33–34, 43–48, 63, 78, 134, 136
Munch, Edvard 126–127
*Munch, Sophie 126
"My first well day since many ill" (ED poem) 39–40

"The name of it is autumn" (ED poem) 132–133
"Nature sometimes sears a sapling" (ED poem) 135–136
"New feet within my garden go" (ED poem) 95
Newman, Anna 81, 110
Newman, Clara 81, 110
*Newman, Mark 81
*Newman, Mary Dickinson 81
Newton, Benjamin Franklin (the blacksmith) 66–68
*Newton, Benjamin Franklin (the lawyer) 14–18, 21, 34, 48–50, 56–79, 80, 81, 82, 91, 98, 100–109, 111, 112, 119, 123, 138, 151, 153–154, 156,
Newton, Beulah 66, 67, 69, 72
Newton, David 66–67, 69
Newton, John Flavel 67
Newton, Lafayette 67–68
Newton, Moses 66–67
Newton, Sarah (the blacksmith's wife) 67–68
Newton, Susan Amelia *see* Lincoln, Susan Amelia
Nicholas Nickleby 9–10
Noble, Marianne 128
*Norcross, Amanda 29–30
*Norcross, Betsy Fay 6
*Norcross, Emily Lavinia 14, 30, 44, 57
Norcross, Frances ("Fanny") 30, 54, 76–77, 137–138, 144, 146, 158
*Norcross, Hiram 30
*Norcross, Lavinia Norcross 13, 29–30, 42, 137–138, 139, 146
Norcross, Louisa ("Loo") 30, 54, 76–77, 138, 144, 146, 158
*Norcross, William 30
Northborough 66–67, 69, 70, 74, 138

"Of course I prayed" (ED poem) 55
"One thing of thee I covet" (ED poem) 97
"An Opium Fantasy" 94–95
"Ourselves were wed one summer, dear" (ED poem) 140, 144
"The overtakelessness of those" (ED poem) 152

*Paganini, Nicolo 120–121
Paglia, Camille 7–8
Petrino, Elizabeth 51
Philadelphia, Pennsylvania 7, 57–59
Phillips, Kate 148–149, 159
Picciola 15–16
Pitcher, Henry Wadsworth 59
Pitcher, Jane Elizabeth *see* Wadsworth, Jane Elizabeth
Pitcher, Mary Ann *see* Wadsworth, Mary Ann
Pitcher, Rev. William 59–60
Pitcher, William, Jr. 60
Poe, Edgar Allan 89, 106, 121, 123
Pollak, Vivian 17
Prescott, Harriet 145–146
Pringle, Mary 98–99
Puffer, Reuben 74
Puffer, Sophia, of Berlin (MA) 74
Puffer, Sophia, of Sudbury (MA) 74
Pulte, J.H. 131

"Quite empty quite at rest" (ED poem) 13

Reveries of a Bachelor 80–82, 98–99, 165–166
Rice, Franklin P. 66
"The right to perish might be thought" (ED poem) 120
Rodier, Katharine 94–95
Root, Abiah 14, 31, 32, 33, 42–43, 44, 45, 100
"The rose did caper on her cheek" (ED poem) 107
Rossetti, Christina 123
Rothman, Sheila 12, 24, 98
Rugg, Asa Warner 70, 75
*Rugg, Betsey Warner 69
Rugg, Sarah Warner (Ben Newton's wife) 18, 64, 66, 67, 69–72, 74–75

"Safe in their alabaster chambers" (ED poem) 101
St. Armand, Barton Levi 105

Sand, George 25–26, 120, 144
Sentimental Love Religion 83–85, 88–92, 96–98, 100–109, 165
Sewall, Richard 2–3, 57, 80–81, 128–129, 156
"Sexton! My master's sleeping here" (ED poem) 106
"She rose to his requirement" (ED poem) 152
"The Sick-Room" 95–96
Snell, Ebenezer Strong 136
*Snell, Martha 136–137, 139
"So has a daisy vanished" (ED poem) 8
*Södergran, Edith ix, 53–54
"Some too fragile for winter winds" (ED poem) 48
"The soul has bandaged moments" (ED poem) 127
"The soul selects her own society" (ED poem) 156
Springfield Daily Republican 18, 24, 61–62, 110, 117
Stacy, John 73–74
Stacy, Sarah (Mrs. Sereno D. Hunt) 73–74
Steinem, Gloria 126
*Stevenson, Robert Louis 103, 134
"A still volcano life" (ED poem) 143
Stoker, Bram 131
Stonum, Gary Lee 140
Stowe, Harriet Beecher 22–23, 162–163
Strong, Martha 13
"Suspense is hostiler than death" (ED poem) 104
Sweetser, Joseph 105
Switzerland 62, 133

"Tell all the truth but tell it slant" (ED poem) 2, 155
"That first day when you praised me sweet" (ED poem) 15
"The distance that the dead have gone" (ED poem) 98
"The lamp burns sure within" (ED poem) 117
"The name of it is autumn" (ED poem) 132–133
"The overtakelessness of those" (ED poem) 152
"The right to perish might be thought" (ED poem) 120
"The rose did caper on her cheek" (ED poem) 107

"The soul has bandaged moments" (ED poem) 127
"The soul selects her own society" (ED poem) 156
"The truth is stirless" (ED poem) 159
"The whole of it came not at once" (ED poem) 23–24
"There came a day at summer's full" (ED poem) 16–17, 148
Thomas, Benjamin Franklin 70, 72
*Thoreau, Henry David 73, 74, 131–132
"Threnody" 91–92
"Time does go on" (ED poem) 158
*Timrod, Henry 134–135
"'Tis not that dying hurts us so" (ED poem) 7
"To die takes just a little while" (ED poem) 102
"To fight aloud is very brave" (ED poem) 27
"To know just how he suffered" (ED poem) 77
"To make one's toilette after death" (ED poem) 100–101
"The truth is stirless" (ED poem) 159
Tuberculosis 2–4, 9–10, 18, 22–39, 102–103, 120–121, 130–137; compared to cholera 3, 10; death watches 10, 25, 30, 33, 45–56, 38, 81, 82–83, 101–109, 120, 122–123, 164, 167–168; denial of 3, 6, 17, 22–25, 27–28, 31, 110, 142, 162–163, 168; doctors and patients 23, 24–25, 26–28, 32, 34–38, 80–81, 85–90, 94, 104, 161, 163, 166, 170; double standard 7, 38, 87–88; fictional accounts of 4, 5, 6, 9–10, 11, 17, 22–24, 25, 26, 37–38, 41, 56, 80–82, 84–85 100–101, 110, 112–113, 118–119, 123–124, 128, 131, 134, 148, 161–170; "galloping consumption" 43, 46, 82, 103; Gothic disease 11, 22; invalidism 7, 22–24, 30, 31, 33, 39, 95–96, 98, 102, 111, 143, 148, 164, 170; mortality rates 3–4, 8, 10, 21, 38, 51, 98, 134–135; "mouse in the breast" 6, 11, 114; *Mycobacterium tuberculosis* 25, 26, 28, 38, 85; Norcross susceptibility 6, 23–24, 29–30, 43–44, 146; religious consolation 9–13, 25, 28, 41, 46–48, 81, 96–97, 98, 101, 105, 116–117, 136, 143, 150, 163–164, 167; remission ("intermittent consumption") 6, 10, 11, 23–24, 37, 79, 88, 96, 103, 115, 136–137, 150, 162–163, 167; resurgence of in 21st century 3–4; spes phthisica 112; stigma attached to 3, 5, 6, 22, 34, 110, 168; survivor guilt 8, 88–89, 96–97

Tuberculosis, 19th century theories of causation: bad air 19, 25, 37, 170; bad diet 26–28, 35, 36–37; chill winter winds 7, 24, 25, 38, 88, 121, 164, 170; contagion 25–26, 28–28, 94, 120; "delicate" constitutions 22–23, 163; heredity 6, 22–23, 24, 25–26, 29, 34, 94, 162, 164; ill-fated love affairs 25, 77–78, 84–85, 119; outgrowth of less serious illnesses 23, 24–25, 28, 37, 143, 168; "vampire" attacks 11, 25, 131

Tuberculosis, symptoms: cough 2, 11, 14, 24, 25, 27, 28, 29, 31–32, 34, 35, 36, 82, 90, 100, 103, 110, 116, 119, 120, 121, 130, 136, 162, 163, 167, 168; difficult breathing 2, 7, 27, 30, 37, 103, 120, 161, 162, 165; hectic cheek 2, 3, 6, 25, 39, 85, 86, 100, 103, 107, 110, 112, 119, 120, 123, 162, 163, 165, 166–167, 168; hemorrhage 2, 6–8, 23, 26, 29, 39, 53, 78–79, 85, 87–88, 103, 120, 130–137, 150, 161, 164–165, 167, 168–169; hoarseness 27, 34, 37, 93, 121; night sweats 2, 29, 119, 162, 165; sharp pain in side 2, 28, 29, 103, 120, 135, 161, 164; sore throat 2, 31, 37, 103, 161; weight loss 2, 11–12, 23, 29, 30, 32, 34, 35, 38, 103, 104, 116, 119, 120, 121, 130, 138, 163, 165–166

Tuberculosis, treatment in 19th century: bleeding 26–27, 30, 36, 100, 167; blistering 26, 28, 36, 37, 39; climate change 6–7, 10, 25–26, 34, 37–38, 43, 61, 62, 81, 82, 85, 87–88, 93, 120, 131–132, 133, 148, 170; cod liver oil 26, 32; cupping 26, 27, 28, 37; exercise 15, 27, 31, 34, 35, 36, 85, 137; glycerin 35–36; horseback riding 26, 27, 31–32, 35, 36, 37, 61–62, 86, 88; leeches 27, 53, 156; medicines 10, 25–27, 28, 32, 37, 100, 167; opium (laudanum) 26, 27, 32–33, 35–37, 39, 85, 88, 94–95, 100, 113, 142, 167; purging 26, 27, 32; special diets 26–27, 28, 35, 36–37

*Tucker, Margaret 90
*Turner, Campbell 138

Turner, Catharine 138
"'Twas like a maelstrom with a notch" (ED poem) 147

*Ukrainka, Lesya 133–134,
"Unable are the loved to die" (ED poem) 79
Uncle Tom's Cabin 22–24, 162–163
Unitarianism 15, 49–50, 61

Vernon, Hope Jillson 94
Virchow, Dr. Rudolf 29

Wadsworth, Charles 57–61, 128–129, 138
Wadsworth, Henry 59
Wadsworth, Jane Elizabeth 59–60
Wadsworth, Mary Ann 59–60
Walker, Cheryl 95
Wardrop, Daneen 106–107
Ware, Dr. John 132, 134, 135, 137
Warren, Dr. John Collins 27–28
Washburn, Asahel Cornwell 45, 47
*Washburn, Emma 45–48, 103, 134
Washington, D.C. 7
"We cover thee sweet face" (ED poem) 90

"We outgrow love like other things" (ED poem) 151
Webster, Noah 12, 45, 78
Weisner, Stephen 61
West Cemetery 5, 8
*Wharton, Araminta 2–3
"What inn is this" (ED poem) 5–6
"When I have seen the sun emerge" (ED poem) 126
Whicher, George 59, 62–63, 64, 66, 68, 69, 75, 76, 80, 107–108, 153–156
Whitman, Walt 27
"The whole of it came not at once" (ED poem) 23–24
Wolff, Cynthia 6, 33, 41, 44, 56, 57, 61, 112, 129
Worcester 16, 17, 49–50, 63, 65–72, 76, 119
"A wounded deer leaps highest" (ED poem) 112
Wuthering Heights 11, 115, 117, 123, 126

"Your riches taught me poverty" (ED poem) 107, 148

Zapedowska, Magdalena 51

www.ingramcontent.com/pod-product-compliance
Lightning Source LLC
Chambersburg PA
CBHW032058300426
44116CB00007B/803